*S*oul

in

*P*rogress

Soul

in

Progress

A
Divorced
Mother's
Spiritual
Adventure

by Dorian Caruso

A.R.E. Press • Virginia Beach • Virginia

A.R.E. Press
Sixty-Eighth & Atlantic Avenue
P.O. Box 656
Virginia Beach, VA 23451-0656

Library of Congress Cataloging-in-Publication Data
Caruso, Dorian, date.
    Soul in progress : a divorced mother's spiritual adventure / by Dorian Caruso.
        p.   cm.
    ISBN 0-87604-336-8
    1. Caruso, Dorian, date. 2. Divorced mothers—United States—Biography. 3. Association for Research and Enlightenment—Biography. I. Title.
BP605.A77C37 1994
299'.93—dc20
[B]   94-32603

Cover design by Lightbourne Images

Dedication

I dedicate this book to my beloved soul companions, my children, whose unrelenting and unconditional faith and love inspired me to push beyond imagined boundaries to achieve what I thought was unimaginable. Also to the unseen, but intensely felt, guides and angels who never gave up on me and who persevered in breaking through all eight feet of my cement armor, no matter how hard I sometimes resisted.

Table of Contents

Acknowledgments

Writing this book has, in itself, been a positive growth experience. Among the many people who have contributed to its birthing are the entire A.R.E. Press acquisitions team, whose creation of a uniquely harmonious environment restored my faith and positive experience in work.

Foremost, Jon Robertson, editor-in-chief, whose repeated requests for my proposal and whose continued enthusiasm and support finally convinced me that perhaps someone would be interested in hearing my story. Also for his clarity about where the story should begin, when I floundered in the muddle of total life events. But for Jon, these experiences would never have become a book.

Ken Skidmore, my editor, whose patience, humor, sensitivity, and forbearance with my unique work mode enabled my process to flow.

Joe Dunn, publisher, whose encouragement and model of dedication inspired me to do my best.

Eileen Wiener, friend and teammate, whose constant faith always boosted my energy to persevere.

My gratitude goes as well to my teachers: "Bill O'Brian," who carefully honed my babble into writing; Yogi Amrit Desai—Guruji—who taught me to treat each person as if God had come to teach me through him or her and whose living example still melts my heart; Edgar Cayce, for the invaluable and still timely wisdom he channeled selflessly; all friends, teachers, and students from whom I have learned to grow; and not the least, to my children, to "Alex," Grandma, and all other members of the cast of my life drama who have moved me forward on my spiritual path.

I am profoundly indebted to you all.

INTRODUCTION

ALTHOUGH THIS book is autobiographical, it is not an autobiography, for many experiences occurred before the breakup of my marriage and many continue since finishing my book.

Most names have been changed out of respect for the privacy of the "cast" of my drama.

My life was not quiet, and events intermingled in a chaotic, seemingly karmic, jumble in my memory until Jon Robertson, editor-in-chief, suggested I begin with the breakup. I suspected he liked the "strength through adversity" theme, a notion which made me uneasy, for I knew privately that it was not all strength—I had a lot of unseen help.

As I mapped my story from the breakup, I saw clearly that this *was* the point where my major karmic chore kicked in. The story flowed from there.

At first my life felt very difficult, but help was always there. Most often I asked (prayed) for it, but even when angst crowded out everything else, assistance came without my asking.

The many rules that parents and institutions invent for us to follow always come with penalties for their infraction. I stand as living evidence that our guides and angels do not impose such conditions. Their help is consistent, unconditional, and without judgment. I can also attest that they are nondenominational, requiring no particular—or no organized—religious affiliation. "Independents" qualify for their help as well as "affiliates" of denominations.

It seems the only thing considered was the intent in my heart. It still works like that for me.

The target audience for my book at first—I thought—was single mothers and its theme, survival. It was never intended to instruct how to rear children. My love for my children carried me through rearing them, mostly by winging it day by day. Considering the uniqueness of each child, I know of no general methodology for child-rearing.

At a point, the book began to take over and a sequence of steps or highpoints fell into place, leading to each spiritual growth milestone and its contributing experiences. I followed that lead. Often at night I would dream of significant details I had omitted or of an oversight that would rescue me from a place where I was stuck. The help continued. I sometimes wondered who was writing this book!

By the time I neared the end, I had a dramatic realization.

The theme of my book is not survival, though I was well trained in that. It is instead what I have spent most of my life learning through difficult scenarios that I must remember I *chose*. It is EMPOWERMENT, and it is for everyone.

I see myself as a "sample human." I share with you the tale of my empowerment. It is my sincere and humble wish that my story will enhance your understanding of your true individual importance and worth to the Creator and to your unseen helpers. Know that your own unique path is worthy of the Highest support.   Dorian Caruso
                                                    Virginia Beach
                                                    August 3, 1994

1

OUT OF CHAOS:
REINCARNATION??

Life is what happens to you when you're making other
plans.   –Betty Talmadge

HIS LONG-AWAITED letter arrived and I tore it
open and raced through it, looking for the flight schedule
that would bring Jen, Sandy, and Alex back for the holidays.
Halfway through the third paragraph, I froze . . .

> . . . I won't be able to come for Christmas. Jen and
> Sandy are disappointed, but Mother distracts them
> with lots of shopping. She tells me they're doing well
> in school. They really wanted to spend Christmas with
> all of you.
>   I've run up some business debt. It's complicated. I
> had to lean on Father for the money I sent you these

1

past months. I'd rather not ask for travel money, too. I won't be able to send any before mid-January. I'll try to send at least part of the rent before the deadline. Hold them off!

I've been thinking about our debt problems. I don't really see how to make this work. I'm really happier here in a familiar milieu. You insist we'd have more problems living here again. Incidentally, yes, I did take offense—I have no drinking problem. We just drink more here than in the States. Nobody is shocked. You're the only one who sees it as a problem.

Maybe the best for both of us is a divorce. We each have a different idea how to live our life. We could get on with our lives better separately.

It doesn't mean I don't love you. You're the mother of my children. I'll always love you. I'd never oppose your having full custody of the children either.

It's not an easy decision but I'm inclined to go with it. You might want to see a lawyer yourself about particulars, or Chuck could handle legalities from this end. I'd see to it that everything is fair. I really think it's the only solution.

Love,
Alex

PS: I'll put the girls on a plane in May when school is over. You and the kids have a wonderful Christmas.

I sat stunned.

A lump of chaos slowly rose from my stomach and stuck in my throat. My cheeks tightened as my salivary glands dripped. I dashed to the bathroom and stood over the toilet retching until my throat and stomach muscles ached, too weary to continue. My chest heaved in a violent wave of sobbing. My knees refused to hold me up, and I slumped to the bathroom floor in a heap of despair.

I dragged myself into the bedroom and fell limp on the bed, muffling the now quiet sobs with the pillow so that the children wouldn't hear me. How could I ever tell them this?

Jay and Dina came running into the bedroom as though we were playing hide-and-seek. "I find her! I find her!" squealed Jay. Dina shushed him before they woke the baby. They believed me when I said I was tired and didn't feel well.

They climbed up to lie beside me. I needed to feel their warm, chubby nearness. I needed their innocence to reassure me that all was not chaos. I settled into a fetal position in the bed and accepted the consolation they lavished to help make me well. We stayed there until the baby woke up.

I got through the rest of the day on automatic. After they all went to sleep that night, I tried to call Alex but there was no answer. I wanted to hear his voice, to see if he could *say* the things he wrote, to see if I could change his mind. Maybe he had written it after too much rum, doing the night club rounds with friends. He couldn't possibly mean what he said. Not without returning to talk things out.

Every time we would argue, he reminded me how I humiliated him at Kelly's party during my pregnancy with Jay when I wouldn't let him drive me home. Kelly had called me a cab because Alex was too drunk. No one ever *said* he had a drinking problem, but everyone knew it. Only he denied it. It was years ago. Why was he mentioning it now?

I tried again to reach him, but still there was no answer. It was late and I was emotionally exhausted. I would wait a little longer and try once more. I needed to hear it from him, to hear why. I sat in the kitchen and read the letter again. It didn't feel real. It felt as if I were standing over the shoulder of an actress, watching her do a scene.

The letter dated December 10, two weeks before Christmas, was the first he had written since he'd left in September. He disliked writing letters, but the months of indifference should have made me suspect something.

We had moved across three states, just signed a two-year apartment lease, so he could start fresh in a new job. After a week, his junior partnership wasn't working. He felt demeaned having a female superior. His parents had come to help us get settled. He and his dad had lots of private conferences over the next two days. The following night I couldn't get Jen and Sandy to stay in bed. They were excited about enrolling next morning in the new school. When we finally got to bed, he pulled me closer and told me the new plan.

"I'm leaving with my parents day after tomorrow. No, don't panic. You don't have to pack anything—you and the kids are staying here. I'll be back so fast you won't have time to miss me. I'll live at home, share Father's office gratis, get a good head start in my own practice through his contacts, and earn more money faster. In six months I can pay off our debts with enough money left to return and start my practice here. I'll have no living expenses, no office rent, all gravy. We'll still have only one set of expenses, and I'll be my own boss. I can be back here and start clean in six months."

I remember protesting, "But we've just signed a lease here. How am I going to do everything with all the kids and no money? I don't even know my way around yet."

"I'll leave the car and get you a street map. I know you can handle it. For heaven's sake, can't you make this one small sacrifice? The time will fly. We'll be back on our feet."

"But why so sudden, why right now?" I pleaded. "I'm not prepared for this. Just when we were going to really work to straighten out our marriage, you run off alone to Santo Domingo and leave us here with no money and bound by a lease."

"I told you everything's taken care of. Look, how'd you like if I visited for Christmas? It would cut the time in half. It wouldn't cost that much. What the hell, if it makes you happy who cares what it costs! Father's giving me money for you to cover expenses and get some furniture. I'll just tell him to add some for the trip. Trust me, everything's taken care of."

"Why did you do that, Alex? You know how I hate taking your father's money! Why can't we live on what you make? All it takes is a little planning. I didn't marry your father—I married you. Every time we run out of money, you get it from your father. I could understand getting a little help while you were still in medical school, but Alex, it's been years. I don't want to feel obligated to your father."

It was one of our biggest sources of contention for years.

Nothing would dissuade him from his master plan. His father believed in his sincerity; his mother's eyes belied skepticism. After living with Alex for ten years, I felt the familiar foreboding of a growing knot in my gut.

I knew he couldn't manage money and that he wouldn't remember we needed to pay rent, buy food, and pay a milkman for the children's mainstay—or he would remember it too late. He always called it "our" debt, but it was his debt that strangled us. In every new town he would open charge accounts in all the fine restaurants and bars to entertain his new colleagues after hours. Meanwhile, the milkman threatened to stop delivery for nonpayment.

One night he took me to dinner at an elegant place, priced so high I was afraid, knowing our circumstances, to order. I wanted to leave and it embarrassed him. Every waiter and maître d' knew him and ran to serve him. Our bill was enough to pay the milkman three times, and he tipped the waiter more than I had spent on myself in months! I was outraged. Somehow the real world had left Alex behind and he existed in Never-Never Land. It would be no different this time.

In a last effort to soften the impact, I convinced his parents to take Jen and Sandy for the school year. "School in another country would be a good experience for them," I insisted, "and I could manage easier here with only three." What I really had in mind was that two fewer would starve.

Jen agreed, but Sandy threw a tantrum and wouldn't go until we assured her that they could fly back to their brothers and sisters for Christmas. "We can all come together to spend Christmas with Mommy and the other kids," Alex promised.

It appeared that everything was settled.

We were nearly evicted twice for late rent and had little left for food. Months went by without a letter. I thought he would at least make the effort to be supportive of us in such insecure circumstances. As Christmas drew nearer, I awaited his call telling us when they would arrive. I longed to cuddle my little girls again! Jen, the eldest, was doing well in school, secure that our separation was only temporary. Yet her lack of protest worried me. Was she always as happy as she seemed? Sandy couldn't adjust, however, and protested to everyone. She missed holding her baby brother, giggling in bed at night with her sisters, and being the tomboy leader of her little cronies. She was miserable in the new school with new teachers and lessons in a strange language.

I glanced back at Alex's letter. Not a word since September and suddenly this. When I took the letter from the mailbox, a sickish feeling went through me before I opened it. I squelched the feeling and forced myself to imagine his tall, right-slanted handwriting that would be happily explaining his arrival plans. I wanted it to be a good, healing visit. I wanted him to tell me that everything was progressing according to plan and that he would be ready to return with the girls when school ended. I wanted this unnerving self-imposed separation ended, resolved in a new start. It really could happen. It would be worth the anxiety and hardship. I wanted us to be together again as before, with all the problems melted away.

Sometimes loving him so much frightened me.

Could this be the end for us? Where did we go wrong? I didn't want this for my children—that was how I'd grown

up. How could we disrupt the lives of these precious inno-
cents and ask them to make heartbreaking choices between
us? No, I wouldn't allow that. I would either keep them all or
never grant him his freedom. I knew he'd turn the children
over to his mother, or worse, to a teen-aged nursemaid—a
niñera—to raise. I wouldn't let that happen to my children.

I went to bed and lay sleepless in the dark, seeing scenes
of our first encounter and the first time I had visited his
magical island birthplace. Why couldn't it stay as it was in
the beginning? We were so young. It felt destined to be the
big forever romance of our lives.

I had been working in a New Orleans photography studio, contracting, billing, and hand-painting portraits. I
communicated with the two Cuban owners in grunts, gestures, and decibels. They liked me and taught me the entire
business—the camera, lighting, darkroom processing, and
enlarging. One evening while experimenting with glamour
poses, a group of Hispanic students came for college ID
photos. When they saw what we were doing, two of the girls
wanted portraits as well. The owners allowed me to do the
sittings under their supervision.

The girls were friendly and easy to work with. When they
returned to see the proofs, they were delighted, and our
conversations lengthened. As I answered questions about
places to eat, dance, and have fun, they invited me to join
them Saturday night to guide them and I agreed.

We became friends, and I joined their weekly jaunts to a
Mexican night club, where we danced all night, ate tacos,
and drank Cuba Libres. We began as a crowd, but ended paired.

One Saturday night twenty of us piled into three cars to
go dancing. I was dancing a slow, sensuous bolero when
my Nicaraguan partner said, "Oh, there's my friend Alex
over by the bar." I spotted Alex and our glances locked as he
made his way, drink in hand, to the middle of the dance
floor to cut in. My partner laughed, shrugged, and returned

to the group. I never saw him again that night.

Alex and I danced all night, oblivious of the others. The attraction between us was intensely magnetic, as if we'd known each other for eons. When the club closed, we noticed that the group had left without us. We moved on to an all-night diner for breakfast before going home.

From then on, we saw each other every night.

It continued intense and dazzling. We could hardly bear to be apart when I had to go to work and he to medical school classes. We would arrive at dawn as my embarrassed grandmother chatted with neighbors. I would sleep two hours, get up, go to work, then meet Alex again. How did we survive it!?

His conversation fascinated me. Some nights we'd sit at the Canal Street pier and talk for hours about our hopes and dreams. He wanted to be a doctor who discovered wonderful cures for terrible diseases. I wanted to study art.

"If we were married and lived in my country, I would send you to our wonderful university to study fine art. We have some outstanding professors, and you would learn very fast. You could choose oil painting, sculpture, water colors, or anything you want. And I would come with you to art history classes. Would you like that?"

"Yes. Oh, yes," I said.

We did a lot of "what ifs . . . " He was so intelligent. We talked about his studies, his country, his climate, his native cuisine, his history, his politics, his travels, the Mayas, the Incas, his beautiful native language, our personal philosophies, the French Impressionists, Beethoven, Debussy, Latin music, what the world could be like in twenty years, what he would do with his life—everything.

When I spoke of visions or dream experiences I'd had since childhood, he found them fascinating. When I spoke of them at home, I was warned to stop the nonsense. I couldn't even confide those experiences to friends. Finally I'd kept them to myself.

My family disliked his ethnic origin. They feared some different racial blood might lurk somewhere generations back. I was attracted to the person he was, not earlier generations. I was "indiscriminate" now. Earlier they'd labeled me "too choosy" when the "nice neighborhood boys" didn't interest me. When I complained that they couldn't talk about anything, the family said what was important was that they had good jobs. That wasn't enough for me. Word traveled the neighborhood that I was a snob who liked only Yankees and foreigners and the neighborhood boys weren't good enough for me, so everyone shunned me. I didn't care. I was working and spent little time in the neighborhood. I had grown up with those boys and knew every nasty little thought in their small minds; it was no loss. The neighborhood had the same mental level as my family and existed in the same rut that had been dug generations earlier. It wasn't the life I wanted.

Alex awakened in me a tremendous curiosity and a surge of intellectual energy never before tapped. At a time when I was ready to fly, he unlocked the boundaries of my mind to things I'd never realized existed and urged me to allow my mind to soar. My mind became as insatiable as a food addict at a Roman banquet.

After five months, we made serious plans to marry the summer after he graduated from medical school—if only to get some sleep, we'd joked—but my family's bigotry, opposition, and ultimatums threw us into high gear and within weeks we had eloped. He opted to tell his parents later, saying they would accept it better if he told them in person. We rented a tiny efficiency apartment and when spring semester ended, he returned to the island, told his parents, and I followed three weeks later.

He met me at the airport in a chauffeur-driven car and wanted to stop somewhere for a drink. I was tired and begged off. I also asked if he'd hired the chauffeur to impress me. I knew he liked doing things on a large scale. He said it was his father's chauffeur. Yeah, I thought! We continued until we came to a narrow driveway that suddenly opened into an elegant carport alongside what looked like the most beautiful tropical night club I had ever seen. It reminded me of the private clubs the Mafiosi frequented in the movies. I told Alex I really appreciated being shown around, it was a beautiful place, but it had been a long day of travel. "Couldn't we do this tomorrow and just go straight to your parents' home now?" I pleaded.

He smiled.

Just then a couple in their fifties came down the tiled balcony stairs to the car, smiling. They weren't dressed for a night club; they wore slippers! They were dressed as most people dress to stay home. Was this really a night club?

The chauffeur opened our door and Alex introduced his parents.

I felt like a princess being ushered into a castle as they showed me around "the house." There was a maze of rooms, most with their own balconies. Italian tile floors gleamed throughout like mirrors. It was not a climate for rugs. His parents had decorated a beautiful first floor suite for us, furnished in tropical mahogany and teak, with soft cerulean blue walls and floral linens and drapes that repeated the island's lush colors. Most luxurious was the long private balcony with cushioned chaise lounges, just outside our bedroom overlooking the white dunes by the sea.

The house faced the sea, its back hidden from the street by a long, *flamboyan*-lined driveway. The front yard led to a private tiled deck that edged the beach. Built-in benches shaded by tall palm trees invited us to relax and watch the bathers, the catamarans, and the moon. Lobster fishermen casting their nets were so close that we could hear their conversation. I was dazzled by the sight of the full moon dancing on the gentle breakers, lighting up the sea amid the fragrance of tropical blossoms. Coconut palms abounded, their silhouettes swayed by trade winds in gracious welcoming gestures. It was a very heady scene that livened all the senses. This truly seductive island with a personality all its own was a paradise that I never wanted to leave. That night, in celebration of my arrival at this magical place, we made love on our own private balcony, deeply immersed in a sensuous tropical milieu.

I had no idea that Alex had grown up in such wealth. When I later wrote my family about this, instead of being happy for us, they were furious that an ethnic person should have such a good life. I was glad to be far from their limiting preconceptions. Here, I was free to discover each new day on its own merits.

His family was very kind to me and appeared to accept our marriage. We returned to the States for his final year of school and graduation, then relocated to the island to pursue his career.

Problems arose with cultural differences. I couldn't adjust to being chaperoned for daytime shopping or limiting my new friendships to the family's social class. When Alex arrived drunk and late, ruining our dinner plans, and I became angry, they despaired that I could never adjust to their ways.

A comic irony happened regarding our suite. It was as flawless as a page from a decorating magazine, and I wanted to keep it that way. No one here knew of my ineptness for housework, but with the incentive of this beautiful suite, I discovered that I could maintain it quite well. Every morning I made the bed, polished the furniture, and put everything back to the perfect picture, until the day Alex's mother called me into a private conference.

"Please don't make your bed or tidy your room, dear," she requested.

"I'm so sorry," I replied. "I was only trying to keep it as beautiful as it was when I arrived. Have I damaged anything?"

"No, no," she continued, "it looks fine but, you see, if you clean your room and make your bed, the servants get spoiled and begin to grumble when they have to do those things for the rest of us."

I loved Alex's beautiful country, his people, and his family. His father always made sure we lacked for nothing, providing us with perhaps too much. When we traveled by train, ship, or plane, he bought our tickets—first class all the way.

"Marrying up" to affluence far above that in which I was reared created problems, too. I chose friends by chemistry, common interests, and philosophy rather than by social or financial status.

There was some uneasiness, too, about the differences in our education. Alex was only a year older than I, but had graduated from medical school. When we met, I had been working two years since high school, paying board at home but living independently. I was bright, curious, creative, and able to interact in any discussion, albeit without a college degree. My family had no money for college. Despite a Southern upbringing and family acceptance of "a man's world," I entered into marriage with a perception of equal rights. That I, an only child, should always be the one to concede was alien to my nature, yet we muddled through ten years with my doing most of the compromising. We had babies every few years during sojourns in the U.S. and during stays on the island. The impact of our differences softened each time we returned to the island, for there was always a new baby to play with and too much to do to bother with trivial cultural differences.

But deeper problems too terrifying to confront crept furtively through our lives. Either I refused to uncover and identify them, or I would eagerly accept Alex's excuses that explained them away. In truth, I lived with panic just under my skin at the thought of breaking up. How would I take care of all these little ones alone? How could I bear to be apart from them or to lose them if I couldn't support them? So I covered every blemish and told myself that it was a good marriage; no marriage was perfect. I allowed only one problem to show, the money problem, probably using it as a safety valve to drain pressure from the others and keep them hidden.

Most marriages had money problems. Priorities caused ours. We were always strapped. Alex spent every penny he earned and the basics went unpaid. Once he said it was only a remnant of a pattern from college days. He was a gangly, fourteen-year-old with acne, a photographic memory, and a phenomenal IQ when his parents brought him to a stateside university. After an uncomfortable year of top grades and freshmen ridicule, he saw a way to be accepted. He need only drink more, womanize more, and pay everybody's bar tab. He was still living the same pattern.

I hated the way he always cabled his father to bail us out. Was he going to continue this for the rest of his life? I couldn't shame him into seeing it differently. He was the genius son of proud parents who had always granted all his desires in the form of gifts rather than money that he might learn to manage. His mother always insisted I learn to be supportive to his genius instead of stifling it, that I learn to cushion problems so that his genius could flower unhampered by daily trivia. She had proudly birthed a genius. She said it so often that I wondered if it served as her validation to exist. He was her testimony before the world. He knew this. He confessed that he resented their expectations, their "shoulds." He never felt accepted for himself, only for his intellect. Since the age of four when they tested his IQ, his life had changed. He was no longer allowed to mingle with other children lest he catch an illness or play games that could result in minor injury. He was constantly reading, learning, rarely participating in life. After years of being an only child, he got a sister. He was very sad the day he told me how he had wished he could be treated as she was, for

when she tested "only average," no one expected anything
of her—they just loved her because she was there.

He never demonstrated open hostility to his parents, but
became instead a master of passive aggression and subtlety,
hurting them in many other ways. The habit spilled over; he
hurt me as well. His mother feared that I, in my youth and
ignorance, would damage him. She couldn't recognize the
preexisting damage.

We did not see eye to eye on fidelity and "natural male
prerogatives." How dare I protest the lipstick on his shirt!
With each incident I withdrew, feeling a little more inadequate, a little more denigrated, a little more trapped. We
had beautiful children who needed care, and I was the sole
care-giver. Our lives began to divide into different tracks. I
had neither time, interest, nor energy to party at night, but
he chose the party track, and the island was replete with
opportunities. The children and I became a sideline to the
main flow of his life.

Two years earlier we had come very close to splitting.
That was how I got pregnant again—the scenes, the making
up. Then he thought of an alternative. Therapy. No, not
couple counseling. I would go alone to work out my problems and learn to accept his way of life. At first I rebelled,
outraged. I was early into pregnancy again, feeling very vulnerable. This was the baby conceived while we were making up after a break. Now we were fast headed for another
break! I didn't feel like rehashing this emotional garbage for
the entire nine months. Then I saw how hopeless the situation was. I couldn't leave him; where would I go? How would
I fend for my children? Maybe I could learn to comfortably
accept his life style and coexist.

There were times when I hated what he had done, was
doing, to our lives. I no longer liked the person he was. At
the same time, strangely, I loved him the same as the day I
first saw him. I hated living with him, but I couldn't live without him. It was an Alex addiction.

For six months a Freudian therapist sat out of sight in utter silence while I lay on a couch counting spots on the ceiling, wondering what to say. The day I mentioned my husband's reason for sending me to therapy, he choked in outrage. It was the first comment I had ever heard from my therapist. From then on he interacted.

Nothing changed at home. The day my therapist announced he would soon discharge me, I panicked. Two weeks later, while ironing Alex's shirts and letting my mind wander to minor problems, I could suddenly see with total clarity each problem's core. I began to see everything as if my mind had just been thoroughly vacuumed clean and not a cobweb remained. Why could I not see this clearly before? I felt a growing strength and confidence that, no matter what happened, I would survive.

At a follow-up session I told the therapist how clear everything had become while I was ironing and, more surprising, how strong I was feeling. I realized it was never the lack of money that got to me, rather the blatant rejection and utter lack of care, as if I and my innocent children had been branded "UNWORTHY."

"Who is he to treat us like this?" I stormed.

My baby was due in two weeks, and I had spent almost the entire pregnancy crying. How would that affect my baby? Surely it would sense the desperation. I was able to think about all this now, hold it all up to the light, and look it square in the eye without crying. I didn't have to hide any of it. Not even the thought of breaking up and the struggle it would bring could make me cry. I somehow knew we would get through it.

The doctor smiled. He had never before displayed emotion.

"Why am I feeling so strong now?" I asked him.

"Because we have worked very hard for exactly that, and we have done our homework very carefully, and now we are being rewarded," he said.

"Will that help me to resolve anything?

"It will help you to *survive* everything." Later I realized he really meant "we." He had thought I was just another bored housewife until the day I told him why Alex sent me to therapy. He had worked very hard with me since that day, within the ethics of his profession, to nurture whatever inherent strength I had. He had no clue what raw material was there. Whatever it was, it had to come forth from me, without prompting. Otherwise it would be too fragile. When we said our last good-by, he looked as if he had just won an Olympic medal. I felt as if I had, too.

Life was not pleasant after the baby came. Alex stayed away longer and was very morose when he came home. The baby didn't interest him. He made no effort to bond. I stayed positive for the children and myself and saw to our needs. If Alex came, he came; if not, then he didn't.

One day he came home elated over a letter he'd received.

"We can leave here now. I have a good job on the East Coast. They want three week's notice here. You go on with the children. It's all turnpike driving. All you need is a good road map. When you get to New York City, my parents will be waiting for you at the Dixon Apartment Hotel with a huge suite. We'll all fit. Things will get better now."

Baby Rafi was then ten months old.

After remembering last year's scene with my therapist, I felt stronger. How could I have slipped back into feeling so vulnerable, so powerless? I needed all the strength I could call upon if Alex was sober when he wrote that terrible letter.

How could he make such a final decree without discussing it? I ruminated again. What was he up to? How could I deal with it? I felt like an empty shell just beginning to fill up on strength. How would I get through this? I must get through it, for if I fell, we would all go down. I would not allow this to destroy my children. A surge of strength relaxed me and allowed me to sleep.

Alex called the next morning to see if his letter had arrived. Yes, it was true. He wanted out. No, he did not want to talk it out. No, he was not coming back. His flippancy was born of guilt. As for me, I didn't want to peek into the guilt picture; not again. I just wanted out. I told him I would think about it and answer soon.

Days of faking good cheer followed while we made Christmas bangles and garlands out of milk carton junk. I wrote asking him to rethink it, but his mind was made up. He wanted out. A close friend suggested that I fight it to create a delay and possibly a change of heart. But there was no fight left in me to save this marriage. It was a parasite eating away at my strength too long. I'd had enough. I wanted an end to this punishment and degradation. If my children ended up with one parent, it would be the one who understood commitment. I could no longer deny ten years of conflict, nor could I live with someone who no longer cared about any of us.

I slept fitfully but awoke feeling lighter. I'd finally gotten the message. I realized it had been given before in ways less clear, but I FINALLY GOT IT. When the kids took a nap, I sat down to write Alex a long letter. I agreed to a divorce, if that was really what he wanted. I thanked him for the past ten years, though some were not great, but I had beautiful children, wonderful memories, and I had learned a lot. I expressed special gratitude for having my mind challenged by living alongside a genius.

It was partly tongue in cheek. His upbringing had warped his genius. He had embraced a pattern that won him acceptance and validation because, at the same time, it made his parents crazy. What he didn't foresee was that he'd get stuck in it and hurt everyone. He wasted his genius and spent his life in senseless rebellion and self-undoing. But the very gift that died inside him awakened me and lifted

me from the pit of utter intellectual stagnation from which
I'd come. He had touched my mind with a magic crystal,
opened it wide, and sparked it to life. He was the fairy-tale
prince who kissed the sleeping princess and awakened her
from the witch's spell of unconsciousness. He had kissed my
mind and it became a sponge. He had kissed my body and
it bore precious fruit. How could I not bless him a thousand
times over for that? He was moved when I told him so.

I also told him to let Chuck handle it. I didn't know any
lawyers and didn't trust them. The car had just been repossessed so I had neither transportation, bus fare, nor sitter's
fees to go for a legal consultation, and I couldn't endure the
retelling and haggling.

"If it is to end, let it end here and now, clean and free. Just
do it from that end. My hands are full already." It felt good to
do that. Now I could shape a brave new life.

The next morning my courage melted away. It was time
to face reality and reality was scary. I struggled to deal with
things the next week, but I was slipping into depression. I
couldn't properly feed my children on the money we had, I
feared coming home from our snowy walks to find the lock
changed if our rent was late again. I seriously considered
finding a job, but couldn't find anyone who would take on
the daily care of five children.

It began to feel as though we would die together or just
fade away. My only joy was having spared two daughters—
now with their doting grandparents—this uncertainty.

As a last resort, I called Alex's mother, distraught over our
situation. She couldn't believe things were as bad as I described and said I was "overreacting."

I couldn't bear to call my mother and listen to her lectures on why I shouldn't have ever married Alex. I didn't regret marrying him. We had some good times, good experiences.
He was the catalyst for my growth and I regretted that we
couldn't continue, but no matter how much I wanted it, I

was only half of it. The other half had turned away. We had taken all there was for us from this marriage and there was nothing left to keep it alive. Despite our hardships and my tenuous grip on things, I knew in the deepest part of my being that I still loved him. And while I could rant over his flaws, I would not tolerate it from my mother. I could no longer live with him, but I knew I would feel a terrible void in my life without him.

When my in-laws learned that the problems were real, they offered to rear and educate two of the children. When I reluctantly told my mother and she stopped ranting, she offered to take two more. Her next offer was for us to come and live in her garage apartment so that she could rear all the children while I worked to save money to buy the plot next-door. She would then find me a husband from among her friends' sons, and he would build us a home on my land. "You should have done this in the first place!"

Their intentions were good, but I meant to keep my children together. When asked why, I answered that I, an only child, had always yearned for siblings and I couldn't separate them. It was one answer, but deep down I felt something larger that I couldn't yet articulate.

If I sent two to my in-laws, they would be well provided for but raised largely by *niñeras*, while the others would feel cheated, not only of their siblings but of a vastly higher standard of living. The two who went to my mother's would grow up in stagnation and mediocrity as I did and hate me for making that choice. If I accepted my mother's second plan, I might just as well forfeit my life.

None offered either assistance or advice to help us stay together. None seemed to understand or care about children bonded to their siblings.

One truth emerged: that I was the only one willing to try to keep us together; the only one who cared enough to accept the risk, the challenge, and whatever it brought; the only one willing to be accountable before God and the world. Alex had clearly said the responsibility would hinder the flow of his life and he would leave them for his mother to rear. I must keep them together, no matter what it took. I didn't yet know how, but I would do it.

Where would I be now were it not for my children? With only myself to fend for, the easier way to escape the pain would have been annihilation. I committed myself to them instead. This was not their fault, and they should not have to take the consequences. I determined to shield them from the haggling.

I carried on every day in normal sameness for them, but every night when they were asleep, I prayed on my knees for help through it all. I spoke with God honestly, seriously, as if I'd spoken with Alex, except that I warned Him that I was going to need a lot of help in the coming years and I expected Him to come through. He was the only source of help left. I asked for some kind of road map and promised to update Him daily. I didn't want Him to do everything, but I needed to know where to go to do what needed doing. We needed too many specifics; I would have been asking for hours. I wanted to understand why this had happened, but now it wasn't number one—I would get to it later. I asked mostly that He get us through the next day, healthy, housed, and fed. And in strange, miraculous ways we got through.

In May, a family friend accompanied Jen and Sandy home on the plane. We were overjoyed. They were all jumping, giggling, hugging, and pulling out every toy they had. In five minutes they had wrecked the living room wonderfully. They ran to the playground to find friends they had made the week before they'd left, and when they returned they all spoke at once about their adventures.

Sandy was quiet, just soaking up being home again. She followed me like a shadow with a wounded-puppy expression, one hand holding onto my skirt, the other supplying the two middle fingers she still sucked in stressful times. I held her close and whispered, "You're home, baby. It's all right. You're going to be home with Mommy forever." She seemed to perk up a little.

Alex had promised to tell them about our split before sending them home, and it seemed they were taking it surprisingly well. I decided to tell the others before Jen or Sandy did, so I called them all into the empty room and sat them in a circle so we could talk. I started by asking the girls if they had any news to tell us, and they talked about everything except the breakup. After several leading questions, I called Jen aside to ask if Daddy had told her he wasn't going to live with us any more. Her "no" came with a very puzzled look.

I asked them to listen to what I had to say, and I told them as softly as I could. I assured them, too, that I would always be with them. A pall of silence hung over our little circle. Dina, the six-year-old, one of the three who stayed, broke the silence, sobbing angrily. When I asked why she was crying, she answered, "Why is he divorcing me? What did I do? I always tried to be good."

My surprise was obvious. All I could say was that he was not divorcing them, only me because we couldn't get along any more. I said they would still visit, only not as often. We would live in two different countries, and he would send them letters. I tried to answer it for the others, too, suspecting that they must be too scared or confused to ask for themselves. During the next days they huddled together and whispered a lot, but school vacation and playmates quickly pulled them into the normal flow of life.

Why was I not surprised that Alex had broken yet another promise to avoid discomfort?

Our apartment was in a high-rise conglomerate of five buildings, fourteen stories high—504 apartments per building, 2,520 in one square block area. Some were medical or

dental offices and conglomerate rental offices. The buildings were spread out with roomy two- and three-bedroom
units. Downstairs were basement laundries and well-
equipped, fenced playgrounds with manicured lawns. I was
happy to have many neighbors and playmates for my children.

When Alex and I leased the apartment, we thought the
corner school was its greatest advantage. Every day we discovered a new advantage now. In the school was a public
library branch and a recreation program for all levels. By
night it became an adult learning center. Next to the school
was the end-of-the-line stop for a bus that went downtown
for forty cents.

Across from the school was a park where my toddlers
found playmates on the swings or in the sandbox. The older
kids played out all their fantasy adventures on wooden "fortresses" and jungle gyms. It was beautifully landscaped with
gardens, shade trees, comfortable benches, restrooms, and
water fountains. The park bordered a university that invited
locals to attend philosophy lectures. That and the library
soon became my treasured recreation.

Four blocks down the street was a series of stores for everything we could need: a bakery, a barber shop, a hair sa-
lon, a bank, a post office, a variety store, a bike shop, a shoe
store, a travel agent, a drugstore, a newsstand, a stationery
store, and a sweet shop. Two blocks farther was a high
school. Three supermarkets competed for the lowest prices
within three blocks.

We discovered them little by little during afternoon walks.
I was grateful for these nearby conveniences, especially
since we no longer had a car. Now we didn't need a car. It
began to seem that there was some strange, wonderful plan
to all this. Everything we needed was at hand, even the doctors' offices. It looked like God was coming through. All our
needs were being provided.

Perhaps, I thought, I should make a grand gesture of giving formal thanks to Him for all this help. Perhaps there was a church nearby. I had lived outside of organized religion since my teen years, but sometimes I had urges to sit in empty churches to absorb the peace. I rather liked my intimate nightly tête-à-têtes with Him, so I opted to go to the library instead.

Scanning the self-help section for books about divorce problems, I couldn't find anything to help with my dilemmas.

Suddenly a book fell from a higher shelf and grazed me on the shoulder on its way to the floor. I picked it up. The title was *Reincarnation*. What the devil is that, I thought.

I took it to a table to browse through it until the librarian returned from her break and could help me find what I needed. I was fascinated by the idea of coming back to live again as another personality. The philosophy made perfect sense. I forgot about the librarian and read on. I forgot that a neighbor was tending my kids so that I could escape for a minute to get a book. When I came up for air, two-and-a-half hours had passed and the library was closing. I had to check out the book.

I apologized to my gracious neighbor and put everybody to bed so that I could stay up to devour the book. It spoke of our spirit being the eternal part of our essence, of the importance of taking full responsibility for our actions and intentions, of the balance of cause and effect, of choosing the time and place of our return, of choosing what parents we would come through and what families we would be part of. That was a little hard to take. I would not choose a mother who would abandon me to a harsh grandmother at two, nor would I choose that grandmother. I would not *choose* to be part of that family; we had nothing in common. The best parts of my character came from total rebellion to all they believed in. Why would I choose to make myself miserable? Otherwise, I liked the concept. It felt right inside, so I began to teach the children this new concept.

I didn't stop to ask myself what Alex would think of it. Reading that book filled whatever it was in me that prompted the urges to sit in church. It felt so accurate, so much richer and truer than anything I'd ever heard. My personal talks with God and this new concept seemed more spiritual than any church. I decided to continue that way.

I wondered why I hadn't found *Reincarnation* years before.

One day in the park Jay made friends with a little boy whose mother and grandmother talked on a bench nearby. I heard the boy's grandmother scolding his mother: "If you had listened to me, it would never have happened," she said, shaking her finger. "You always had to have your own way. So now how do you feel? You should have listened to me. You should never have married him. It would never have happened."

She used the exact words of my mother and grandmother. To her, it should never have happened, but how could she know what good things had happened in that marriage that had made it all worthwhile. The pluses might have outweighed the minuses. Surely the grandmother couldn't know that, for what goes on between two married people is never totally revealed to a third. I could feel the rage swelling inside me as I identified and watched the older woman's shaking finger!

I hated hearing my mother and grandmother say that to me. Why don't you answer her, I thought-transmitted to the young mother; tell her about the things she made sure would never happen in your life!

She sat passive, ashamed, and silent, so the voice of my own rage sprung forth to answer inside myself.

"Suppose I hadn't married him. I would never have known another country nor experienced that all people are essentially the same. I would never have become really fluent in another language, nor seen how different races can live together respectfully. I would never have experienced gratitude for people who tried to make my life pleasant, nor had the chance to live a wealthy life style under the protective umbrella of a good and generous father. I would never have been able to attend a foreign university to study art— that's one promise he kept, Mother!—nor discovered that I could learn anything that I studied. I would never have learned to read a road map, find my way across four states, design a budget, resolve problems, cook a meal, clean a house, or make an independent decision. I could never have interviewed a principal to see if his or her school was suitable for my child or lived my own life style without caring what the neighbors think, and many, many more things that I never learned at home. Remember my beginnings, Mother. You didn't care if I didn't know how to shampoo my own hair when I eloped or that my husband had to teach me how to cook. And, Grandma, would I ever have discovered I had a mind I could be proud of when it was so undervalued in our family? Remember the art scholarship you wouldn't let me accept because it would cost trolley fare and a box lunch for four years? It was high time, you said, that I started bringing something in instead of wasting time on more school. College would be wasted on a girl—we only get married. Better I should get a dime-store job and contribute five dollars a week at home. Did you think how much easier life would be right now for me and my children if I had that fine arts degree?"

My rage began to dissipate as I went to the next phase of the litany. "What if indeed it had never happened? I wouldn't have these beautiful, innocent children to love. I might have married someone else and had other children, but they wouldn't be these particular children, these special children whom I love so much. These are the children I want, the ones that I had with Alex, and the only way I could have had them was with Alex. So let us have an end to these nonsense syllables 'What if it had never happened?' and accept that it did indeed happen, and for the good fortune and the ill fortune that came of it, I am now a stronger person."

I felt drained, but cleaner after playing out that scene. What anyone said about Alex loomed much larger than what he did or neglected to do. There were many more positive instances in my marriage than in my childhood, if one really began to compare. We were both immature in different ways, perhaps also egocentric, but never vicious. What hurt after the breakup was not only the bad times but also the special times that I knew would never be again. I had done a lot of growing up within the marriage, but in some things I had been incredibly naïve.

Most damaging was one of my misconceptions.

I had seen a zillion movies during my most impressionable years. Grandma paid a teen-ager ticket and candy money to take me to the movies three times a week so that the family could get a few hours' peace. I remember at seven being quite taken with biblical movies where women would follow their men saying, "Whither thou goest I will go, and thy people shall be my people and thy God my God." I got very emotional. I took it out of context into my relationship with Alex, immediately embraced his country, his people, his language, and made an honest attempt to embrace his atheism. The atheism lasted for two experimental months until Christmas Eve when I got dressed, called a cab, and went off alone to the heady ritualistic splendor of a Catholic midnight mass to plunge into the incense of God and fulfill my longing.

He received me with open arms from my short vacation. He knew I'd be back.

It didn't matter that I wasn't Catholic.

Why were all these memories coming up? It felt as though I was getting ready for a trip and had overstuffed my luggage. Some of this stuff was no longer useful and I had to release it. But, like old clothing, I had to take just one more look, perhaps just try it on once more to see why I ever liked it, to feel the last mote of nostalgia, and thank it for whatever good I had gotten from it before I threw it away.

Discarding the "Whither thou goest . . . " myth was overdue. I was ready to meet the world on its terms and negotiate with it for our best good. No more following, no more surrendering power. I blessed the part of me that thought it was a good myth to live by, but I had grown a notch and it was too small for me now to fit into.

2

One Day at a Time: Testing, Testing!

If you do not change direction, you may end up where
you are heading.   –Lao Tse

A S I rearranged my closet to hang the children's better
clothing, I discovered Alex's Harris tweed overcoat. I'd forgotten it was there. When we had last talked, I'd groped to
make conversation, asking if I should send it.

"In this climate? I have no use for that coat," he insisted.
"Do what you want with it."

The faintest trace of his aftershave wafted from the lapel,
conjuring images of us in happier times. I pulled it closer
and snuggled into it, wrapping it around me as if it were his
arms. The yearning for times that could never again be retrieved mixed with loneliness and fear of the enormous task
ahead of me. How would I ever be able to do it? Why hadn't

my life proceeded on a carefree course like the lives of my friends? Why was I getting all the hard stuff to handle?

Uncontrollable sobs erupted. I clutched the coat sleeves as relentlessly as I clutched the memories of better times. If I surrendered those memories, only the wrenching, tearing loneliness would remain.

His scent evoked the scene of our elopement. I had rushed home from work, bathed, and put on my nicest dress—the azure blue silk that I'd sewn the year before. I styled my hair and make-up carefully and packed some clothes in a suitcase. Grandma confronted me, threatening me to abandon my marriage plans, but I prevailed. I was old enough—all of nineteen—and I'd asked her to accept it and come along. She'd followed me out to the cab where Alex waited, shouting, "You'll pay for not obeying me. I hope you have all girls so you'll know what misery is." I raged back at her, "You're the one who's made life miserable, for Mother and for me. We're the only girls you've raised. We know you hate girls. Now your misery's over. Mother left and I'm leaving. But I'll tell you this: no matter how many girls I have, I'll love them and teach them to be proud to be girls."

I pulled away, shaken, from her slurs at Alex, and we set out for Algiers.

We weren't sure where we'd end up. Algiers was one of a row of towns across the river, notoriously bulging with justices of the peace ready to marry anyone with a license. We planned to knock on doors until we found one who would marry us late that Saturday night. The taxi driver—our cohort and witness—loved the adventure. He patiently chauffeured us until we found a JP in pajamas willing to marry us. His wife, in robe and curlers, was our second witness. It was a scene from a '40s' movie!

The memory of that wonderful time pained me. It was gone, never to be recaptured. If Alex were to call now, I thought, I'd probably go running to him! Why couldn't I get over him? Every time I thought I was free of him, some half-forgotten memory would surface and pull me back. When would I ever stop crying over him?

I muffled the sobs so that I wouldn't wake Rafi.

Drying my tears, I thought of sending the coat to the cleaner's in case he changed his mind and wanted it again. Without his cologne scent, it would be less likely to trigger memories.

I emptied the pockets and found what looked like a wad of receipts. I opened them to see if it was something important that I should forward to him. "Mr. and Mrs. Alex Ortega" caught my eye. They were different hotel bills with dates during the three weeks that he had sent us ahead to the East Coast. Slowly the truth dawned. Slowly I began to understand how pitifully naïve I was to expect Alex to change.

I felt as if I'd had the breath knocked out of me. I sat down to keep from reeling off balance. I closed my eyes to blot out the images the memories had evoked, and as I imagined erasing them all from a blackboard, they disappeared, and the space began to fill with quiet rage.

I snatched the coat off the hanger and emptied the pockets. I washed the tears from my face and changed into a clean jumpsuit. My neighbor tended Rafi for ten minutes, while I took the coat downstairs to the superintendent's office.

"Can I help you, Ma'am?" a janitor asked.

"Sure," I responded, "do you know anyone who'd like a fine, expensive, almost new, British tweed overcoat?"

He was thrilled to accept it.

The part of Alex that was left inside me finally died.

We settled into a new way of life. School was opening and the children were excited. Jay started morning kindergarten, Dina went to first grade, Sandy repeated second, and Jen went to fourth. Their playmates kept them happily busy on weekends. I was the unchanging constant on home base.

Rafi was not yet two, and it was a relief having quiet

mornings with only one toddler. The others sensed, without understanding why, that he was my greatest concern. He was an infant when Alex left. Alex had hardly looked at him since birth. He would grow up without even a memory of his father, deducing from the silence his father's total rejection.

Alex wanted no more children, yet he took no precautions. When he realized my pregnancy was real, he approached several colleagues seeking an abortion. When he found a willing cohort, he insisted I go along "just to talk." I warned him I wouldn't do it, but he felt sure he could coax me to do what *he* wished.

They were very patronizing, laying out the advantages for me. I interrupted to tell his colleague I was into my fifth month. He paled, went silent, pressed his lips together angrily, then turned on Alex for not telling him this.

"Don't you care that I could lose my license if she had complications? Dammit, Alex, count me out of this."

Alex smoldered at me, but the more he manipulated, the more determined I became to protect this child. Someone had to care for this little one!

No matter how I had tried to make things right in our marriage, nothing worked. I had spent the entire pregnancy despairing for the fate of us all. I feared for this little child more than for my other children. When they reminisced about Daddy, Rafi would not even have a mental image from which to draw.

I hid the scars that Alex left on my heart so that the children wouldn't be reminded of theirs.

Who could guess that our lives would fall apart so suddenly? That he would leave his job? Leave us? That the car would be repossessed? That the kids and I would be stuck here alone?

Alone—amid more than two thousand families!

Although our needs were now within reach without a car,

we lacked money. It would become a familiar refrain, for
what Alex sent barely covered rent and a meager food supply. No extras. Caring neighbors donated outgrown clothing
and my great aunt filled the constant need for shoes. Nothing remained for medical expenses.

I had learned medical terminology and symptoms by listening to years of conversations between my doctor
husband and his doctor father. I was grateful, too, that Alex
had left his PDR—*Physician's Desk Reference*—behind. I remembered treatments for various children's conditions, but
allopathic medicines were unattainable without prescriptions and money. I had to become resourceful.

I scanned the library for alternative home remedies. I
learned a lot, but the first time I had to use the knowledge at
2:00 a.m. for Sandy's raging fever was one of the scariest
moments of my life.

Years of observing my family worship doctors as gods of
healing, years of brainwashing about the dangers of self-
treatment exploded in my mind as I held onto her burning
little hand. I coaxed her out of her feverish lethargy long
enough to feed her honeyed saffron tea, and I sang her a
soothing song as I held her on my lap and sponged her
flushed little body. She fell asleep in my arms. The suspense
was terrible. I didn't know how she would respond. We were
alone with neither encouragement nor consolation. Finally
she awoke in a drenching sweat, pushed off the covers, and
asked for water. The fever had finally broken. I felt triumphant, humble, grateful! What an awesome responsibility!

I kept vigil and continued the treatment round the clock
until the fever ended.

Doing it once did not raise my confidence. For a long
time it terrified me, for my child's life hung in the balance. I
began to relax into it after about a year. I began to sense a
familiar, guiding presence. I was not alone.

Even if we'd had money for a doctor, my trust was low. I
remembered complaining to Alex when I took Dina to a

pediatrician for an earache, "He forgot to examine her ears and became irked when I reminded him." Alex had replied, "Oh, he might have been just a little hung over. Anyway, that's why they call it *practicing* medicine. He'll learn eventually."

I found a competent and committed doctor who surprised me by extending professional courtesy to us by not billing us because we were a physician's family, despite our divorce. Many times, however, we had no money to fill prescriptions. Sometimes he gave us sample medication, sometimes not. For serious conditions, I'd borrow money for prescriptions. For those less serious I used alternative remedies and prayer. My alternative approach steadily improved.

My therapist was right. I'd been rearing the children alone all along, even before the divorce. It was beginning to look like my big job in life, and I was getting progressively better at it.

Alex remarried on the island almost as soon as our divorce was final. I realized why he wanted a quick divorce and why he refused to face me. It was someone else's turn now. I was glad mine was over. He never took time to write to his children.

One day a neighbor suggested that I put notices on the laundry room bulletins for tenants who needed sewing services. Before I finished posting the notices, my phone was ringing. At first I earned small amounts of money that supplemented what Alex provided. Word of mouth soon brought a steady stream of work. I was glad that I'd stood firm against Alex's pressure to sell my sewing machine with the rest of the furniture when we moved east!

It was more than "luck." Everything we needed was put before us. Again!

I was so moved to gratitude one night that I even gave

thanks for my rigid upbringing. Living nineteen years under Grandma's reign with no margin for error proved useful now. How would I have managed this without rigorous training? The memory evoked a feeling of resistance and childhood rebellion. I remembered *Reincarnation*. The big lure was that if I really did well this time, I would *never* have to return as a child again! That would be worth *any* effort!

Despite years away from Grandma's domination, the residual anxiety persisted. I seethed every time I remembered the scene of her final rage. Now she urged me in letters not to be permissive with the children while they were little, to be sure to lay down laws. I'd had enough of laws. We had enough to deal with now. There was no time to worry about permissiveness or laws. We had to live each day as it came. I strived to simplify our life, not to complicate it.

Since I left her stronghold, I lived in fresh air, breathed freely, moved and grew into my own beingness. She had mothered me since I was two, nursing me through illness many nights, sparing my body only to wither my spirit in other ways. Life under Grandma's reign was a daily struggle for survival, and I had learned well. She ruled by fear, never understanding the kind of child I was. In her obsession to break my "willfulness," to do a better job than my mother could, she was attempting to annihilate my very creativity. My strength of will was my survival.

I was determined not to pass my neuroses and fears onto my children. They didn't know that the night light was for me—I was still afraid of the dark. When I walked them three miles to swim classes and cheered them on to win trophies for breaststroke, relays, and butterfly races, they didn't know I couldn't swim. I hid from them my irrational fear of snakes and my monthly anxiety when the rent money arrived late. My friends lived comfortably without fears of darkness, water, poverty, or snakes, and I wanted that tranquillity for my children. I would deal with my own childhood wounds in time, quietly. I would rear my children with minimal damage.

Rebellion led me to reject Grandma's methods and do the opposite with my children. It worked well, but a haunting dream intruded. She was a Gestapo captain assigned to train me to be astute and thorough, to walk a narrow line with no margin for error for a crucial, demanding mission. I remembered snickering when I awoke.

Privately, I had to admit that her training saved our lives. What I couldn't understand was how a traumatic process could turn into a plus. I couldn't quell the gratitude I secretly felt.

"Mommy, why doesn't Daddy come here any more?" asked Dina one day.

It was a test. I was angry at Alex. I could easily have demolished him with words. Leave it to Dina to come up with prize questions!

Should I tell my children the truth so that they could see which of us really cared about them? Should I make him look good by making excuses for him? I wanted to tell the truth, but I couldn't bear for them to feel abandoned or unloved.

Feeling abandoned by my mother to an overstrict grandmother was devastating. I felt a great void of yearning for my mother and had made a conscious decision to be the kind of mother to my children that I would have wanted. In doing that, the void filled somewhat. As I lovingly nurtured them, I felt I was getting some of the mother love I needed.

So I opted for a fabrication that, though defending Alex, left their self-esteem intact.

"Daddy would love to visit, but he has a lot of very sick patients who need his care. It might be a long time, but he can't leave until they're well. He might not even have time to write letters." I covered the absence of letters, too. "You know, Dina, sometimes it makes you feel better when you miss someone if you write them a letter first instead of waiting for them to write to you. It makes you remember the fun you had together, and it almost feels as if it brings them back."

It wasn't total fabrication. Alex really cared a lot about his patients. Nothing was too much trouble for them. I remembered envying them.

It satisfied her. She ran to tell her sisters to write Daddy a letter so that he wouldn't feel lonely, and they did.

The important thing was that they still felt loved.

I walked Rafi up Irvin Street one afternoon and discovered a photography studio. I liked the showcase samples, so I went in to ask if the photographer needed help in painting his portraits.

In New Orleans I had learned to paint portrait photos to make them look like oils on canvas. During Alex's final year in medical school, I'd also found extra piecework in a French Quarter studio that added to my skills. The photographer had occasional bridal portraits that needed painting. Otherwise he worked in color film, photographing entertainers whose racy lives had prematurely aged their faces. Since color negatives could not be retouched, a make-up artist applied greasepaint to cover the facial flaws.

One day he called me, frantic. His make-up artist had fled to avoid retaliation for gambling debts. He had four sittings booked, and no one to do their faces. He begged me to come in and try to do on faces what I did on portraits. I went.

It worked. I had learned another skill, and he was happy. Later when I enrolled in oils at the island university, both skills carried over into portraiture.

The photographer wanted samples, so he supplied two portraits, paints, brushes, and solutions. I stayed up late painting after the kids' bedtime so that I could deliver them quickly. They were not completely dry, but he liked them and promised me work. Two weeks later, he brought a steady flow of work, picked up finished work, and left a check. It was enjoyable work that paid well.

When word traveled, another photographer brought me work, and my sole overhead was paint.

About the same time, the school needed teachers for the adult program and asked if I could teach knitting. I agreed, despite stage fright. My forte was adjusting dimensions on intricate patterns for a perfect fit. I gained respect and confidence in this initiation into teaching, and my family and I were almost self-supporting.

The lure of health insurance dredged up thoughts about a "regular" job. If I tried harder, maybe I *could* find someone brave enough to care for five little kids every day. When I factored lunch, transportation, child care, and clothing into entry level take-home pay, I had twenty dollars a week net. It wasn't worth the stress and problems it would create. My little jobs worked better and kept me on the scene. I opted for the status quo.

After a year I began a relationship with Mike.

It boosted my self-esteem to have his attention focused on me, to have someone to talk with, to feel in rapport with, to go to the movies with, and to share simple things.

I went into this liaison knowing that Mike was married. He'd assured me that it was over, that he and his wife hadn't communicated in months and were "in process" of filing for a divorce. It was only a matter of months, he'd said, for a quick no-fault divorce and a year for it to be final. I liked the year's wait. It would give us time to know each other and time for me to see how he got along with the children.

I made it very clear to him that my children came first in my life and that I had very specific ideas about rearing them. My children would not be disciplined by every male friend I had, as was the case with my divorced friends. My children would know that I would be the constant in charge. I needed to nurture each child's individuality, each one's own kind of creativity, and each one's way of learning. I didn't want a string of paper dolls; I wanted individuals, and I was willing to make whatever effort it took.

"Are you sure you want this involvement, Mike?" I asked

him one day. "It's not as though I'm the only one who has to like you. It won't work unless we all do. I won't play referee. It's a lot to take on and I wouldn't blame you if it shakes you up, but I'm the only stability my children have and they come first."

Mike knew where I was coming from and accepted the terms.

When his wife needed surgery, he couldn't see how he could initiate divorce proceedings until she recovered. I agreed, telling myself it was only a matter of two or three months more.

Six months into the relationship I was pregnant. I couldn't believe it. I waited weeks before I told him, to be sure it was true. When I told him, he was furious.

"I thought you said you couldn't get pregnant any more!" I was as puzzled as he. Three years earlier after Rafi was born, I'd had a tubal "ligation." The doctor who performed it wanted to save me the trauma of a cutting, in deference to his colleague Alex, so decided to *tie* off my tubes with fancy little sterling silver clips. He assured me that they would do exactly what a ligation did. I didn't think it was possible to get pregnant again. Obviously a clip had slipped! I didn't know what to say to Mike.

He became increasingly defensive.

The next week was an ordeal of silence between us.

"What do you plan to do about it?" he asked one afternoon, as though it were my problem. "You're not going through with it, are you?"

I walked over to the window and gazed out into infinity wondering what to answer. The faith I'd put in him—in his intentions, in the plans we'd made together—was slipping away. He spoke as though we were strangers who had come together one night and had an accident. I was surprised and hurt, but face to face with my naïveté once again.

When would I ever learn? What had I stepped into?

I knew Mike had yearned for a child of his own, but there

was a fertility problem. I remembered how he'd criticized Alex for "not appreciating a wife who could give him children." His defensiveness now was an abrupt about-face.

He accused me of contriving the pregnancy to force him into marriage. He didn't know I wasn't sure if I wanted to marry him. Seeing this side of him made me wonder even more.

My mind wandered through a blurred maze. My eyes traced the shapes of raindrops that trickled down the window. "How would I manage with yet another child?" I asked myself. "Maybe I should consider ending this eight-week pregnancy. Isn't it better than to bring in a child I can't take care of? It certainly looks as though I'd be doing this alone again. But I feel so bonded with this child already. Why is this bonding happening so early? When I go to bed at night, I can almost feel this little child, happy, filling me with love, hanging on, so glad to be here. How can I end this? I feel as though I know this little one already."

I turned to see Mike waiting for my answer, expecting me to comply with his wishes. For a moment I was tempted to say whatever would postpone the issue, to keep peace, but I had promised to be true to myself even if it meant disrupting the quiet and confronting the consequences.

"I know what you want me to say, Mike," I heard myself saying, "but I can't. There's a lot going on that you don't understand. I hardly understand it. It's as if I already know this baby. It's never happened like this before. I know you're going to be upset, but I'm keeping this baby. We would both appreciate your taking some responsibility to help in some way, but if not, we'll handle it."

"Why are you doing this to me? You can't do this," he shouted. "It'll complicate my life."

"I didn't hear you worrying about that before! It's *my* body, Mike. I make the decisions about it and I'm keeping this baby," I repeated. "I can't be guided by what complicates your life."

He panicked. "Then you can't name me as the father. You've got to make up something. If that should be announced in the newspapers, I'm finished. I can't be named; that's all there is to it," he insisted.

"All right," I said, "you won't be named. I have a perfectly good name of my own to give it, and I'll be happy to do so. Just think about what you'll answer when this child grows up and asks you why it doesn't have your name. Can you handle that?"

Should I have said that? My pride wouldn't allow me to accept something not given from the heart, but here I was making that decision for my child as well. And pride wouldn't let me retract it.

A very sheepish look came over his face, as if he'd exposed a side of himself he'd rather keep secret. He turned slowly and left in silence.

I had no way of knowing whether or not he would return. It surprised me that even without knowing what the next step would be, I didn't go to pieces.

He was back after four days, repentant, but things were never the same again. I had seen something in Mike's reaction, beyond his words, that made me uneasy, though I wasn't sure what it was. I held it in reserve for later, knowing that in time I would understand it.

He was disappointed that I wasn't overjoyed over his return. It was good to see him, but I had a lot to do. He was an adult who could take care of himself. I had to look out for my children.

The times were not tolerant of out-of-wedlock pregnancies. I didn't want to be the cause of my children being targeted with demeaning remarks. Also, if Alex's family found out about this, I feared they would try to get custody of my children on moral grounds and the courts would probably grant it. I had no idea how to hide this pregnancy from friends and neighbors. I needed help, but I didn't know specifically what to ask for, so I asked God to handle it.

Once I got past morning sickness, it proceeded as all my other pregnancies. I blossomed. My energy increased. My hair became thicker and glistened. My complexion glowed to translucence. My eyes brightened, my lashes grew thicker. I beamed with good health. My feelings, however, were very raw and tender, my vulnerability quotient quite high. Knowing it was hormonal didn't ease it.

Near the end of the pregnancy, I got news that my grandmother had died. I preferred that my family not know of my pregnancy. They knew I didn't have money for child care and airfare to go to New Orleans for the funeral, so they didn't expect me. Why hadn't they told me she was so close to dying? I would have liked at least to have talked to her while she was alive. I still hated her harshness, but I wanted her to know I appreciated her efforts. I wasn't interested in her funeral. Though I never had a chance to say good-by, I knew I would have a lot to say to Grandma.

My mother gave her the best of care when she left the hospital. She described the dress she had bought for Grandma's burial, "a beautiful gray and pink chiffon dress like she had always wanted." I asked why she'd never bought that dress while Grandma was alive to enjoy it. That was my family's pattern. They bickered daily and at the final moment made a grand superficial gesture to numb their guilt for being hateful and vindictive to each other in life.

I was glad to be far from their entanglements.

When I went to bed that night, I began talking to my grandmother. I had a feeling she could hear me even if she had died. I lay in the dark and imagined us face to face. I told her of things I remembered, things I hated, and things I appreciated, of my three lovely little girls who filled my heart with joy. I was sorry she couldn't see her girls that way, but I thanked her for doing the best she knew how, what she thought was best for me. I felt lighter. Her face softened into a loving smile.

I returned my focus to dealing with my pregnancy.

It was unusual that I didn't "show" until the final four weeks, so I continued my activities unnoticed. The children knew, but we kept our secret to surprise our friends. I had managed to get discreetly to and from the doctor's office and when I finally began to look pregnant, I told everybody that I had a windfall of work that would keep me out of circulation for a couple of weeks.

Late one night in the final weeks I had Mike take me to a food store in a different neighborhood to stock up for the duration. The laundry and the dog's walks were the only chores to be done outside. Jen agreed to do the laundry if I sorted it. The others agreed to take turns walking Skipper, our dog. I then settled in to await the onset of labor.

Mike was glad I took those precautions. He feared talk would reach his wife if I was too visible. It created more friction between us because I refused to lead my life to guard his secret. "Doesn't your wife ever ask where you go all the time?" I inquired one evening. "Between work and the time you spend here, she must notice your absence."

He pulled himself up to his full height and proudly said, "She wouldn't dare. She was raised never to question her husband's whereabouts, never to ask about his business."

"I'm not like that, you know. I'd ask. I'd want to know. Who would raise a daughter that way?"

"She knows she's better off not knowing," he said cryptically.

"Why does she know that, Mike?"

He didn't answer and I dropped the subject. I didn't like seeing him play the big man when I knew how he evaded responsibility.

My fear of losing my children made me particularly vulnerable during that pregnancy. I had to take precautions. Not for him, for them. I knew that as soon as the baby was born I would have my body back and my hormones normal, and I could stand strong before anyone.

As my due date drew near, the last thing I prayed for was

to get out of the building unnoticed to get to the hospital. I prayed to the Blessed Virgin Mary for this because I thought she would better understand a mother-to-mother condition. I felt her nearness when I prayed, and I was sure it would be answered. I imagined going into labor late at night when everyone was in bed, escaping to the hospital in the dead of night, unseen. Instead, I awoke early one Sunday morning, the day before my birthday, in labor a week early.

What happened to my prayer? Was it because I wasn't Catholic? Or because I chose someone I thought could best relate to my problem? Was that wrong? I was disappointed.

It was broad daylight. Everyone would be out on a Sunday morning. Mike called early and was surprised that it was already time to go. I was upset. After getting through the entire pregnancy without any repercussions to my children, now that it was about to culminate, the whole neighborhood would see me leave for the hospital.

Mike brought my suitcase to the car, then returned for me. I stepped into the elevator, apprehensively, only to find it empty. Now I only had to face the prying eyes on the sidewalk.

By the time we got outside, a thick cover of fog hung so low that I couldn't recognize anyone who passed by me, nor they me. I exited clear and free, once again protected.

Lisa was born eleven hours before my own birthday, a beautiful eight-and-one-half-pound, dark-eyed beauty with thick, black ringlets covering her head. I wondered where she had hidden during eight months; however, I was grateful. A taxi brought us home two days later to welcoming siblings.

Yes, I thought, she had to be here. She'll blend right in— one more is hardly noticeable. We'll make it just fine.

Mike beamed when he saw her. He never again mentioned the outcome of his wife's surgery or the divorce status. I no longer felt guilty about seeing someone else's husband—I was no threat; the attachment was too weak to last. I suspected that Mike had never intended to file for divorce. He might have wanted to—I think he liked our life style better than his clannish existence—but he lacked the courage to take the step.

I was beginning to understand what I saw in him that repelled me the day we argued over the pregnancy. It was a lack of courage to confront life. We continued in a bland friendship as I reclaimed my energy and focus.

Three years later, when the sewing work had slowed, I responded to an ad offering samples of a California cosmetic line. I liked them. The company needed door-to-door salespeople. With another child, extra money would help. Lisa was not yet in school and was delighted to come with me to "visit" the people on our block—all two thousand-plus families! We did rounds in the morning, came home for lunch and a short nap, and did more rounds until the kids came home from school. Weather never deterred us. We were always sheltered.

There was an endless supply of customers, but after several months I felt restless with the same routine. I began to organize afternoon cosmetic parties to do on these faces what I had done in French Quarter studios with stage make-up. It was more creative than simply selling, and I sold more in a party than in two weeks door-to-door. With one or two parties a week, I could spend more time in the park with Lisa and still earn surplus money.

I wasn't deceiving myself that I was doing prestigious work. I simply needed money for our expenses, and the children were too small to be left alone while I earned it away from home. Mike never seemed to have any money for Lisa's needs.

I began to notice signs of a habit of his—not alcohol like Alex's, but gambling.

He bet on everything—hockey, football, World Series, Little League, Olympics, and especially horse races. Couldn't I pick men!? He was looking more and more like Alex, just a variation on the theme. Once he arrived with a bandaged hand, severely lacerated from putting it through a radio that broadcast a winner he hadn't bet on. I had never seen this violent side of him. He had always been very gentle, soft-spoken and protective, except to those who created problems for me. Then there was the contradictory cowardly side of him.

I was concerned about his hand until I learned how it had happened.

"You couldn't care less what happens to me," he complained.

"It looks to me like you're what's happening to you, Mike. All you have to do is walk away from it."

"But you used to care," he continued.

"I care, Mike, but I can't do it for you. I'm too busy trying to meet our needs. I already went through my own pain of growing up. You've got to stop postponing yours."

"You don't understand the fascination of this. I'll tell you what. Why don't we go to the track next weekend? You'll see how easy it is to catch the fever."

I had always liked horses, though not in the way that he did. I'd rented horses with school friends to ride along the levees just outside New Orleans, where we raced them full speed. The levees were artificial walls of earth built around the city and its neighboring parishes, like the Great Wall of China, to keep the Mississippi off the land at flood stage. The levee tops had wide, flat surfaces, free of obstacles, ideal for racing horses.

Riding was incredibly freeing—like flying through the universe. That is, until the day something frightened my horse and he reared up, dumping me off his back. I went limping home with a damaged coccyx. My grandmother's ire came swiftly for ignoring her rules, but despite her threats, I was riding on the levee again as soon as my back healed.

I humored Mike and went to the track. I was curious to see exactly how he was when he caught the "fever" and how powerful was its pull on him.

He ridiculed me for taking four dollars. It was all I could afford to play with, enough to bet minimum on two races. He insisted I couldn't possibly enjoy it that way.

"How much did you bring?" I asked.

"Never mind," he chuckled, quickly changing the subject. "Let me show you how to review a racing form."

He explained the form and the odds, then told me to choose a horse for the second race. I chose one whose name I liked, completely disregarding the statistics.

"Why did you choose that one?"

"I like its name," I replied.

He tried to hide another chuckle.

I bet two dollars on my horse. Mike secretly placed his bet at a different window. It seemed part of the mystique.

Watching the race through binoculars, it was hard for me to keep my horse in view. I enjoyed seeing all the horses run in top form. When it was over, my horse had come in second and Mike's had come in sixth. I had fun. He was disappointed.

I decided to wait until the afternoon races to bet my other two dollars and just enjoy watching the other races. Mike studied the form intensely and bet on every race. Each time another horse won, his silence deepened. I could feel an explosive energy building as the day progressed.

With only three races left, I bet my last two dollars on another horse whose name I liked. He saw no humor in it at this point and again placed his bet at a different window.

"Are you losing a lot, Mike?"

He shot me a look that told me I'd asked the wrong question.

"This one will make up for all my losses," he answered. "Just be quiet and let's watch the race."

I dreaded his attitude if his horse didn't win this time. I

was getting tired of his gloom and anger every time he lost a bet. Why couldn't he just quit?

My horse came in first and I won twenty dollars. I was jumping up and down with excitement while he became more angry. His had come in fourth.

"Pick this horse for the next race," he advised. "He's a sure win."

"I'm not betting any more, Mike. I spent my betting money. I'm taking my winnings home."

He mumbled about it being no fun to go to the track with me, and he made another bet. His mood became blacker and blacker as he lost that race and the last. I don't know how much he had bet, but he lost every penny of it. It seemed to me the worst way to have fun at a race track.

By the time we left the track, he had told me very emphatically not to speak to him on the way home. When I got home on safe territory, I told him to leave. He was too enraged, too intense, too negative, and I didn't want him in my space.

So that was his "fever." It seemed pretty masochistic to lose all your money and get madder and madder all day. It might have been fun had he not become so impossible. He didn't see it as a problem, but I wanted no part of it. It didn't have me in a stranglehold.

The next day I gratefully went back to my routine—the photography painting that exercised my creativity, the evening classes that challenged my mind, and the cosmetic parties that were fun—all of which provided for us. My track winnings bought three pairs of shoes on a sale.

Materially, there wasn't much that I needed to ask for any more, so I prayed for the children's health, for mine so that I could take care of them, for energy, stamina, and clarity, and for an occasional day off from head-counting. Again, I was grateful.

I began sensing that Alex's health would not hold out

long, so I got an office job to cover child support should he become seriously disabled. His life style took a heavy toll.

Home circumstances were changing. Lisa, six, was in school all day. Jen was in high school nearby and agreed to pick up Lisa and Rafi on the way home and tend them for an hour and a half until I got home. It worked well. I continued the other jobs after hours. The money helped and for once we had health insurance.

While I was visiting my mother the following year, Mike called to say that he had intercepted a telegram that arrived for me with a brief message: *Alex died at 6:00 p.m.* I stood numb, waiting to see what my reaction would be, but there was none. I decided to tell the children after the visit. I didn't want to hear Mother's litany about Alex.

He had married three times and fathered three more children. I knew how he lived, and over the years his mother had mentioned his health in her letters. He suffered four coronaries at different times, but each one occurred when he was on duty in the hospital and he was quickly revived. He succumbed to the fifth, which happened at his home. Liver damage and artery problems, alcohol related, finished him.

I felt sad, but I didn't sink into old memories. I felt worse for the children—they wouldn't know how to react. They hadn't seen Alex in so long that they probably didn't remember what he looked like. Rafi even had never had a memory of him.

I had pleaded many times with his psychiatrist friend Manuel to help him get therapy for his alcoholism.

"Sometimes it's better not to tamper with it," Manuel replied. "When you eliminate one way of acting out, you risk opening up a worse one."

It was very cryptic. I wondered why, if one condition could be treated, whatever it opened up couldn't be treated as well. The consensus was that it was better to have a drunken genius. Well, now they had a dead one. What a terrible waste! He had been a good, caring healer for many patients.

Weeks later we were informed that Alex had left nothing but debts. No will, no insurance, no provisions whatever for any of his children. I wasn't surprised. I had learned not to expect anything from him. But I was angry at this final indifference to our children.

I was promoted to a better position and was soon able to buy a car. Nothing fancy, but an attractive, mechanically sound car that would fill our transportation needs. The kids became very cooperative in helping take care of it after I suggested they name the car. Having a name made it, for them, more than an inanimate object.

When summer came, we piled into our car and spent my vacation week at a seashore beach house just off the boardwalk. It was my first vacation in eighteen years and the first the children had ever had. We had a glorious time. After that we drove every Saturday to a nearby beach to soak up the sun and relax in the sea air, filling our lives with simple pleasures.

I ended up with surplus money and saw a chance to claim my dream of college, a dream I'd saved for for many years since I quit school in a rage when Grandma destroyed my scholarship.

College admissions required that I pass GEDs first since I had no diploma. After two full days of GED testing, I passed and was admitted to the spring semester. I could hardly wait the three months until January.

The kids caught my excitement when I told them. Mike, however, became very sullen and made sarcastic remarks about going back to school.

"You didn't tell me you were planning to do this. Are you making plans in secret now? Don't you think you've been out of school too long to go back now? Do you want to fail and make a fool of yourself in front of all those college kids?"

I wasn't concerned about making a fool of myself. I didn't care who saw me stumble! I wanted this too much to fail. Failing wouldn't make me want it less. I would do it or repeat it until I succeeded.

I knew Mike wouldn't know how to relate to me if I had a college degree and he didn't. Did he think I'd turn into a different person overnight? Did he expect me to give up my dream to spare his ego? It began to seem a lot like Alex leaving the junior partnership rather than answering to a female boss. I was tired of men with ego problems. I refused to be held back.

When his objections failed to alter my plan, there was more overt friction between us. He began to lecture me.

"It's your place to stay home and raise your children, not to chase after college degrees," he insisted. "What kind of a mother are you? Men need college degrees, not women. You need a man to take care of you. Have you forgotten what it's like to be a woman?"

Mr. Hyde again! He followed me around nagging until I could no longer stand it.

"Mike, I'm not interested in your ideas about what men do and what women do. I've been doing men's and women's things for so long that I'm no longer sure about gender headings, nor do I care. Colleges are full of women, and men are cheering them on. I take care of myself and my children; that's the kind of mother I am. And I've decided to gift myself with this opportunity for a long-cherished dream."

In my mind's eye I saw Grandma ready to slap my face, "You willful child!" But the scenario changed; I was responding. "My willfulness is saving us in difficult circumstances, Grandma. It isn't always bad, you know. When Uncle Lucas does it, you call it determination, but when I do it, it's willful! You must agree it's served us well since Alex left."

The relationship deteriorated into two or three visits a

week. Mike would visit Lisa and make sarcastic comments about "Lisa's coed mother" as though I were not present. Lisa tensed, realizing something uncomfortable was going on.

All evening I would hear, "Lisa baby, get Daddy that pen" or "Get Daddy that ashtray."

It drove me mad. I finally asked, "Mike, can't you relate to Lisa in any other way? Maybe you could read one of her books to her or look at the finger paintings she made this afternoon."

"That's your job. You're her mother," he snapped.

"And what are you—her master? Are you grooming her to be your servant?" I stormed. "Are you teaching her that she exists to wait on you?" It was obvious I wouldn't permit that.

The frail fiber on which the relationship hung finally broke. We both knew it was doomed. We ended it without fanfare.

The only thing that troubled me was that Lisa never asked about her father after that night. I probed and prompted, just to get her to talk it out, but she always ran off to play when I brought it up.

I felt no regrets about leaving Mike. I couldn't help him learn to relate to a little girl when he wouldn't open enough to admit he didn't know how. I was on a roll, growing fast. Mike was static, cemented in a hung-over pattern of an earlier century and trying to pull me in with him. He was a traditionalist, except when it wasn't convenient. The relationship would have ended earlier had the pregnancy not occurred. It was never strong. I had lost respect for him for his cowardice.

I could go forward alone now or slide back. It was my call. I no longer feared doing it alone. I was well practiced.

I chose to go forward and began to savor the feeling of total freedom.

That night as I lay in bed looking out the window at a full

moon, I thought about all that had happened since Alex and
I broke up. The pattern was familiar. I was devastated and it
had taken me so long to get over it, to let him go. Too young,
too naïve, I was caught up in the myth that I wasn't complete without him. Then I couldn't pull out of the loneliness.
The same loneliness made me yearn to feel complete again.
I didn't know how to stop feeling lonely unless I found
someone to fill up the void and complete my life.

It was a myth of an earlier time, when two halves came
together to make a whole. The same codependency led me
to enter into a relationship with Mike, so that our halves
could come together to be completed. How strange this
sounded now! How did I ever get the idea that I needed another person to complete myself? Awareness of all the
things that I'd done myself strengthened me. I wasn't feeling needy now. It was time to begin growing into completion
by filling my inner voids with self-esteem and reaffirming
my worthiness to do so.

Mike never returned or called, not even to see Lisa.

Several months later I was still introspecting to sort it out.
Had we each come together to learn courage to face our
lives and follow our hearts? I chose to participate; nobody
made me do so. I chose to believe him, though I knew he
was married. I accepted the responsibility for my choices. I
believed that Mike sincerely wanted a better liaison than
his marriage provided and he said that he had found it, but
he lacked the courage to confront the issue and make the
change, as well as the courage to be honest with me. I believed he cared about me and he loved Lisa, but we were at
the back of a line with too many people or issues ahead of
us in Mike's list of priorities. I was alone again, but it didn't
frighten me this time. I was through with dishonest rela-
tionships. Everything had to be out on the table under
bright lights or I wouldn't touch it.

I would continue my life and wish him well with his.

I couldn't be so generous with Alex. My feelings toward

my former husband were anger mixed with hurt that dug deep, despite his death. It stood as an obstacle on my path. I knew I had to eventually forgive and release him to go forward, but the wounds were still raw. Just as I couldn't let go earlier of memories of our good times, I couldn't let go now of memories of his deception and abandonment. It hung before me, begging closure, but I needed to see it in a different context and it wasn't yet time.

Nevertheless, I refused to brood on it.

Life was exciting. I had no complaints. We were all healthy, modestly prosperous, learning and growing into the flow of life. The children were doing well in school, happy in their activities, winning swim trophies, making friends, occasionally visiting Alex's parents in New York or on the island, and thriving with one caring parent.

I was rearing them without gender roles. No "men do this and women do that" in our house. People were people, and one did what needed to be done. Jay had learned to cook on scout camp-outs and loved cooking at home. He was also good at child care, as Lisa quickly realized. He learned to adjust his new pants on my sewing machine by watching me. The girls and I could hang shelves, install door locks, assemble furniture, and rewire lamps. They were learning resourcefulness and self-sufficiency. My girls would never have to marry to be taken care of, and my sons would never need wives just to keep house for them. They could all marry for much better reasons.

We had no church affiliation. I had taught them about humanitarian values, reincarnation, and a loving Creator. I taught them to talk to God whenever they wanted to, but I never imposed it. I taught them that there was some good in every religion and to respect others' religious beliefs. They knew that they could tell me if ever they felt they needed a church affiliation.

Jay was the first.

"Mom, I want to be an altar boy with Scott."

When I told him that he had to belong to the church for that, he insisted on joining.

Next, Sandy and Dina wanted to join. They, too, had friends who attended the same church.

Jen wanted to join the synagogue where Sheilah went.

We conferred about "church" and how going should be more than wanting to do what friends were doing. When they seemed to understand and insisted they really wanted to go to church, I allowed them to follow their promptings. I insisted, however, that they not forget God as I had taught them, and I assured them that they were free to change their minds if they needed to. In my teens, I had left the Protestant church I attended since age four because of hypocrisy and dogma. My childhood friends had left their churches, even the most devout in Catholic New Orleans, and guilt had permeated every aspect of their adult lives. I did not want guilt for my children. I had always had a direct inner connection with my Creator that continued uninterrupted after I left my church.

The church required me to take catechism instruction if Jay and the girls were to be accepted. I agreed, making clear that I would come for instruction, not conversion. Father Reilly, a young priest just out of seminary, was my instructor. I must have been a major thorn in his side!

We each survived, neither changing the other.

Late exposure to a church was better for my children. Occasional debriefing reduced the problem that dogma could have been.

I noticed a subtle change in myself. I was enjoying my autonomy. I used to wonder why the people I knew could put their lives together and marry, or remarry, have a family, a nice home, a secure job, a good car, and grow old comfortably together—everyone except me! Now, more often I was excited about my fantastic health, despite problems and stress. I marveled at my constant high energy. I delighted in my beautiful, wonderful children. I remembered how terrific it felt to have an abundance of unseen guidance that made everything we needed fall exactly into place at the crucial moment. With Alex, my life was subordinate. It was his life; I was an adjunct. There were arguments about roles, priorities, discipline. With Mike, it would be the same, for Mike could generate crises with his jealousy, his ego problems, and his gambling. It might consume all my energy. Instead of focusing on what I'd lost and been limited to, my focus now was on what I had and how far I really could go. I began seeing in my situation undreamed-of opportunities to take command of my life, to live it without coordinating with anyone or asking permission or seeking approval from anyone to make decisions and take responsibility for the results. It felt a lot like *power*, but because I didn't yet understand the difference between power over others and empowerment, I wrapped this awareness inside of a cocoon of privacy, confiding it to no one, saving it until I understood it clearly.

Jen got a state university scholarship. Sandy and Dina would soon finish high school in fine arts, Jay was in the nearby high school, and Rafi and Lisa were in the elementary school on the corner.

It was satisfying to see the wisdom of my decision to nurture and preserve their individuality rather than taking the easy way and cloning myself. Each was beginning to find a special niche in life. There was more to do, but it was getting easier. The pattern was established, the worst was over.

Part of my emerging pattern was to move when I felt the energy of movement. No longer would I argue about not being ready or not understanding it well enough. I would act, and soon—well into the next adventure—I would see the last one clearly. Most important, I began to understand the pattern, to trust it.

I was on the threshold of realizing my dream of higher education.

I could feel the guidance again, embracing, encouraging, never judging, allowing me to grow at my own pace.

It was profoundly satisfying.

3

GETTING EDUCATED: 3D:101

Experience is not what happens to you; it is what you
do with what happens to you.   –Aldous Huxley

ARRANGING FOR someone to cover at home while
I attended classes worked out easier than I thought it would.
Sandy and Dina picked up the younger ones on their way
home from school and agreed to limit weeknight dates to
nights when I had no classes. At other times, a neighbor
covered. The girls prepared simple meals or Jay sometimes
did. I occasionally left precooked meals that needed only
warming. When I had no classes, I cooked meals they especially liked and spent extra time with them, helping with
homework or just being there for them.

I was ready to celebrate when I fulfilled my math defi-
ciency and finally got into college-level work. Because I had

entered without the usual diploma and was holding a full-time job, I was on automatic probation, allowed to take only two courses each semester. I would be home-free as soon as I successfully completed twelve credits, and my determination was high.

I found a new job in an insurance company. The salary was higher, they gave partial tuition reimbursement for any degree program, and it was three blocks from my urban campus, a great convenience.

Evening college included all age groups, highly motivated either for personal fulfillment or career advancement. Many of my classmates were young corporate managers completing their bachelor degrees. One was a supervisor at the job I'd just left; we chuckled at our Psych 101 encounter.

One night in English composition class I felt eyes on me. I turned to see a classmate copying my homework and angrily covered it. He did the same in every class. When I became annoyed enough to complain, he cornered me in the hall at break, apologizing for copying my work. He asked how I studied to get high grades. I told him the subject seemed easy for me. When he asked for my help, I started to say no. I assumed he was like the arrogant fellow I'd overheard in the registrar's office refusing to do the math requirement because he had a secretary to do it.

"Look, I'm Jerry Damiano," my classmate began, "and I work for Litton. Please," he pleaded, "I really need help. This is the fourth time I'm going through this course, and I just can't understand all these rules and terms. If I don't pass this time, I'm out, and if I'm out, so are my job and ninety-six credits. Please, can we meet in the cafeteria before classes once or twice to see if you can help me? If you think there's no hope, then I won't pursue it, but please give it a try. It means a lot to me."

His honesty moved me. I agreed to try.

We met every class night in the cafeteria. I tried to simplify grammar rules and helped with exercises he didn't understand. He was well spoken, but got bogged down in the mechanics of terminology and rules.

"It's kind of like my mother," he said one night. "She's a good driver, but she doesn't know what to call what's under the hood of the car. She knows how it works, but she can't describe it. You know, I wonder if she ever studied English like they teach it here. I'll bet if she did, she'd find the car real easy to describe!"

It made sense. It seemed to bear the seed of a solution.

I went home and questioned the kids, asking how they remembered learning to speak our language. They thought it was a joke. It came down to "what we heard everybody else speaking, Mom. We copied you and Daddy." They went on to say that they sometimes imitated the books I read to them, movie scenes, and teachers they liked.

Ruminating on this helped me figure out how to work with Jerry. I had him read the exercises aloud and listen to himself, then choose the form of the word that sounded and felt correct. In most cases he made the right choice. When he didn't, I would read the sentence correctly several times and let him listen, then repeat it until he got the "feel" of it. In that way we discovered an important key for him.

He meant business. He was very open and cooperative. For scheduled quizzes and finals I gave him extra weekend help and he finally passed. He was so excited, he took me out to dinner in a gesture of gratitude.

Teaching seemed to come naturally to me, and Jerry and I had become good friends during the weekend study sessions in my apartment. He related with ease to the kids, and it was a new experience for me to have a man for a friend instead of a mate. It felt very comfortable to interact in an open, honest, natural way without cat-mouse games.

We went our separate ways after a year of English. Neither our courses nor our paths crossed again for some time.

I was apprehensive when I began literature and philosophy courses. My family's put-downs and Alex's mother's insistence that I didn't know how to live with a genius echoed in my brain, causing me to privately doubt that I could really do this. I reminded myself that I was exploring my mind to see what was there, testing its limits. Despite my fear, I forged ahead, fueled by years of intellectual deprivation.

My course work was exciting. I entered as a math major, but quickly found it was not my forte. I then changed to psychology and changed again when I saw that it required statistical math. I knew then that I needed something not geared toward career, but that would impassion me and offer endless variety.

How could it not be literature? I could tap into the greatest, most impassioned minds of all time with an endless stream of ideas. If I exhausted the field in my own language, I could tap into the literature of my second language, for I was, by then, fully bilingual. It proved to be the best choice.

My teachers expected me to parrot a certain body of material. What I wanted was different. I satisfied my teachers with one and learned another for myself. It took more study but it didn't matter. My mind was, by now, a voracious entity that required constant nourishment in order to be at peace.

When I completed forty A-minus credits, I qualified for a full-tuition scholarship, renewable as long as I maintained a B+ average. I took on the challenge with gusto. My job had reimbursed half of my earlier tuition and the motivation to qualify for this scholarship was to have my entire education paid without having to do extra work for tuition money.

I was now ready to intensify my course work once I covered child care. While at the insurance company, I worked compulsory overtime, went to school three evenings a week, and came home to tuck the kids in and get our things in order for the next day. When everyone was asleep and the house quiet, I'd study until 2:00 a.m. My energy abounded. I wouldn't dare express surprise. I accepted it and thanked my angels again.

One day at work, a young woman approached me in the rest room. "Hi, I'm working here for the summer. Somebody said you go to the same college I attend, only at night. I chair a committee to raise women's consciousness and I'm looking for people to help me organize a women's lib chapter. Are you a single mother?"

"Yes, I am."

"You're just the kind of person I'm looking for. We'll have good speakers once we're organized. You'll learn a lot of helpful things to make your 'ex' pay up and to stop being taken advantage of. We'll organize marches on the mayor's office and picket the university for catering to business majors. We'll put them all in their place. You'll really want to be part of this," she ranted. "You do know about the lib movement, right?"

"I admire your energy," I said, "but I can't spare a minute. I'm already fully committed."

"What do you mean? You're not committed at all unless you make time for this! You're a woman, aren't you? What kind of a life do you think you'll have without this? This male-dominated society is already out of hand, and it's because of apathetic women like you who want to maintain the status quo. Oh, I know your problem. You don't want to lose your meal ticket, right?"

Were there words for this onslaught of assumptions? Did it deserve a response?

"Sorry," I said simply and left.

How could she presume to know what I was doing even before the movement had an official name? What did she know of responsibility—for a family, a job, college, scholarship grades? I was apathetic? I could challenge her to do as much. I didn't have a life? I had all the life I could handle! An important life! I wondered who had made her angry enough to lash out blindly at all males. The mayor had nothing to do with my life, and the university had generously given me all the help I needed.

I didn't see myself as a victim. I was given many wonderful opportunities, by both seen and unseen "angels." I always thought of myself as an equal person. I was also my own meal ticket and much too proud to marry for that reason.

I wouldn't take part in random hostility spewed to all men, nor was I ready to dismiss men. They were the only other gender in existence and I rather liked them. I just had to be more careful in my personal choices. Lacking the ideal match did not mean good men weren't out there. Statistically, two bad choices do not make a valid sampling. If I included my premarital boyfriends—wonderful, honest, open people—it tilted the sampling in favor of the good guys.

I was already doing my part by the way I reared my children. Equality was the only way of life they knew, as soon as I became their teacher. I refused to lend support to someone's unresolved anger by indiscriminate bids for attention.

After my first year I couldn't idle through summer waiting for fall classes, so I enrolled summers in carefully chosen electives that would be exciting, creative, and absorbing. Living theatre, constructivist art, film-making, silk screen, and classical mythology kept me happy. Having waited almost twenty years for college, I was determined to make it pure joy.

A classmate in silk screening read my palm during a break one day and told me some accurate information about the flow of my life. "You broke off a relationship fairly recently during a full moon. I see a bunch of children, unless some of these lines are from handling chemical solutions." She had to dash to another class and invited me to her house so that she could read more in depth. She wrote down her address for me, and I saw that it was the same block where Mike lived. I made up a story.

"My boyfriend's best bowling buddy lives on your block. His name is Mike."

When I told her his last name, she immediately recognized it.

"Yes, I know him. Well, actually I just see him a lot. I rarely see his wife. They seem very nice, very quiet, but in my neighborhood it's hard to tell. A lot of families with old mob connections live there. It's best to be nice but not close. She rarely leaves the house. My neighbors say she's from one of those families, and her brother collects gambling debts—you know how! They really hang together. I wouldn't want to cross any of them."

I looked at my watch and made up an excuse to quickly leave. I drove around to a different campus parking lot and sat in my car, shaken, trying to process the information I'd just heard.

No wonder Mike was afraid to end his marriage. If his in-laws weren't pleased, he could very well end up in some alley. I remembered when he said that his wife wouldn't dare ask where he went every evening. I felt outraged for her. "She was brought up not to ask questions," he'd said. "The less a woman knows, the safer she is." It sure seemed to fit.

Poor Mike! He was stuck in a hole from which there was no easy escape—like the hole I'd escaped from before meeting him. How trapped I'd felt, how slowly the wounds healed, how long the fear lingered! I was sad for him, but glad to be free of it.

I gained a new respect for myself for perceiving something wrong and heeding my feelings even before I understood them.

Mike really couldn't be a full participant in our relationship; he was almost forced into stagnation. But his stagnation threatened to tear me from the impetus of my growth. When I realized this, I left the relationship. It felt callous, but I was driven. I could neither stop nor tolerate an obstacle in the path of my growth.

Of all the extracurricular opportunities available, theatre

workshop most intrigued me. I participated in all its facets. I took an acting part to force myself to overcome stage fright. After six months, the director left and I undertook the responsibility of reviving the organization. I became immersed in reorganizing it to surpass its former brilliance, and it proved to be an enriching and creative outlet for the next three years.

Two years later, it was time for the economics requirement. Like the young man who wondered why he needed math if his secretary did it, I wondered why I needed economics as an English major. I attended the lectures and focused my attention, but economics would not penetrate. Its terminology sounded to my ear like hybridized nonsense syllables and corporate jargon. Soon I was in deep trouble with a shattered ego. It was my time to learn humility. I had already calculated the grades I needed to graduate summa cum laude. This course could ruin me, maybe ruin my scholarship, too!

The next week our class was shuffled. I had been struggling so intensely with economics that I never noticed the faces in my class. I wouldn't notice the new ones either.

Someone in the row behind me chewed loudly on corn chips during the lecture. Who could be so nonchalant in economics? When I turned to see who it was, I saw Jerry Damiano!

At last! A friend to whom I could confide my despair. How wonderful to find Jerry again! Now I would surely have a sympathetic ear to complain about how I suffered in this course.

"Jerry," I whispered, "what are you doing here?"

"Hey, look who's here," Jerry whispered loudly, "my English teacher. Say, wait'll you see me in this class. Not at all like in English. I'm in my final year. I saved the easiest stuff for last. What a haul! Long but fun, and I'm glad it's over. How'd you end up here?"

"I'm dying in this class, Jerry," I pleaded.

"Well, now, isn't that interesting! This just happens to be my forte."

Students were glaring at us from all directions, but he paid no attention.

"Weren't you smart to pick this class before I graduate! Now I get a chance to show off! I'll have you acing it in no time."

"Let's move to the back row so we can talk," I suggested, noting the disturbance we were causing.

He was already up out of his seat, stumbling over knees and books to reach the aisle of the huge lecture hall. Then we climbed the stairs to the back row.

"Say, how are those great kids of yours?" he asked when we got settled. "Shall we start meeting in the cafeteria again?" We met regularly for tutoring—a thankless struggle, for my brain was impenetrable to economics. Jerry worked much harder teaching me economics than I did tutoring him English. That year, I learned more about humility than economics.

"Say it aloud," he insisted. "Say it aloud."

Trying to comply, I said some strange phrases aloud, without understanding what I was saying.

He burst out laughing. "You're so tense," he laughed harder. "Don't you remember teaching me English that way? I know you can't learn economics like that, but you're so wound up over it that you didn't even catch the humor. I just did it to break the tension. I thought you'd die laughing!"

He tried his best, but I barely passed. If I had been fantasizing about becoming a valedictorian, economics brought me sharply to reality. With shattered plans for a summa cum laude, I would now have to recalculate for a magna cum laude.

I went to Jerry's graduation to celebrate his achievement and his relief. Grateful for the freedom from economics, I also thanked him for helping me learn humility and self-acceptance by his example. After the ceremony we agreed to stay in touch, but Jerry called the following month to say that he was promoted and was transferring to another state.

Two or three Christmas cards later we lost touch and never saw each other again.

It was as though a helping angel had dropped into my life to fill a need and teach a lesson about giving and receiving, and just as suddenly dropped out. Again, I was grateful.

With economics in the past, I focused again on creative studies. My friend Gary's professor allowed me to audit his art of India course during my free period. I couldn't fit it into my schedule, but it was so interesting that I did the assignments and papers and derived all benefits except the credits. The final exam was a term paper describing the significance in Hindu mythology of a Hindu icon, which we were expected to buy, then to draw its picture on the cover.

Gary and I set out one wintry Saturday morning for an import section of New York City, where many shops sold Indian artifacts. The variety was amazing. After browsing through five shops, I was so drawn to a Shiva Nataraj statue that I badgered Gary to get it. We bargained the shopkeeper down to twenty dollars.

All I knew about Shiva was that he was the Hindu god of destruction and creation, death and regeneration. It sounded contradictory. Shiva destroys illusion and falsehood to rebuild in its place reality and spiritual truth. The Shiva Nataraj, or Dancing Shiva, depicted Shiva in the dance of life, the unending cycle of death and rebirth. I learned that Shiva is connected with reincarnation. I knew a little about that. It is also connected with kundalini energy. I knew nothing about that!

We each completed the assignment independently. When the professor heard that I had done this assignment, too, he invited me to submit my paper for an unofficial grade. I was moved. It was very unusual for a teacher to add an unofficial fifteen-page term paper to countless others that he had to officially grade.

When the course ended and Gary went on to other studies, he said I could keep the Shiva statue. I somehow knew I would end up with it. We seemed strangely bonded. I didn't know at the time that I was to learn much, experientially, from living with Shiva in my window.

Next semester I officially enrolled in an aesthetics course with the same professor. He offered the class an alternative to the usual fare of reading Ruskin and other traditional critics. We opted for the alternative: experiments in extending the five senses so that we could be our own critics and make our own judgments.

Throughout the semester we stretched our senses until we developed an incredible range. In the sight exercises, he taught us techniques that made it easier to visualize. He made vague references to that word again—kundalini, the life force energy—and the third eye. Since none of us understood to what he alluded, he dropped the topic. The most dramatic advances we made were in the olfactory and tactile exercises. We learned to distinguish the difference in scent between the flower end and the stem end of an orange. We learned to recognize blindfolded whose orange it was, among fifteen owners. Then we recognized which end of whose orange it was. Next, moving on to people, we learned, blindfolded, to recognize each other's unique fingertip scent and to distinguish each of fifteen persons' particular scent from the others.

The final exercise involved the sense of touch. We lined up in the hall outside a darkened classroom where secret preparations kept a volunteer crew busy. When everything was ready, the crew came out, blindfolded us, and led us one by one through the aisles where desks had been replaced by tables piled with fabrics of every possible variety.

We would touch these and say what type of fabric they were. After sewing for years, I expected it to be too easy.

I passed each table, feeling the fabric and saying, "This is satin, this is eyelet... piqué... voile, etc."

As I touched a piece of voile, I got a visual impression of pale pink with a diffused imprint of mauve and purple flowers. I laughed, "Who ever heard of *feeling* colors?"

Next, as I felt a satiny fabric, a mental image of a bold, energetic design impressed me. I reported this to the volunteer helper, adding, "I'm sure you must think I'm nuts!"

"What do you think you see?" she asked.

The picture became clearer when I focused to describe it. "I can 'see' a kind of South Sea Island design with masks and totems, outlined in thick black lines."

She pursued it, "Do you see any colors inside the outlines?"

"This is absurd," I said. "How can I touch this cloth and 'see' its design? And you're asking if I see colors?" I thought she was ridiculing me. "You must be as nutty as I!"

Suddenly I saw brilliant pinks, turquoises, golden yellows, and bright greens set in a kind of mosaic between the thick black outlines.

The helper got excited as I described it.

"No," I interrupted. "This can't be so. The fabric feels like satin. I have never seen a satin fabric in such a bold design. Usually satins are in solid colors, either pastels or brights."

"Would you like me to remove your blindfold now?" she asked.

"Sure," I said. "It feels like it's getting late and I have another class to get to."

She untied the blindfold and asked me to turn on the room light over by the blackboard.

I was in a hurry and headed straight for the hall after turning on the light, but she called me back.

As I approached the table where she stood, she held up a piece of voile and asked, "Is this the pale pink voile you saw with the mauve and purple flowers?"

It really did have mauve and purple flowers, very diffused,

as though brush-stroked in water colors!

Then she pointed to a bold island print. "Is this your satin?"

Yes, that was it! Exactly what I saw. Or felt. I was confused trying to talk about it. Did I see it or did I feel it? Whatever it should be called, how exactly did I do it? I thought and thought about how this could happen, but couldn't come up with an answer.

I turned to her and asked, "Did I really do that? Are you sure the lights were out? Did anyone else have that experience?"

"Only two others," she said. "And yes, not only were the lights out, but when you were feeling this fabric, it was underneath a pile of pastel satins. There was no way you could have seen the design when you were describing it."

I couldn't dismiss the experience, yet intuitively I knew it would be best not to discuss it with just anyone. I went to my professor instead.

After the discomfort of contriving an excuse for requesting an appointment with him, I blurted out, "I had a strange experience down in the fabric room."

"Can you describe it to me?" he asked.

I told him about the two fabrics whose colors and designs I had perceived through my fingertips, bracing myself for ridicule. "It was exactly what I had hoped would be your experience. I am disappointed that only three of you experienced it. The entire course was designed to sharpen your senses, to teach you to turn inward to seek messages, answers, and to teach you to trust the messages you got. It is difficult to know now if only three of you experienced it or if others did, but felt it was too strange to talk about. If that was the case, they probably blamed it on imagination. I will never know, for I cannot ask the class members if they saw colors through their fingers. I congratulate you on your intuition in being careful whom you chose to confide this experience to. Especially," he said, "in academia."

It was another mind-opener for me that made me rethink a lot of things I believed to be so. I could never duplicate the experience at will, but many times since then it happened spontaneously. I stopped believing in limitations that day, especially of my mind and senses. The hardest part was not being able to talk about it and having to contain the excitement of each experience.

In the final year of my course work, I enrolled in a writing workshop. Word was that Professor O'Brian was so outstanding that we would be lucky if we got into his class. Twenty-five of us reported with great expectations.

Shock ran through the class as he spewed sarcasm and disdain. Some left immediately to drop the course. He assigned us a one-page report on any topic to be written in twenty minutes, then called on people to read it to the class, and goaded the class to critique it. After being thrown to the lions, more students deserted by the second class.

By the third class we die-hards conspired to fight our way through this course and show him we would not tolerate his verbal abuse, but after the roster count, he broke out into a warm, enveloping smile, surprising us all.

"Welcome to writing workshop. I am always happiest working with students who refuse to be antagonized," he announced. "Not only that," he continued, "I am now left with the cream of the crop, the elite! All the 'prima donnas' have fled, leaving me with the strongest, most seriously committed of the lot, and in a number conducive to the most dynamic learning experience. I welcome you with all my heart. You may call me Bill outside the classroom. I would be happy if you would consider me at eye-level with you. Teaching is, after all, a sharing of knowledge."

Silence blanketed the classroom, then we suddenly burst out laughing. Mr. Hyde had just exited through one door and Dr. Jekyll came in through the other. His unorthodox way of whittling the class down to a manageable fifteen compensated for the university's refusal to limit enrollment.

He detailed his course method: we would still be thrown to the lions, but gently and anonymously. He followed with advice to defend our stand and hold to our truth. Several of us had never heard of "our" truth before, only "the" truth, so he patiently elaborated.

It didn't take us long to realize our good fortune. Bill O'Brian proved to be better than the rumors about him.

We had to bring unsigned, typed copies of each assignment for everyone, and we had to learn to listen straight-faced to all criticisms. We never knew whose paper we were critiquing and, of course, we were at liberty to accept or reject the suggestions for our work. Some criticized spelling, punctuation, and syntax. Others criticized digressions, characterization, approach to the subject, and even the philosophy.

One assignment was to find any short book and write a review on it. I'd had an unusually busy week and postponed it until late, so as I scanned short books, the red cover of Sybil Leek's *Diary of a Witch* caught my eye. I was fascinated by her childhood in England, her interactions with the Black Forest gypsies and their use of healing herbs. I thought the review I wrote on it was good. He gave me an "A" with a red-penned note: *Your work fulfills the criteria for an excellent review; however, kindly refrain in future from submitting occult material in this course.* I had carefully refrained from revealing my agreement or opposition to the subject, so I probed for the deeper feeling that prompted O'Brian's objection to my topic. He was too disturbed to discuss it. I could have held my ground. After all, it was a short, published book, and I had fulfilled the terms of the assignment. But this was a teacher whose nurturing I valued highly. Just because of a hint of human foible, I wasn't willing to antagonize him and taint the good I could get. Instead, I apologized and agreed to honor his preference to omit occult topics from his class. I think he forgave me for unintentionally uncovering one of his sensitive areas.

Another assignment was poetry. After twenty unproductive attempts at writing verse, I went to bed with my notebook under my pillow.

That night I dreamed I was back in childhood, three years old, a time when Grandma would put me to bed before my energy had dissipated. My fear of her wrath made me pretend to be asleep. I would busy myself until sleep came by creating what seemed to be verse without rhyme. Then, still dreaming, I was in my teens, hearing someone say that the verses were beatitudes. Next, I was face to face with a figure of light. I put my finger into the light and felt love, and I wanted to stand in it and soak it all up. The light-being allowed me to stay as long as I wanted, and I couldn't seem to get enough. It was lifting me higher and higher until I felt compelled to utter a stream of so many words—words, words, and more words that came out in lines that rhymed in the softest, most beautiful way. Then I remembered I had to complete an assignment.

Half awake, I groped for my notebook while streams of poetry spilled from my brain almost faster than I could write them down. Words I'd heard in the dream and words I was now hearing merged through my pen as though I were doing automatic writing. My heart was overflowing. When it was all down, it was love poetry, moving and intimate though not erotic, raised to a much higher dimension of passion. I wasn't sure I'd turn it in. Could I risk baring this depth of feelings? Then I remembered our anonymity. Only O'Brian would know who wrote it. Would he realize it came from a dream? Were dreams part of the occult that he would not accept? Would I really blow it this time? I decided to risk it.

The class gave it excellent reviews. O'Brian criticized it privately, however, saying its intensity provoked the reader to wonder who was "the beloved."

"Who was it?" he demanded to know. It startled me. His

demeanor was that of a father who had just discovered his daughter planning a love tryst. I decided not to mention the dream.

"I don't really know," I said. "Maybe it was the music I was listening to while I did my homework. I'll do it over."

"Yes, do that. And don't spend so much time with St. Teresa of Avila and St. John of the Cross."

"I'm not Catholic, you know," I said. "I don't read the church's list of approved books, and I don't read about saints. Who are they?"

The only reason he believed me was that when he told me what they wrote, I asked densely why monastic saints would write love poetry if they weren't allowed lovers. He shrugged impatiently.

I went straight to the library after that class to find the works of the saints he'd mentioned and discovered the most exalted love poetry I had ever read. St. Teresa "met" God during meditation, in the inner sanctuary of her Higher Self. She expressed her ecstasy through poetry as a lover and was almost excommunicated. None of her bishops had had this experience. Even her family thought she was losing her balance. St. John's poetry went further in its eroticism, although he was never threatened with excommunication. He simply made everyone nervous.

Reading their works, I understood why they expressed themselves as they did. I couldn't yet articulate why I understood it and I wasn't yet sure what meditation was, but the feelings evoked were the same that I'd felt in the dream which inspired what I wrote. I knew then that I had written it to God.

A classmate, Marie, approached me one evening during break. "I'm an astrologer," she said. "Have you ever had your chart done? I keep feeling drawn to you, and I feel it's somehow connected to astrology."

I told her I hadn't, but I always checked out the newspaper astrology column. She offered to do my chart at no charge, if I wished, so I gave her my birth information.

Two weeks later we met in the cafeteria and she showed me my chart. It was a complete mystery of circles and colored lines, mathematical calculations and strange random symbols.

"I was surprised by your birth date. I thought you were younger. Maybe that's better because you won't be as vulnerable to the pitfalls in the chart." It was beginning to sound dire. "You should forget about marriage and having a family. With Saturn in your fifth house you'll either never get pregnant or you'll never be able to carry a pregnancy to term. It'll be only grief. And with Venus in the tenth, you're really cut out to be a career girl. None of this domestic stuff for you! You're on the right track getting a good education with Mercury ruling your Sun, but the Moon rules your Ascendant, making you very soft. You couldn't handle hardships in your life."

She continued giving information that had little relevance to the real flow of my life and finally asked for feedback. I tried to be tactful without seeming unappreciative of her efforts, but nothing she had said applied.

"Well, I was married."

"But you're not now?" she quickly added.

"No."

"O.K. And you have no children, right?" she asked.

"Well, I do."

"And you had a lot of trouble during the pregnancy?" she persisted.

"Well, not really. In fact, my pregnancies were fine. And my children were healthy and fine."

"But you lost them. Your husband got custody, right?"

"No, I did."

"Wait a minute. Something's wrong here. Did you give me the correct birth information?"

We checked my information against the calculations for

the chart she had erected and found no error. She was embarrassed.

"Wait a minute. You said 'pregnancies.' How many children do you have?" she asked.

"Six," I replied.

It was an uneasy moment. She was momentarily stunned, but broke into laughter, "Well, if you're not angry at me, let's talk more about it so that I can understand what I missed. And If you're really interested in astrology, when the semester ends, you can come to my house once a week and I'll teach you how to calculate charts. After my botched reading, I wouldn't presume to teach you interpretation. I'll give you a good bibliography so that you can learn that yourself."

So it was that I began to learn astrology. Soon I could calculate charts, and a few good books started me toward interpreting my own chart, for I was most interested in understanding myself. Later I would move on to others.

The more I learned, the more I understood why Marie had misread my chart. She had assumed that astrology showed specifics rather than potentials from which free will could choose. Also she had simply not gone far enough synthesizing the planetary interrelations in my chart.

Saturn in the fifth house could indeed have shown what she thought it did, but it could also show heavy responsibility for children, which was the way mine manifested. My Moon-ruled ascendant was not weak and vulnerable, for Pluto, planet of power, accompanied it, bringing strength and intuition to survive hardships. I had started out soft, but quickly found the strength potential in my chart.

True, I was born under Mercury-ruled Gemini with the hunger for learning everything! Perhaps that was why I enjoyed my education so much. I would never have time to learn all that I'd like to learn. And while I felt no affinity for the career-girl image, I could comfortably accept the career-student image.

I became aware that horoscope charts were pictures of

situations and the options available to deal with them. They
were not fixed pronouncements.

Mr. O'Brian caught me discussing charts with Marie during a later class break. I didn't want that to happen. I would
rather not remind him of our discussion about the occult.

"You're doing astrology now?" he asked, looking me
square in the eye.

I could feel the flush rising up my cheeks, but before I
could think of an answer, he was asking me to do his chart.
I couldn't believe my ears!

"What do you need to know?" he asked. "I can call my
mother to get the time. I've always wanted to know what
was in my chart. This should certainly be interesting."

I agreed to do it, as I stood there dumfounded! Why was
Sybil Leek occult to him but astrology wasn't? Maybe it was
the word "witch" that pressed his button.

Astrology so fascinated me that I became deeply involved in it. It fulfilled a need in me to become impassioned
with a thing of endless variety. There was an element of
mystery to it that I intuited would become profoundly important to me. I had just embarked upon a lifelong interest
that would be an important step on the magical ladder to
my higher spiritual growth.

Our class had become unusually bonded. The very thing
that had threatened us all at the beginning—having our precious writing torn to shreds by our classmates—was what
brought us closer under the guidance of this unusual mentor. Near the year's end we gathered at a classmate's home
for our final class and a potluck meal.

During second semester, I had found myself hanging on
every word O'Brian uttered, not hearing the content so
much as the voice. I had developed a crush on a teacher. I
spent hours, days, sorting this out at home. Getting crushes
on teachers was not my pattern, but this man was unlike
any other instructor I'd ever had. I wasn't lonely. I had my

share of male friends, class comrades and dates, a nice social life. I wasn't feeling a need to be steadily dating or
married, and I wasn't feeling "incomplete without a mate."
So what was this???

I guarded this secret awareness and ruminated over it for
months until I finally figured it out. It made perfect sense to
me, but I feared it would sound dramatic or silly if I verbal-
ized it. I was learning, nevertheless, to be true to myself and,
in its squeaky-clean innocence, saying it could harm no
one.

Now at our final gathering when Bill concluded the class
material and everyone clamored around the barbecue trying to get the coals to burn, I cornered him.

"Did you ever have a student get a crush on you?" I began.

He braced himself as though for an onslaught!

"Well, it would be pretty immodest of me to say yes,
wouldn't it?"

"No, not at all. It happens. I know students who get
crushes on teachers because they're good-looking, or sexy,
or tyrannical, or because they give them A's."

"Well, since I don't fit any of those categories, especially
the tyrannical one—now that everybody knows me—I just
don't qualify as crush material, right?"

"No, on the contrary. I had a crush on you."

"Oh, you *had*? But you found me unsatisfactory?" he
countered. "I just hope you don't write that on your faculty
evaluation form."

I could see he was trying to be funny to defuse a declara-
tion, but I continued.

"No, you weren't unsatisfactory. You see, it felt like any
old crush at first, but I don't jump into things suddenly any
more. I have to dance around and turn it over on all sides to
get a real good look at it, to see if it really is what I think it is.
I don't act on every impulse any more. I know that if it is to
be, it'll wait for me, and if not, well, maybe it wasn't meant

to be and another opportunity will come along. Anyway, I asked myself if I'd be willing to give up the male friends I now know, and it didn't feel like a 'yes.' I'd miss them. So I set it aside to see what would happen, to see if it intensified. And it did, but only while I sat in your classroom."

"So you're asking me to be your classroom paramour?" he asked in a devious whisper, choking back the laughter.

"No, silly," I replied, "I'm saying that it was not a romantic crush after all."

"What the devil was it then?" he feigned offense.

"I was in love with your mind," I confessed. "Still am. It's like your mind devised these methods you used in teaching us, and I grew so much under that guidance. It's more important than a romantic attachment. It's like a mind-meld, more lasting. Romance never lasts as long as what a mind embraces. Sometimes it felt as if you pressed your fingerprints into my mind and the imprint is there forever, like Omar's potter. Not many teachers can do that, and when I find one, I realize it is even more—it is a soul-meld. What I'm really saying is 'thank you,' except that 'thank you' is so inadequate. You're the best teacher I've had. You're my greatest influence and I have only the deepest gratitude for what you've given me. So, yes, I have a tremendous crush on your mind, O'Brian."

He was moved. He was blushing. His eyes were glassy.

He quickly collected himself and started joking again.

"Well, I shall expect my fourteen-carat Oscar within a week for that year-long performance."

"Consider it done," I said, and in my mind's eye I saw him surrounded by angels who blessed and celebrated him.

My classmates came from the barbecue with filled plates, plus one for O'Brian and one for me. Each looked for a place to sit near him. Sam suggested we put his chair in the center and sit in a circle around him. He blushed again, but we wouldn't accept a no. Someone found a swivel chair for him so that we each could see him as we spoke.

He began to joke flippantly, but Sam wouldn't allow it.

"Cut it out, O'Brian. It's our turn. You've had all year to chew us up and your time is up. You have to just sit there now and let us have our say. The sooner you quiet down, the easier this'll be for you."

It was a roast. Each took a turn saying something about him, but no one could think of anything brash.

We kidded him about his guillotine method of trimming the class down to size, and he swore us to secrecy. We told him how his dedication had inspired such a level of trust in us that we were able to completely open to the learning process. We cited our gratitude that he never violated that trust and that he always nurtured us in the purest sense, giving unstintingly of his time beyond the classroom. We concurred that there were times when we felt like disciples at the feet of Socrates, and, though he didn't teach philosophy, he gave us the space to formulate our own. It was unanimous that everything he taught us proved valuable. We all felt like children equally loved.

A few tears spilled around the circle. He had allowed us to share in the wisdom of his soul. It was a profound experience that we would never forget.

He shot me a quick glance when it was over and said, "Does that mean they all have a crush on my mind?"

I smiled. It was his way of saying he understood. I was sad and happy at the same time.

Graduation approached and I was depressed. All that I'd learned was small compared to all I would never have time to reach in this lifetime. I was utterly frustrated. I didn't want it to end. I hadn't had enough. How could I walk up to accept a degree that most considered to be the finishing touch when I did not feel finished? It was hypocrisy.

I received notification that I would graduate magna cum laude in the top three percent, ninth in a class of 320. I didn't want to attend the ceremony. I planned to make an excuse to the administration and request they mail my diploma.

The fever for learning had excited me, but I wondered if it was good for the kids. They would wake up around two in the morning to go to the bathroom and they would see me finishing homework. When finals were near, my insecurity level was so high that they would see me studying to the point of overkill. It did not paint a tempting picture of college for them. I explained several times that not everyone has to study so hard to get through college, but one day Lisa asked, "So why do you, Mom? Don't they like you?"

"Of course, they like me, Lisa. It has nothing to do with liking. It's that I had to wait a very long time to do this and I need to do it well. I want as many A's as I can get so that I can graduate with honors."

"Will that mean you're smart, Mom?"

"Well, it's not exactly that. You don't need A's to be smart; you know when you're smart. It's that . . . Oh, Lisa, go to bed, honey. You have to get up early for school. Let's talk tomorrow."

What did I almost say? I almost said, "A's show the world that I'm smart."

Suddenly it was as if a voice inside me spoke to me: *So go on . . . it's that you're validated, approved, that you now have the right to participate in life on planet Earth, that you can walk alongside instead of ten paces behind, that you got even with Grandma. What do you think you'd look like, waving your honors around and shouting like a five-year-old, "See, I can, too, do it!" Whom would you shout it to? Who do you think cares? Who do you think you are anyway?*

There it was, rearing its ugly head again—the self-worth ogre. I certainly didn't want to pass that on to the kids! As soon as finals were over and the graduation dilemma resolved, I determined to slay that dragon once and for all, but I knew it wouldn't be easy.

Back on campus, I ran into Carlos, who said he would be

presenting diplomas to the honor graduates. He congratulated me for being on his list.

"I might not be there for the ceremony," I said.

"Is there a problem?" he asked, looking closely at me. "Do you need a ride? You know, I haven't had a chance to grab a bite to eat yet. Come with me to the cafeteria, and we can talk there while we eat."

I confided my feelings to him over a cup of coffee.

"Is that all?" he asked. "Do you think you're alone? Didn't anybody ever tell you that's what graduate school is for?"

"But I haven't the money for graduate school. And the time. How am I going to go to an even higher level school and work a full-time job again? I have children to support. There won't be enough money for tuition, nor enough time to study."

"You did it for this degree. What's the big deal? You'll apply for a teaching assistantship," he countered.

"What's that?" I asked.

He explained what it was and why he felt sure I'd get it. We talked for a long time until he finally convinced me.

When I left the cafeteria, I had decided to go to my graduation ceremony and apply for graduate school.

Gary noticed me in the parking lot one evening and yelled, "Hey, are you taking care of my Shiva?"

We walked to the cafeteria together and caught each other up on the latest developments. When he learned I was graduating, he wanted to come to the ceremony.

"How are you going to get all your kids to the graduation?" he asked.

"I haven't figured that one out yet. We'll probably need another car."

"I have an idea," Gary went on. "I've been driving a school bus part time and the supervisor's a nice guy. I'll bet he'd let me use the bus, especially since it's a Saturday graduation. Shall I ask him? It would be big enough for scads of people.

Would you go in a school bus?"

"Gary, you've got to be kidding! Isn't it kind of silly to show up for my college graduation in an elementary school bus?"

"Doesn't seem silly to me," he replied, disappointed. "All your family and friends would fit."

He was serious.

As I hesitated and thought more about it, the humor of it struck me. It expressed exactly how I felt. When I was determined not to go to my graduation because I didn't feel "finished," someone came to tell me that this was only the first step and I could go on to another step. Yes, it was appropriate. I had finished my first grade and was simply going to pick up the pass to my next grade.

"I think you're right, Gary. It's not at all silly. It's quite appropriate and I really appreciate your help."

Fourteen of us piled into the big yellow school bus and set out for the main campus stadium, thirty-five miles away, for the ceremony. It wasn't until we arrived and I met with some of my classmates from writing class that I began to feel the excitement of the event.

We stood around in clusters waiting for the ceremony to begin. It was a steamy May day and the sun shone brightly on the stadium. It felt at least fifteen degrees hotter in caps and gowns. Some students removed the gowns until the ceremony began, exposing beach shorts, halters, and jeans. If I had been a little more imaginative, I could have been a lot more comfortable. Instead, I walked to the platform in a wilted gown with perspiration gluing the mortar board to my head.

Carlos gave a supportive wink when he called my name for my diploma, and I could see my children waving from their seats when they saw me going up to accept it. I felt very loved seeing their pride in me. It healed the rejection I felt at my mother's silence weeks after sending her an invitation.

As I accepted my diploma and left the stage to return to my seat, I passed several people I knew, people who had once seemed quite tall. I wondered why they suddenly seemed to have shrunk. Then I realized they were still the same; the change was in my perception.

I was as tall as anyone now. At eye-level.

4

GRADUATE SCHOOL
OF MIND AND SOUL:
HIGHER AND HIGHER

You need only let go. The universe then begins to
create life for you, effortlessly, because you have gotten
out of the way. —Yogi Amrit Desai

GETTING INTO graduate school proved complicated. The grad English director, a highly specialized
Anglophile, criticized my "meager years of Chaucer and
Shakespeare" despite my other British lit and classics credits.

"The focus was not intense. Time was wasted on contem-
porary American lit." She visibly winced! "An MAT is the best
I can offer. It won't qualify you for Ph.D. candidacy, but you
can teach high school with it."

I could teach high school without graduate study. If I became a teacher at all, I would teach—not discipline—at
college level. It wouldn't do.

Besides, if this was a sample of grad English faculty, I knew I would be suffocated.

I accepted an academic counselor position on my home campus, resolving student problems and getting students needed financial aid. I was part of a congenial, creative team doing something worthwhile and fulfilling. Being bilingual broadened the range of students I could serve.

The university was enormous. Eight campuses stretched across the state to include a law school, a school of medicine, and several graduate schools.

Soon I was invited to teach an evening Spanish class on a neighboring campus. Though I had only a B.A. in English, they had based their selection on my Spanish grades, my fluency on the job, and the high praise from the English faculty for the years I tutored Hispanic students. I felt honored by their confidence in my teaching ability and I wanted a taste of college teaching, so I accepted. I could not foresee that, fresh from my B.A., the first class I taught would include eighteen police lieutenants and sergeants. What a test!

When Carlos contacted me, he wasn't disturbed over my experience with the grad English department. It didn't look good, but he was excited that I was teaching a Spanish class, doing well, and enjoying the experience. If I focused on teaching well, he said they would probably keep rehiring me.

"Have you considered applying to the Spanish department?" he asked.

"I can't handle graduate lit in Spanish," I snapped. "I can't conceive of reading entire Spanish novels and critiques, then writing a zillion-page thesis in Spanish."

"Why not? You can handle it. I remember the novella you wrote in Spanish for a term paper. You're as bilingual as anyone I've heard. I'll give you an excellent recommendation."

He described how nice the main campus was. "You'd be living there for grad Spanish. It's much nicer than this urban commuter campus. There is good, affordable housing for grad families, separate from undergraduate dorms, and a gym, tennis courts, excellent libraries, free cultural activities, and a good high school half a mile away with bus service. A free campus shuttle takes you anywhere on campus or in town."

Living like that sounded great, but getting in was another matter. It meant taking yet another exam. Basic grad entrance exams were an ordeal enough; the English and lit parts were easy, but had it not been for Dina's perseverance and infinite patience tutoring me in math, I would have failed it. Undergraduate math had been agonizing!

Lisa, noticing my tension over the new test, offered her usual support. "Relax, Mom. You always get nervous, but you always end up acing it. You'll do fine." Lisa's intuition was finely tuned. I needed that positive reinforcement and she was always there with it. How could I not succeed?

Reporting for the advanced Spanish exam, I noticed it was only more literature. I understood my second language well; nevertheless, scoring higher in Spanish than in my native English surprised me. I applied to grad Spanish.

The grad Spanish department promptly invited me for an interview. After discussing my application, the director asked in Spanish, "Which Hispanic island do you come from? I can't quite place your accent." I was as flattered as he was puzzled.

I told him I needed a teaching assistantship, but he had only recently awarded the last one. He asked if I had tuition money without an assistantship, for if not, he would rather admit someone on the waiting list who had it.

"Of course," I replied without thinking, as if to an absurd question. It was as easy as slipping into a theatre workshop acting role. I had no idea where I would get tuition money—

only a gut feeling that it would be there when the time came. He remembered a possibility and made a phone call.

"I spoke to my colleague, the chairman of foreign languages, on our sister campus. He has awarded all assistantships but would like to interview you anyway. I said you could be there in fifteen minutes. I must warn you, however, that his campus is considered more prestigious, so assistants must work harder than on our campus, although the stipend is the same. You would still have time to attend courses and study. Could you handle that?"

"Yes," I answered, certain that I could do whatever it took.

When I reached the other campus, the chairman apologized that no assistantships were left, but he expected to have one or two next semester when some students completed their Ph.D.'s. We had an interesting interview. He asked if I were from Peru or Ecuador. I softened my answer, but as I left I chuckled at how I had baffled them all with my "accent."

I returned to my near-empty home and my job, feeling slightly down. Jen had left college and married. She lived several miles south. Sandy was weary of my complaints that everything I touched or sat on at home had paint on it, so she'd moved down the street to a studio apartment and continued commuting to art college. Dina had also married and lived with her in-laws, and Jay shared a basement apartment a few blocks west.

Sandy and Jay had their own unique life styles and wanted to live them in their own place. I missed them all. I had reared them to be self-sufficient individuals, to make thoughtful decisions, and now they were testing it. I had to respect what I had engendered. We agreed on one rule: when they got sick, they would come home to be taken care of; when they recovered, they could return to their apartments. It worked.

It felt as if my four best childhood friends had moved away. We had struggled together for so long that it seemed we'd grown up together. Even though I was the responsible adult driven to make a good life for them, a child part of me seized the opportunity to find the playmates I lacked in childhood, and I was rewarded with many wonderful lessons from them about seeing things each time as if for the first time, not being self-conscious, speaking my feelings, and crying when I hurt. I learned to stand up for myself by standing up for them. As they grew, we talked, we shared, we philosophized, and found things in common and things in conflict. We were already so bonded that we could support each other even in conflict. So we had grown to be very close friends as well.

Lisa and Rafi, both in high school, were the only ones left at home.

Carlos responded to my tales about my interviews, "I have a real gut feeling you'll get in with the help you need. You never know with these things. If it's meant to happen, it will, even if you can't see how. Just go on living your life and let it happen. You have all summer for things to change."

"Fat chance," I mumbled.

As soon as the words were out of my mouth, I realized that I'd slipped. When I was totally broke and didn't know where to turn, it was faith and that feeling of walking hand in hand with God that got me through everything.

Here I was, not in such straits as then, slipping so far from faith over something like tuition. It was time to regroup and recover that connection.

I resumed my nightly "conversations" and remembered all the things for which I was grateful. All my important needs were met, the most difficult things I had to do were done, and we had come far! How could I make such a faithless remark about something like tuition, as though my life depended on it? If I didn't get it, maybe I couldn't go to graduate school; and if I couldn't go, it wouldn't crush me. I would find something else to do.

Settling into the daily routine more positively, I shifted my whole perspective about school. Somewhere deep inside me was an excitement that brightened every time I wondered about the tuition, as if to confirm that it was all set. Where did this crazy against-all-odds feeling come from?

A problem arose at home. Rafi had dropped out of school and recruited himself into the peacetime army three months after turning eighteen. I was devastated. He'd had such a delicate nervous system throughout his childhood and more than his share of problems in school; now he had privately decided that the best way to escape academic discipline was to go for military discipline. The recruiters had guaranteed training for a highly paid occupation, without study, and he would have a ball. He knew I would insist that he stay in school, so he signed up secretly and told me only days before his induction. I recognized it as another in a long series of impulsive actions by which he hoped to gain the identity his father had denied him, and it tore at my heart each time. In this instance he lunged blindly into the very thing he hated—discipline. I could do nothing but accept the inevitable and pray for him. I saw him off with a deep sense of foreboding.

My acceptance to graduate school Spanish arrived, but I saw no tuition coming my way. I opted to wait until the very last minute to withdraw my application. Deep down I still felt sure the money would appear, so I didn't seek a loan. I felt no guilt about the "diligent student able to pay tuition" being denied admittance because of me. Rather, I knew it would happen. Whenever I closed my eyes, I saw myself teaching on that campus.

Summer was over and only five days remained before school would begin. I stopped by the grocery to buy snacks to relieve Lisa's misery from a cold. When I returned, she said that a very impatient man with a heavy accent called.

She didn't get his name but wrote down his telephone number. When I called it, the chairman of foreign languages on the "prestigious" campus answered.

"Yes, yes," he said excitedly, "I now have a teaching assistantship available for you. My best student just wired me from Europe. She fell in love with a Frenchman, got married, and is staying there to live. I tell you . . . these students. They do irresponsible, crazy things! They don't care what plans they upset. Her classes have already been scheduled, so we must have someone to teach them. Are you still interested?"

"I think so," I replied. "Can you tell me about it?"

"Yes, of course." He recounted all the benefits of a "TA" as well as what was expected of me in return. He also explained how to ensure its renewal for whatever duration I was studying. " . . . and you can bank all the money you have saved for tuition and have a nice little nest egg when you get your Ph.D. Do you follow me so far?"

"Yes."

He was very thorough and doing a good sell. Carlos and the other director had already told me much of what he explained, but now that I really had it, I wanted to hear it again. My mind was running on two tracks at once. One was following the sales pitch, while the other was observing the unfolding of what I, at another level, had *known* was going to happen. Part of me was playing very cool and grinning impishly about the "nest egg," while another part of me was totally awestruck.

His voice cracked almost imperceptibly as he went on, "I do have to tell you one thing about my school. Here, a 'TA' must teach two courses, twice as much time and work as on the other campus. Are you willing to do that?"

"I think I can handle it," I said.

"A final little detail: My student was a Ph.D. candidate, so she was scheduled to teach intermediate and advanced Spanish to sophomores, juniors, and seniors. Do you know your Spanish, especially subjunctive tense, well enough to handle that?"

"Yes, of course," I said, refusing to reveal that the "little detail" left me slightly shaken. The other teaching job had kept me on my toes, but I would have to cram subjunctive.

"Well then, if you accept this assistantship, you must come to pick up your schedule and textbooks today and be prepared to teach those two classes in four days when the semester begins. Can you do that?"

"Yes, I'll be there, and thank you, sir."

I hung up the phone and let out a primal yelp that embodied all the joy and exuberance I had been holding back during the conversation. Lisa came running from her room to see what was happening. When I told her, she became excited, too, and insisted on going with me to get the books. We sang silly songs in the car all the way down to the campus. It was good having her along.

On arriving home my first impulse was to phone Carlos to thank him for his constant encouragement, but he had not yet returned from his vacation.

I was beside myself! I had my teaching assistantship for graduate school! I savored what it felt like while I cooked, while I relaxed in a bubble bath, and while I lounged around daydreaming about living on campus. It was a dream come true. It meant all my tuition and fees were paid for the duration. We could move to a comfortable two-bedroom campus garden apartment. I would not have to split my focus by working in a different field. My job would reinforce my field of study. And as if that weren't enough, I would receive a stipend—a paycheck!—that would enable Lisa and me to live modestly well. Everything was now in perfect sync.

I now knew what it felt like to want something so much, to *know* I'm going to get it, and to really get it. Now I had four days to cram Spanish subjunctive and teach myself how to teach advanced Spanish.

I knew I could do it.

The first month was hard. With no housing vacancies I had a long commute. Difficult course assignments kept me studying long into the night. It was imperative that I know without hesitation the material I taught. Commuting, lesson planning, paper correcting, studying, and traffic delays consumed huge blocks of time. I was always rushing and always tired. I did little else but commute, teach, study, and sleep. I pushed myself mercilessly the first weeks until my body finally adjusted to the new schedule and balanced my energy against my needs. One Monday morning when I panicked because I'd fallen asleep without doing the laundry, Lisa had done it all, guessing which clothes I'd need. I was moved by the many ways she supported my efforts, often before I even asked for help.

Finally I adjusted to the new schedule. I had reviewed so intensely what I had to teach that I now knew the entire textbook. My grad Spanish course work was so interesting that my study speed greatly improved. While the inane literature of Franco's censored Spain left me cold, the vibrant, earthy magic realism of Latin America excited me. Its infinite variety, its differences in vocabulary, region to region, fascinated me. In pre-Colombian studies, I felt strangely familiar with certain Incan folkloric tales, but stranger still were the panoramic visions that flashed across my forehead like a movie of the Mexican Yucatan. I was unaccustomed to such "movies" and had no time to ponder these phenomena, so I dismissed them as probable scenes from the many movies I had seen in childhood.

Two months into the fall semester, I learned I had an apartment in grad family housing for January. With that news, I relaxed into the commute, knowing it was temporary.

We moved on schedule into campus housing. The well-kept academic community of garden apartments boasted commonalties of intellectual pursuit, limited funds, and pets. Our roomy apartment cost less than $200. There was a Swap Shop for used clothing, books, toys, and other items next to a food co-op two blocks from our unit. Across the court were a library and tennis courts. Lisa's school bus and the campus shuttle stopped at our corner. Everything we needed was nearby, just like our first apartment after Alex left.

Lisa found as much baby-sitting as she desired right in our building, and I soon offered evening adult classes in Spanish in a nearby middle school.

As spring approached, the university allotted several acres of nearby unused land to graduate students for gardening. The School of Agriculture instructed us, distributed gardening pamphlets, piped in water, and set up spigots for hoses. We sectioned off plots in desired sizes. Our only expenses were a modest tilling fee and fence wire. It was my first gardening experience.

The plots were separated by narrow walkways. When it became a mosaic of sprouted seeds, we named it "Plot City."

I centered a strawberry pyramid on my double plot like a mandala, rising in four tiers, and I grew compatible flowers and herbs. I talked to the garden while I worked, at times to individual plants. Soon I had bumper crops, including weeds, but after the first weeding, I learned to mulch.

One day I pedaled to Plot City to harvest squash and tomatoes. I also found peppers, beets, okra, and late radishes. I had to make two trips to get everything home. We kept what we could eat and gave the rest away. Several months later Lisa asked, "Mom, can we go to the supermarket and buy some chicken or meat?"

I realized we had almost totally subsisted on the garden for three months! We had slipped very naturally and quietly into a healthy vegetarian life style, rounding it out with milk, bread, rice, beans, pasta, and cookies.

One afternoon a Plot City neighbor asked what special tricks made my garden yield such large crops.

"I have no tricks," I replied. "I do what everybody does."

"No, no," she said, "I don't mean that. We all do that. I see you here before sundown sometimes standing around looking at the plants. Once or twice I thought I heard you talking, but when I looked up, you were alone."

"Oh," I answered, "well, when I come down to see how the plants are doing, I always feel a kind of presence in the garden, as though the plants themselves are alive and they understand me on some level, and I guess I end up talking to them. I'm excited by how beautiful they are and I tell them so and always thank them. When I talk to them, I feel something happen inside as though someone is pouring love into my heart. I feel it expanding me until I'm standing there with tears in my eyes. It's love overflowing, and it feels like it's coming from the plants. I guess we're a mutual admiration team."

She shot me a suspicious look and inquired what I was studying. I answered and asked the same of her.

"Biology," she scowled authoritatively. "And I want to say that if you want to keep your gardening tricks secret, it's up to you, but as for talking to your plants, you're wasting your time. I can guarantee that they can't hear you."

I let the guarantee fly past me. I shrugged and left without trying to explain. My relationship with my garden needed no tampering.

Occasionally I would see her in her garden casting dark glances my way. As I continued my horticultural conversations, my bumper crops flourished every season throughout graduate school.

Life was smoother than when I was an undergraduate. I was focused on one area of study, more intellectually mature than when I was an undergraduate, and had no big problems in my life. My TA limited me to two courses each semester, so my teaching quality could remain high. I stretched the normal two-year master's program over a longer span and became a more experienced teacher. It was a respite after chaos.

I added two more teaching jobs for income and experience. The dean of the medical school needed a medical Spanish course. I was the only student with a medical vocabulary, acquired in my father-in-law's living room. A nearby international corporation also needed a Spanish course for the engineers who coordinated their South American branch activities.

At this point, I was studying my graduate courses, teaching my TA courses, plus teaching Spanish weekly to adults, to medical students, and to corporate engineers each two afternoons a week. It gave me a wonderful array of course designing and teaching experience, but left time for little else.

A TV talk show aroused my interest in meditation. I had heard of it since I started college, but every meditator I knew on campus was also heavily into marijuana, so I shrugged it off, assuming it was esoteric theatrics. The guest was an author whose honesty and integrity I respected. He spoke of meditation as a method to relieve stress and recharge energy.

Two days later at a local center, seven of us learned to meditate. Each was asked to describe the first experience.

I saw myself as a twelve year old in a long, flowered dress and a wide picture hat with satin ribbon streamers blowing in the breeze. I made my way through a field of high grass and wild flowers. As I looked at each flower, its colors became brilliant, unlike any earthly flowers I had ever seen. The colors would break out of the flower outlines and diffuse toward me into the air. When they collided with my head and torso, my pores seemed to open to absorb them. Then I left my body to stand aside to see what it looked like, and I could see it filled with swirling colors that blended until all converged in my head and became the most brilliant white I had ever seen. As the dazzling white approached me, a voice interrupted, ordering me to "open my eyes and gently come back from meditation." I came back prematurely, very annoyed at the teacher for aborting my meditation before I had seen the entire scenario.

At home, I tried to duplicate the image, hoping to recapture what had been cut short, but I couldn't. Meditation mellowed my stress and energized me, however, so I continued.

Rafi returned from his three years of volunteer service. We were happy to have him home, but he seemed different now. Very secretive, very angry. He was restless to get back into the mainstream of civilian life again, but insisted he needed a rest after what he'd been through. He was very scattered about whether he wanted to go to college or get a job. He seemed almost afraid to seek a job.

In June I took him to an artist colony an hour away, hoping he would get some ideas. We spent the day weaving through blocks of studios to see if anything fired his interest. When it was nearly dark, we ate in a vegetarian restaurant before heading home. We discussed what we had seen and, though he enjoyed the day, nothing motivated him.

As we left the restaurant, I dropped my car keys and stooped to retrieve them. When I straightened up, I came face to face with an outdated poster and stood transfixed by the picture on it.

It was a man with long hair, deep eyes, and exotic good looks, whose energy still reached out from the faded picture. The rains had blurred his name and the poster information; only the address remained intact. I felt compelled to write to this "ashram"—whatever that was!—and inquire what their programs were about, so I copied it. Rafi teased me about "the long-haired guy in his nightgown" who put me in a trance!

At home I couldn't get it out of my mind. I sent a letter.

Dear Friends,
Please tell me what an "ashram" is. I saw your poster in Newport announcing a Memorial Day program. Please send me information about your programs and tell me what your organization does . . .

A handwritten answer arrived within a week. They explained that an ashram was the home of a guru, that theirs was a yoga center offering programs based on yoga and that the man pictured was their guru. They sent a brochure describing current programs. I became more curious to see this place, but it was three months before I actually went for an introductory weekend.

One Friday in September I set out for the ashram with Mario, a curious neighbor. Neither of us knew about yoga, and we wondered what this ashram was like. It seemed like an eerie adventure of leaving reality to investigate make-believe.

We talked a lot during the three-hour trip. I remember saying that I liked my life, that I had nearly everything I wanted, and I'd soon have a great faculty teaching position with long, exciting vacations—then I could find a mate to feel complete. I really said that! Shades of Alex and Mike! Of course, I didn't mean it in a subservient sense, but I did say it and I thought I wanted it.

Mario didn't like life much then. He felt pressured by his doctoral dissertation and marital problems. He wasn't sure which was worse.

Finally pulling into the ashram parking area, we noticed several women in diaphanous garb walking along the paths. It seemed just right for make-believe, but in contrast to our jeans and sweatshirts for this rural setting.

We entered through a room with shoes piled on long, low shelves and were asked to leave ours. As we waited in line to register, we saw the women in the flowing gowns and realized they were residents dressed in white Indian saris. The male residents wore loose white cotton shirts and what looked like white pajama pants. It was strange, but we determined to keep an open mind.

We sampled a yoga class, toured the grounds, watched a video guru lecture, and just explored. They informed us that they separated the genders on either side of the room for yoga practice and for evening services, which they called *satsang*. It seemed childish to impose such rules on adults. I went, however, to the segregated yoga class.

Guru pictures were everywhere, and whenever residents passed us, they made a gesture that seemed very nice, although we could not understand their words. They all had Sanskrit names which were hard to remember.

Everywhere we turned we found surprises, as well as many other gaping mouths besides our own. Curiosity mounted to see this guru in person, and everyone talked about it at dinner.

Satsang was a spectacle for us. There were excellent musicians playing drums, cymbals, and tambourines in addition to the harmonium that the guru would play during chanting, but before he arrived, residents led the service. I decided to sit with Mario on the men's side of the room despite the rules. The general strangeness made me feel unsettled, and I needed to stay close to my support system.

Chanting was a new experience. We sat cross-legged on the meditation room carpet repeating strange Sanskrit syllables to drumbeats and music. Suddenly two women in saris stood to sway to the beat and uttered strange sounds during the chanting. It triggered a reaction in me that manifested as a stream of uncontrollable giggles. I could do nothing but try to muffle it, without success, and to wish for the proverbial hole in the ground to open and swallow me. It was just too strange, too much strangeness packed into one afternoon.

I was relieved after the giggle attack and finally calmed down when the chanting stopped. It was as if the sounds the women made had triggered a release of tension I was not even aware I had. To my delight, I learned that everyone was so caught up in the chanting frenzy that no one had noticed my giggling. In my impatience to see this guru I looked around to spot a "Restroom" sign where I might hide out until he arrived.

Suddenly the music softened, the rhythm slowed, and all heads turned to the back of the room where the guru was making his entrance.

He was a tall man, about six feet, handsome in an unusual way. His thick, dark hair cascaded over his saffron robe past his shoulders. He walked tall and proud, his hands in prayer, and made eye contact with as many as possible, stopping here and there to give a special blessing. Our eyes locked for a long "instant." I immediately felt self-conscious on the men's side of the room, but his eyes held no judgment. They were the same eyes that had gripped me from the poster outside the restaurant last summer, eyes that invited a clear view of the soul inside. Words were not necessary to perceive the purity of this soul.

The service was reverent but joyful. The chanting became more familiar. The ashram began to feel more hospitable.

Activities ended at nine o'clock. In the female dorm, as we placed our sleeping bags side by side, we learned that Saturday's program began at 4:30 next morning and a sister would come by to wake us. We would begin the day with a jog in the valley, then a yoga session, *satsang*, and breakfast at 8:30. That would be a feat for me! Eight-thirty was my normal waking time. But the first feat would be to get to sleep so early!

Saturday at 4:30 was a cold morning. We proceeded on schedule until it was time for *satsang* again. The guru gave a moving lecture and invited questions. A woman challenged, "What exactly is a guru, and why do these residents bow down to you? Who do you think you are, anyway?"

"A guru is simply a guide," he responded gently. "Some-one who is going where you wish to go and knows the way. I am, for some, an external guru or guide. You each have an inner guru who speaks to you and guides you if you learn to be still and listen. Some people honor me because they see me as a symbol of their inner guru. When they bow to me, it is not to honor the man before you in robes; it is to honor the symbol of their inner guru, that guru who dwells within each of us, guiding and cherishing us, leading us back to God-source. I, too, seek God. I am but a few small steps ahead carrying a lantern, lighting the way."

We sat in silence, absorbing the profundity of his words.

After breakfast, there were more tours. The grounds were beautiful. It was a Shangri-La, bordering a placid lake, tucked in a valley surrounded by green mountains. As I be-gan to get the feel of the place, it occurred to me that saris blowing in the breeze were appropriate in this energy.

They were very aware of health, believing that the body was the temple of the divine soul. To eat what did not en-hance health was to throw garbage into your temple. To neglect to keep the body flexible and well cared for was to inhibit the function of the soul. In keeping with that phi-losophy, they grew most of their food and ate carefully combined and balanced diets. Many worked together in their huge, cheerful kitchen, singing and laughing, prepar-ing the next meal. I noticed that my energy level was decidedly higher than when I arrived. I could certainly use that at home, I thought.

There was a lot of talk about expressing feelings instead of hiding them and "processing" problems while they were fresh instead of allowing them to fester. This was new to me. The pattern I had learned was to hide hurts or risk appear-ing weak and inviting the next blow. This was a little frightening. Processing problems was something I wanted to learn, but I felt I would need someone beside me to poke me whenever I slid back into old patterns.

Before lunch I attended a guided meditation session. I liked yoga, but it was the first time I had experienced guided meditation or visualization, and I fell into the deepest relaxed state I had ever known. I was amazed that I could retain so vividly images I created during visualization. They seemed more real than those I saw with my eyes wide open. I participated in every subsequent guided meditation that weekend.

Lunch was gourmet vegetarian, incredibly wonderful.

After lunch, I walked alone in the woods to digest the new experiences. I needed quiet with my inner self to figure it out and to see where it fit in the context of my life. A very subtle change was taking place. I was no longer feeling strange. I felt more mellow, balanced, relaxed, and I loved the whole world. I was amazed that I had been awake and active for nine hours and still had lots of energy. I couldn't understand exactly what was changing, but it felt important. I couldn't name it yet, but I knew I must trust it.

By mid-afternoon I had an urge to be with the kitchen people, so I walked over and offered to help. I spent two wonderful hours chopping salad veggies to fill the enormous salad bowls and joining in *bhakti* chants. "*Bhakti* chants," they explained, "are Sanskrit devotional chants. Musical family members have written some very beautiful chants in English that you can learn or listen to on tapes. They are chants of adoration. You can just sing out your love for God."

Yes, I felt it. I left the kitchen in an endorphin high, made my way to the dorm to bathe and dress for evening *satsang*. My jeans felt too crude. I approached a young resident to ask if I could borrow a sari anywhere. She led me to an adjacent building that housed an endless supply of clothing of all kinds.

"We try to live simply and not accumulate too much stuff like we did outside. Everyone brings one's surplus here. You can probably find a sari somewhere. I'll help you wrap it. If you need a sweater, a shawl, or a blanket, you'll find that, too. Please help yourself."

I found a sari and a shawl, both white. I felt more integrated into this special energy now, so I returned to the dorm to prepare for *satsang*.

The chanting seemed less strange than the night before. The guru arrived later, so the residents stepped up the tempo of the chants. Soon he made his entrance as he had the night before, this time in a saffron-trimmed white robe.

He proceeded to the altar, sat before the harmonium, and began to lead chants. It was a replay of the night before, except for one thing. Encouraged by the presence of the women up front who seemed very natural dancing to the speedy tempo, I joined in, swaying and clapping to the rhythm.

Suddenly I felt something welling up inside my chest, making its way up, up, up, until it all came out through my eyes—tears, pumping from my tear ducts, rolling down my cheeks, salting the corners of my mouth, sobs forcing their way up from the very tips of my toes, from the most unfathomable depths of me, heaving, wracking my body as uncontrollable sounds burst forth, while I stood by as a spectator, unable to stop, unable to explain to those who came to help that it was happiness, bliss, not sadness that overflowed from my being. And I stood there, tear-soaked, marveling at my capacity for joy.

When it stopped, I sat in trance, feeling the deepest peace that I had ever felt. Through my closed eyes I saw the seat of peace as a brilliant, unearthly light with flashes of color filling my chest. What seemed like an eternity later, I returned to the here and now, aware of the guru's voice as though from far in the background. I perceived millions of threads connecting me to everyone in the room, everyone in the universe, like lanes interlaced, incessantly sending-receiving, and I understood in a flash of knowing that my heart chakra had opened wide.

I walked to the women's dorm in a cloud of bliss, meditated deeply amid a room full of scurrying guests, then fell promptly asleep.

Sunday morning I overslept. The sun came up as I opened my eyes. I remembered the experience the moment I awoke, and it came alive again. I felt differently inside now, and I simply couldn't wipe the smile from my face. I wanted to get out into the sunshine and the cold morning air, so I dressed quickly.

"You're looking bright this morning," commented my dorm neighbor. "That was quite a heart chakra opening you had last night. I had a similar experience the first time I came here. Is this your first visit?"

"Yes," I replied. "I think I'm still in the experience. How long does it last? It still feels very alive and beautiful."

"It varies with the person and the circumstances. It's not something you can manipulate. It just is, and it is for as long as it is. A lot depends on attitude. Just accept it, enjoy it."

"I feel a deep peace after every meditation here, yet there are no meditation rules. I could never reach this depth before, and I could never meditate at bedtime."

"You're right. Here, meditation is simply melting into the energy of God and letting go. Intent determines whether it will energize or relax. It's really easy. Just keep your spine straight, don't grab your passing thoughts, and intend to feel the presence of God in your special inner sanctum. There's no one correct way."

She was right. It felt like a melting into God. I wanted to ask more questions, but she had to coordinate her travel plans for the afternoon departure, so we hugged and said good-by, and I headed toward the main building to join the program.

I had never had these experiences when I first learned meditation. The trainers had not taught us to melt into the energy of God nor to feel His presence. God was, in fact, never mentioned. My first meditation was so beautiful, but those that followed were flat, and I eventually abandoned that center.

When I first learned to meditate, it reawakened a childhood longing for God. I recalled how I felt when I was small and would compose poems to God while I pretended to be asleep. *Bhakti* chanting filled me with that same feeling. They were like beatitudes set to music.

After a wonderful final day, we headed home in an aura of melancholy. Having pursued different interests during the weekend, Mario and I had uniquely personal experiences. Sharing them shortened our trip back to the campus.

We agreed that we had experienced the greatest reality we had ever known, and we were leaving that reality now to go play out our lives on a huge game board.

Mario had new attitudes about his priorities. I no longer felt incomplete. Something had changed that made me absolutely certain that I was complete just as I was. I had also once said that if I ever found Mr. Right and he was not on a spiritual path, I could find a way to accommodate that. My feet were set firmly on my path now. There would be no accommodations, no compromises.

We chatted about the ashram program with the same affection as we would have spoken of a happy family reunion. We completed the trip home in relative quiet, each calmly within the energy of the treasure we had just discovered within ourselves.

We didn't understand how to resolve the dilemma of living our lives in Earth's dimension while longing to be in another. We knew only that we must allow ourselves to grow into insights at our own pace as we continued our daily lives.

As I stood in the campus parking lot Monday morning juggling my briefcase, lunch box, and tape recorder, someone called me from across the field. I looked up and saw my colleague Victor running toward me.

"What have you been up to?" he asked. "You look different. Did you go on vacation? You look radiant! But it's more. It's something intangible. Did you fall in love? What's going on?"

I stood smiling, unable to keep up with his questions.

"If you can slow down," I said, "I'll try to tell you. The 'me' you used to know went away to a wonderful place for the weekend, and a new and different 'me' came back last night."

"But where is this place? You look so wonderful. There's a kind of glow. But it's more than the way you look. I could feel it from across the campus. What is it?" he insisted.

"I don't really know, Victor. I wasn't aware anything was noticeable. I just had an amazing inner experience that I don't fully understand yet, but I thought it was all on the inside. I had no idea anyone else could see it . . . or feel it . . . sense it . . . whatever."

"I know you have a class to give and I see you brought your lunch, so can I come to your office for lunch and talk about this?" he asked.

"Sure, see you at lunch break."

By lunch time, Victor arrived to find three students in my office, just sitting. It seemed everybody was sensing something. Nobody had a problem to discuss or a schedule conflict to resolve; they just wanted to be around me. I wondered privately if I had stepped in catnip on the way, or if I suddenly resembled the Pied Piper. What I really wanted was to be alone. I still felt the full essence of the experience, and I wished to wallow in nectar as long as possible, but I couldn't do it in an office full of people.

When I arrived home, I was happy to find Rafi out somewhere and Lisa on the phone with her friends. I knew that was good for two or three hours. I quickly slipped into my room, shut the door, sat cross-legged on the bed, and visualized being at the ashram meditating. It felt as if waves of nectar, of love, were sweeping over me, and I lost track of time.

Six days went by like that. I continued to feel as if I were swimming in a pool of nectar during every waking moment. I thought it would last only a day or two but, after a week, it showed no sign of abating. I began to plan my days around this feeling. I would plan lessons as fast as I could for four days at a time so that I could be free for days. I would plan match-ups and multiple-choice quizzes that required minimal time to correct. I would review assignments for my graduate classes and spend hours speed-studying ahead. At home, I would spend as much time as possible meditating in my room. Food didn't interest me. I'd forget to cook, and Lisa would prepare something simple, thinking I was too tired. I was grateful to eat whatever she prepared without complaint, for it was so full of love.

A week later I pondered, "How long can I go on like this?" I had come down to a slightly lesser level that allowed me to function in a more grounded way but, nevertheless, it continued. Wherever I walked, it was as though I waded through a pool of joy. People I hardly knew were showing up, standing around, hardly knowing what to say. No one understood it.

"Is there some kind of energy around me," I wondered, "that attracts people like a magnet? The woman in the ashram said it was a heart chakra opening, but should it feel like this? I was so entranced by the meditations that I forgot to ask about chakra openings."

I decided to call the ashram that afternoon to see if they could throw some light on what was happening to me.

The resident I spoke to seemed very knowledgeable. I posed my question and described the reactions.

"Sounds right," he said. "It's a very potent, irresistible love energy. It has filled up your aura and they're feeling it. Your aura must be enormous if they can feel it across a campus. It's an energy of unconditional love. You needn't worry about uninvited advances because it's not that kind of energy. But tell me, how do you feel about these people? For that matter, about everyone, especially people you met here?"

"I haven't thought much about it," I said. "I like them all, I guess. Especially the guru."

He probed for finer details of my feelings, and after several tries, I was saying, "It feels as if I'm in love but without a focus. I love everybody, but I love them all the same. It's stronger than romantic love; it's deeper or better—oh, I don't know, in some way it's different. I think it's the way the guru loves everyone and the way I love him. What's strange is that the more he loves everyone, the more I feel loved, and I overflow to tears, happy tears." I was getting very emotional. "You must think I'm really crazy, talking like this."

"No," he assured me. "You're not crazy. You've been zapped by the guru's *shakti* energy, and it has caused your kundalini life force to rise in its upward path through the energy centers called chakras and blasted your heart chakra wide open. Don't be upset; there's no damage. If what you're experiencing is 'all nectar,' as you put it, then it appears you had no serious blocks to obstruct the kundalini's rise. You were in the right place at the right moment for it to happen. The people who are attracted to you are feeling your aura that is now filled with divine unconditional love from the open heart chakra. They intuitively want to be close to that energy, so bear with them. Just keep meditating, keep doing the best you can in the world, and keep a positive outlook. Remember, God is always there for you, and you're growing ever closer. Come back to see us soon, and call if you have more questions."

I felt better after calling. I understood now what had happened and the big attraction that was drawing people. It was humbling.

When it leveled off another week later, it had continued for three weeks. I came down grounded. I understood my path; I understood the game board. I understood my direction and my unseen support system. I understood the importance of playing out my daily earth routine, and dreams assured me that the reality at the end of the game was undeniably splendid.

I knew I'd never be the same again.

The German department director, Dr. Negus, taught astrology in his campus office to interested students. He invited us to join the Astrological Society of Princeton, which he had founded in his home town.

At the first meeting I attended, everyone wore tags showing not names but their Sun, Moon, and Ascendant signs. There was an interesting lecture and a delectable snack table for afterward. It was wonderfully freeing to mingle with people with whom I could speak "astrologese" without being called a witch or a weirdo, for astrology was accepted here as a wonderful tool.

I met many interesting people and well-known astrologers there. I made friends with a tiny, ninety-year-old Englishwoman named Nell, a direct descendant of one of Geoffrey Chaucer's characters from *The Canterbury Tales.* "Don't think they were characters, my dear," she warned. "They were real people."

Her fragile body housed a lucid mind, a sharp wit, and a heart filled with love. She feistily called lecturers on errors and she fearlessly rocked boats.

She began a serious interpretation of my chart one day, pinpointing flaws I thought were well hidden. She invited me to visit her to talk more about it. I couldn't afford an astrology reading, so I made excuses about my busy schedule. She quickly intuited my reason and said, "I never charge for reading charts, my dear. Do come so we can talk."

I made time to visit her and found her full of surprises. As we sipped tea, she spoke of earlier studies with Krishnamurti, tours with her musician husband, renowned celebrities, and teachers she'd met. She always added Krishnamurti's words, "it is all on the inner plane" to her good-bys.

She called Earth "our free-will planet" where our choices determine everything. She said time did not exist in all dimensions. She spoke of reincarnation and lives in series connected by the same lessons.

She mentioned having had a life reading by a psychic

named Edgar Cayce in 1943. "It's about a past life," she explained. "I was known as Zermada when the Essenes were educating the Child Jesus. I traveled from my native Phoenicia to confer with my dear friend Judith about some of those decisions, for I was a respected astrologer in my own land. If ever you visit the place Mr. Cayce founded, you must read the transcript of my reading. I would show you my copy, but I have temporarily misplaced it.

"I would like you to call me Zermada," she continued. "I dearly love its vibration. The ancient languages have a stronger spiritual vibration than the modern ones and sound has a very strong vibration in itself. Every time you call a person by his or her name, you energize the vibration of that sound. Zermada is of an ancient, holy vibration, and I would like to energize it for myself. I have asked you to do this for me because you are so open to these truths. Will you do it, my dear?"

I couldn't refuse her simple request. It made her happy.

"My Saturn is at your Ascendant, my dear," she said. "It indicates that in a prior lifetime I was your teacher, and we have come together with this connection because I owe you something—something I have yet to teach you. I haven't been able to intuit yet what it is, but when I do, I'll teach it to you. Let's continue meeting. Don't be smug about what you learn. Things have a way of being correct on one level but wrong on another. Keep an open mind. Things are not always as they seem."

I had heard that in the ashram.

She was the most fascinating person I'd met in years. Whenever I left her home, I'd think how extraordinary that a woman her age had such independent, offbeat ideas.

I didn't yet recognize it as wisdom.

With my course work completed, it was time to begin studying for grad oral exams. I had four months to cram every book on a four-page list of titles—literature as well as critiques, all in Spanish—many of which were not included in my courses. I groaned in resistance.

I set up my bedroom as a study and sorted, labeled, and stacked books from the list. In a corner, I fashioned a tiny meditation altar with a small white candle to symbolize divine light, an incense burner, a supply of saffron and sandalwood incense, and a tiny vase with a small wildflower. To complete my personal "shrine," I taped pictures on the wall above it of my most inspiring spiritual teachers. This room became my sanctuary; in this vibration I would claim my dream.

Then I treated myself to a pre-cram movie fling, *Close Encounters of the Third Kind.* I would knuckle down to business the next morning unless, I joked, a UFO dropped by to take me for a galactic cruise.

That night I dreamed I relived the emotion I'd felt during the movie when the UFO communicated in colors and musical tones. As Richard Dreyfus approached in astronaut garb to board the mother ship, I accompanied him, feeling the indescribable wonder of making the ET connection. We were going for a cruise and I knew the territory. It felt very real.

The next night late, I sat by the window studying. I heard a humming sound outside. The mother ship?? A cruise?? I was excited/terrified but refused to look to really see. I sent a strong thought: Not now, my friends. Later, after my orals.

"Why didn't you go?" Victor asked, when I told him.

"I couldn't leave without an explanation. And you know how Lisa would take that kind of explanation! Also I want my degree, evidence of the hard work I've done here. When I return from a cruise, I'll still have to work, you know. Life goes on."

Maybe I was a little too grounded!

The following morning, I browsed through the Co-op Swap Shop and saw a book, *Edgar Cayce's Story of the Origin and Destiny of Man.* It was about the same man who had given Nell's past-life reading. The jacket spiel called it "a psychic's vision of history." Tucked under the flap was a chronology of each amazing psychic milestone in Mr. Cayce's life and a brief about his over 14,000 trance readings on health and past lives housed in the A.R.E. Library in Virginia Beach. The contents showed chapters about the Mayas, Incas, Atlantis, and reincarnation. Would the psychic's view of the pre-Colombians match the historians'? I took it into my study to browse during my breaks. The history chapters were tempting, but when I saw "Reincarnation: The Continuity of Life" and "The Human Destiny," I could not resist.

I was particularly impressed by a single line embedded in a Cayce quote, "*Mind is the builder ever, whether in the spirit or in the flesh.*" The author expounded upon it by saying of karmic patterns:

Mind is the builder, and no effort is ever wasted. Thought upon thought, line upon line, we build that which we are and will be in the future . . . and what we do today will be meted out to us in like measure in some future life, for man is indeed the captain of his soul, the creator of his fate.

I had witnessed these concepts in my life already. My mind and my will seemed intricately connected. It said I could create happiness or disaster. Out of love for my children, I had built much. They deserved my best and seeing them happy and healthy was my sweetest reward. This seemed to say that I had created rewards for next time. What about all the rewards I had already received?

Cayce spoke often of karma, the balancing of cause and effect. "*The evasion of a law puts off that condition which must eventually be met.*" I could relate to this. Before I knew about the karma concept, I usually preferred to face issues when they came up rather than put them off until later.

Further on it stated, "... *any close relationship of long standing is almost certain to be karmic, good or bad.*" Alex and I were a prime example of that. From the time I first learned of reincarnation and karma, I had that one pegged.

The parts about the Incas and Mayas felt truer than what I had studied. The historians claimed to be limited by lack of written records before they had broken the hieroglyphic codes. They dared not lend credence to anything suggesting dates earlier than Egypt. What would my professors call this book!

The "Atlantis" section tore me from my studies for days. At times I forgot I was reading and could "see" clearly what was described, as though I were reliving it. I felt that I had been in Atlantis, but not as an Atlantean. I had seen these things before. The descriptions quickly brought them forward in my consciousness again. Had I been a guest, an observer, a visitor from some other place?

I had to force myself to put this book aside for later investigation and carefully put it in a very special place.

One sunny April morning I reported for grad orals. A thesis would have been easier, but Rafi wasn't doing well and I anticipated too many interruptions to a written work.

I waited exhausted, not nervous, in the outer office. For four months I had studied from 10:00 a.m. to 4:00 a.m., except for three teaching jobs. I felt a numb, light-headed fatigue and worried that it might create blocks, but now there was no turning back.

For three hours, six tenured professors would cover every literary genre of Spain from Visigoths to the present and of all Latin American countries from pre-Colombian era through our century. My head was literally stuffed! I had no way of knowing which questions they would ask, but if I didn't answer correctly, years of effort went down the drain.

After three hours of poker-faced grilling, I wanted to know my fate immediately, but they asked me to wait outside. As I thought about the answers I gave, I realized that when I visualized the question written across my forehead, I "saw" the text section and sometimes the page numbers and could almost read my answers. This was a new awareness, but I would soon see if I'd read the correct pages.

When they came out to congratulate me, it was somewhat anticlimactic. I kept my promise to myself to celebrate in a warm, bubbly tub, followed by twelve hours' sleep.

The next day I regretted that after years of work I could not feel excited about its successful climax. Studying it was more exciting. In the quiet under a willow tree, I pondered what my master's work had taught me. I realized it was much more than Hispanic studies—and more important.

The university generously granted us the apartment and garden through July. The Spanish department on the main campus generously contracted me to teach an intensive summer course throughout June and an intermediate course for the fall semester.

I exited with my foot still in the door.

5

THE ASHRAM EXPERIENCE: SPIRIT, MY LIVE-IN LOVER

There are more things in heaven and earth than you
have dreamed of, Horatio . . .   –Shakespeare

SUMMER WAS half over. Marketing myself was not as easy as studying, teaching, or designing courses! The fall course I had contracted for was my only employment prospect. It would barely cover rent. I had not found an apartment either, only a place on a five-month waiting list. Meanwhile, Dina and her husband rearranged their basement to accommodate Lisa and me, and Rafi got his own place.

One sizzling morning after teaching a class, I trudged across campus to a frigid air-conditioned Spanish department office where everyone worked in sweaters. As I sat cooling off, a student assistant who was sorting mail dropped two letters in my lap. One bore the familiar logo of the corporation where I had just taught. They now needed a culture course and their pharmaceutical affiliate needed medical Spanish. The EPA also needed Spanish for their Puerto Rican operations. By lunch time I had called them and negotiated three contracts for September classes. The corporation had spread the word as had an EPA employee from my evening class. With these, plus the university course and another evening course, the year's financial needs were covered in eleven classroom hours per week. The contracts had literally dropped into my lap. I discreetly bowed to my unseen angels once again.

The heat seemed less oppressive as I headed to my car with a bounce in my step. I heard Dr. Cortez's voice behind me.

"I haven't received your application yet for Ph.D. candidacy. Why are you procrastinating?"

"Dr. Cortez, I've decided not to pursue a Ph.D. now," I said. "I must do something else, though I'm not exactly sure what. I might apply later."

I watched his face change from a smile to an angry scowl.

"Had I known when you first applied that you didn't intend to pursue the Ph.D., I would not have approved your entry into our program. Why did you come here at all?"

"But I had intended . . . "

Before I finished, he stormed off in another direction.

I took the long way home to ponder it, yearning for someone to help me sort it out. I regretted that he assumed I was ungrateful or too dense to appreciate his interest in my career.

Why indeed had I come here at all? I wanted an upgraded career—intellectually challenging, important, enjoyable. I wanted college for my children, financial security, a comfortable life, and nice, long summer vacations. I deserved it after years of hard work, and for that I needed a Ph.D.

But something had subtly altered along the way.

Could I live my professors' life style? An honored position teaching, administering departments, traveling to research important authors, creating analyses and critiques to fulfill the "publish or perish" edict to guard my tenure.

Tenure was the "carrot"—lifetime positions, advancement guaranteed. It was approved or rejected by peers, and I had seen gifted teachers rejected for not conforming to expectations of jealous colleagues. It was a supportive, sheltered existence.

Why couldn't I want that life now as I used to want it?

I had what it took. I was a good teacher and I could write. I cared enough about my students to motivate them to greater achievements than they believed they could reach.

Could I conform and abstain from rocking the conservative boat of academia, given just cause? I knew I couldn't. Subjective tenure decisions would be the first boat I'd rock! Could I return every fall to classrooms to continue the same routine? Not I. I would rebel, insisting on teaching experientially, dragging my students to another country to learn language and culture by immersion. Could I spend *all* my summers in the same place in myopic focus on another's writing instead of creating my own? This tore at my heart!

My professors taught a stunning array of literature with compassion and commitment although none had lived the hardships of human drama about which they so brilliantly expounded. Few had friends outside the discipline they taught. The campus had become their world, a good world indeed—prestigious, neat, dignified, comfortable, secure.

I silently reprimanded myself for not being able to conform to this nice, tidy world. I felt like a fly blemishing a bowl of gourmet soup.

My history was one of rebellion, not conformism. Rebellion had saved me from stagnation; conformism would decay my soul. My family had a low threshold of ambition, with no hope of education and, as if in some unspoken pact to defend their own helplessness, labeled it snobbery. They feared censure for attempting to rise above the mire of mediocrity that engulfed us; that fear caused my grandmother to reject the scholarship I was offered. They felt unworthy and assumed I was part of their unworthiness.

"Stop the foolishness!" She had slammed the lid down on the stew pot. "It's time for you to get work and bring home some money. We've supported you long enough. Girls don't need college. They end up married and it's a waste. If you were a boy, it would be different."

In a fit of rage, I'd quit school. No penalty could make me return. Humiliation before the neighbors was the only vengeance I could levy to make her feel how deeply she had hurt me. I swore I would leave at eighteen, break her patterns, and live my values and life on my own terms. Leaving the birthplace was sacrilegious to my family. I watched the furrow deepen in her brow as she countered that I lacked courage to fulfill that unthinkable threat. It was not a threat; I did it for me.

Books were taboo at home, except for German fairy tales and textbooks. "A waste of money. Adults must work," Grandma stormed. "They can't waste time reading books!"

She collected my certificates from summer library programs and used them and my report cards to prove her parenting skills. When I showed off the books and bookcase I'd spent my first teen-age paycheck on, she condemned the effrontery of "foolishly wasting money while everyone struggles to make ends meet."

I became a closet reader. When I married Alex, I was expected to read and happily complied. Wherever we lived, I enrolled in the local college or university, but frequent moves and increasing child care forced postponement of my education. Finally, years after our divorce, my drive having never diminished, I pursued my dream of higher education.

Freedom from responsibilities came late. During the child-priority years, I grabbed any available job or created work to support us all. After years spent grappling in the material arena, I knew firsthand its twists and turns. The unexpected always developed in my life and forced me to deal with it. I had learned to live life that way, to solve problems, make friends at all levels, explore ideas, and discover truths. In this way I had become aware of unseen guidance.

Would a tenured life style dissipate my resourcefulness? The sweet security of a placid life might quickly become stagnation. Could I live so insulated, so proper, so conservatively? Was I willing to limit my friendships to colleagues? Could I live straight-jacketed, however secure, in academia's cloistered world? I couldn't.

I was different; it was as simple as that.

I would miss the magical spontaneity and the element of surprise that threaded through my life. As an "authority," I would lack the freedom to explore, as a student, undergraduate physics or whatever struck my fancy. I might even miss the challenge of occasional struggle.

While part of me wanted security, a stronger part wanted adventure and spontaneous interaction with life. The drive to be true to myself was most compelling. I concluded that a secure, conservative life style would, in the end, cost far too much.

At the deepest level I knew this was not to be my kind of life, at least not now. I knew I had to experience this schooling even if I went no further. It was also time to come to terms with letting go.

But why had everything fallen so neatly into place to open the way for me here?

Since my ashram experience, I had begun to quickly intuit an order of priorities in my life. A sense of certainty made me obey the signal blindly. To be bound, I sensed, to the tiny part of the world I now walked away from was no longer important in the larger scheme of my life. It was a closing phase in an interim preceding change.

I thought of it now as a sideline rather than a career. I had teaching skills I could apply to anything I knew with great flexibility, more than academia allowed. I could always contract to design special courses or teach in the university. But I had come full circle to the same question of why my guides had opened the way so dramatically for me to be here if this were not to be my career.

Why here?

Certain experiences required my physical presence in this location. I encountered a mentor who advanced my knowledge of higher astrology. I found Edgar Cayce—whose imprint on my life would last forever—in the campus Swap Shop. And one magical, priceless day I was zapped by a guru's shakti energy and my heart chakra opened wide. None were ordinary coincidences, any more than the quiet synchronicity with which all our needs were met from the moment we came here.

Perhaps I would not have found them had I not been on this campus. Perhaps I needed the focus of grad school to clearly see opportunities, to open to receive and act upon them.

I appreciated my education, but it trained my mind, not my soul. In their intricate connection, opening my mind led to opening my soul. Soul learning's greater good surpassed that from any academic institution on earth. Now was my time for it.

I made no apology. I felt at peace with my decision.

For the next two years I enjoyed designing courses for various groups, though it required more work than straight teaching.

My continued visits to the ashram deepened my understanding of Eastern philosophy, and I marveled at how similar were the concepts to the principles in Cayce's readings. The similarity shouldn't have surprised me, for both stemmed from universal spiritual truths that existed long before religions or churches abridged the ancient teachings and divided the people.

Meditating on those truths led me quickly into higher
states and, while my first impulse was to share that state
with friends, my friends were not interested in "the weird
stuff." I soon learned to hold what was sacred sacredly inside myself. Years spent rearing a large family and cram-
ming so much into each day had often kept me out of the
mainstream. Responsibilities sequestered me somewhat
from peer influence. Having long been forced to make decisions alone, carry out plans alone, and take responsibility
for my actions alone, I had high confidence in doing things
myself. Peer pressure did not make a dent. I liked acting independently, going my own way, being who I am.

My guidance came more and more from inside, often
from dreams. It was my most reliable guidance since early
childhood and I began to listen again. Dreams came more
frequently now.

For some time I had yearned to live at the ashram, to im-
merse my days in a yogic life style and have it become so
much a part of myself that when I returned I could walk
through the world in a bubble of spiritual peace. I wrestled,
however, with the dilemma of generating income in a depressed rural area. If I left a job to go there for a year, I would
have to struggle again upon returning to find a teaching position in a downhill economy.

I vacillated. All the résumés I sent came back with apologies. As the urge to go became stronger, making a decision
became harder.

One night near the end of August I meditated and prayed
for guidance.

My eyes shot open unusually early that morning, just after the final scene of a dream. I sat up in bed, unsure of
where I was. I looked around the room, trying to sense any
familiarity of furniture, curtains, books on a window sill,
clothes carelessly thrown over a corner chair. Yes, I was here.
It was a dream and I was back, amazed that what had hap-

pened was so real, so moving, so significant. Here is the dream:

> I'm going on a trip. Alex's mother phones to ask if I
> can give Alex her love. His place is on my way so I agree.
>   I arrive at a large brick building and make my way to
> the entrance past a garden party of beautifully dressed
> people under tall trees.
>   A matron knows why I'm there. She signals me to
> follow her through a wide, well-lit hall that grows dim-
> mer as it slants steadily downward. Finally we're in a
> basement so dark that I can hardly see.
>   I perceive the outline of barred cells with depressed,
> sad men inside. Openings are where cell doors would
> be, but no doors. Nothing holds the men there except
> themselves!
>   The matron leads me through the cells until we
> come to Alex's tiny barred cubicle at a dead end. He is
> alone with a book, reclining on a bare bunk.
>   "You came!" he glows when he sees me. "You really
> came." He extends his arms to hug me and I respond.
>   He's so happy to see me! He makes room for me to
> sit beside him.
>   "I'm really so sorry." He's very sad.
>   "It's really all right. We're fine now," I say.
>   He keeps saying he's sorry and peering into my eyes.
> He looks so hurt, as if he has punished himself a mil-
> lion times over. I can't stand to see him suffering. The
> hurt and struggle I experienced from his abandon-
> ment seems nothing now. All I want to do is console
> him and heal his hurt.
>   "We're all fine now. The children are grown and we
> made it through fine. Please don't feel so bad."
>   "But it must have been so hard." Such sadness fills
> his eyes. "I'm so sorry for the hardship. It wasn't fair to
> you."
>   "It's really O.K. We all became much stronger for it.

It was hard at first, but we can do anything now."

"But how . . . ?" he insists.

"We're fine. Really. Maybe you were meant to play that part. I mean, the heavy responsibility for children is in *my* horoscope, not yours. So is doing it myself, doing it alone, getting my education, and all that. It looks like that was the way my soul wanted to do it. Please don't feel bad. It really came out all right. We're fine."

He relaxes and we chat like old visiting friends who care a lot about each other. He seems calmer.

It's time for me to leave. He takes my hand in a reluctant gesture, but I must go back.

"Call me when you get back," he asks and I agree, assuming that he wants to be sure I get back all right.

When I call from home the next day, I see through the phone as the matron answers. I ask to speak to Alex.

"Who—? There's nobody here by that name."

"Of course, there is," I argue. "I just visited him yesterday. You took me to him."

"Oh, him. He's not here any more. He left right after you did. But he left you a message—something you need to know."

She fumbles to pick up something from the floor and holds it up for me to see.

It is a torn-off side of a cardboard box with a message printed roughly on it in large, block letters:
                    MOVE CLOSER

An immediate *knowing* told me it said YES to the ashram question. I decided to go as soon as I completed the fall class and other December commitments. I would spend Christmas with the kids and leave right after the new year.

But why did I dream about Alex? It had been years since I had even thought of him. Why was Alex entangled in the message about the ashram?

It felt real, straightforward, urgent, as if Alex needed to visit and it was the only window he could get through.

I could still feel his hurt, his remorse, his disappointment in himself, his sincerity. I had never seen him like that. All the anger I'd ever felt dissolved the instant I sensed his anguish and pain. The old love resurrected in my heart and all I could think of was to console him, to ease his suffering.

Everything I'd told him was true. We had really grown from it. We were all fine and getting on with our lives. It amazed me that my astrological chart came up in the dream. In my waking state I had never thought of its connection to Alex. I was too busy using its strengths to mask my fears about life. It all made sense now. Alex played a role, as did we all, in my drama. How could that be? Nothing in my spiritual studies had referred to this. I had never before felt the emotions in a dream so strongly. How would I ever understand this?

By November we had celebrated Lisa's wedding and I was preparing to leave for the ashram. The university liked my teaching evaluations and had extended my contract through spring and the following school year. I declined, saying only that I was moving to another state, and once again I appeared to shun a kindness with ingratitude. I would not submit to their judgment nor seek their validation. I would stick to my plan and go.

I arrived at the ashram one snowy January afternoon with some clothes, books, notebooks, pens, tape player, and my Shiva statue. I stored furniture I hadn't sold, put some valuables in safekeeping, and left the dog with Lisa.

My daughters' supportive calls and visits helped me to adjust to the new place and the new routine. Lisa told me during a visit that my mother had called her to ask why they'd allowed me to join a cult that would take all my money.

"Grandma," Lisa had told her, "Mom wanted to go. We

couldn't stop her. And she didn't bring money with her. It's a nice place, not a cult. I visit her some weekends. She's fine."

One day I shared lunch and an interesting conversation about reincarnation with Chandra, an older resident. She knew much more about it than I did, so I listened attentively. We then shared tidbits about our dreams. I told her about the dream that led me to the ashram and the scenario about Alex before the message came. When I finished, she sat staring at me.

"Do you really think that was a dream?" she asked. "Or was it a contact? Could you have actually contacted your ex-husband?"

"Are you serious?" I asked, dumfounded.

"Very much so," she continued. "That was why you felt the emotions so acutely. Don't you understand why the woman said he'd left right after you left?"

"Not really," I answered.

"He needed your forgiveness before he could forgive himself and move on. Only then could he be released, but he couldn't come to you until you were ready to forgive him. When you released him with true forgiveness, he flew out of there in a mini-second to get on with his own evolution. The people whose cells you walked through had created their own prison and were free to move on at any time. That's why the cells had no doors. They would stay until they worked through their stuff and would no longer be bound by it. Then they could release themselves and leave just as Alex left. Does it make sense?"

"It makes sense," I reflected.

"Had you not sincerely felt utter compassion for his pain, despite what it appeared he had done to your lives, he would not have achieved that release. He would continue to be stuck there. You answered your own question about why your chart came into it; it added a glimpse of how things work. Perhaps you were not a strong person before, and you decided at a soul level that now was the time and you needed the help of a friend to do it. You two souls probably knew each other already and had contracted to come in at the same time to play out this scenario that you think of as your life. You already know that horoscope charts show what you came to do and what you brought to do it with.

"Another thing," she continued, "he left the door open. He told you to call him when you got back," she commented.

"Yes, I did call. I let him know I got back all right."

"That wasn't what he meant. He wants to get back together again at some future time," she said, impatient with my density.

I felt edgy. "I don't know if I want to get together with him again," I said, remembering the hard times we'd had. "I don't want to go through that again."

"I don't think you will. You just did it, and I suspect you did the whole thing well, despite the hardship. You've learned that lesson or passed that test now. Next time might be much more pleasant. I remember the story of how you met. Your meeting had all the earmarks of a karmic relationship in which you knew each other before. You might be very happy next time."

"Maybe I'd rather try a different cast in the next scenario. I need a rest from problems. We had a very intense relationship. He was very jealous. I like my freedom. I'm afraid to expose my feelings to it again. I forgave him and I love him, but I'm afraid to get that close again."

"You see," she said, "a string of lives is like an anthology of short stories. Each one is complete in itself. Each has its own beginning and its own ending; each is different. One of the strengths in your chart is courage. It might be next time, the time after that, or later. When the time comes, you'll do it."

I asked where she learned so much about reincarnation and other dimensions.

"I've researched it for a long time. My husband was a Unity minister before he died, so I was exposed to it then. I missed the ministerial interaction with people after he passed, so I trained for the ministry myself. The deeper I delve, the more fascinating it becomes. I see it as a larger picture. The flow of life is truly beautiful. We would all know these truths if the early churches had not deleted them from original teachings to insure their power over the masses. But these truths are coming more into general knowledge today, and people are hungry for them. We are in a very exciting age."

I lay awake many nights pondering what I had just learned from Chandra. It made much sense. Maybe Alex had agreed to help me. In the deepest part of my heart I knew that had I experienced a trouble-free life of affluence, I would never have gotten off my cushion to educate myself or to learn all that I had learned from problems. I would not have liked that useless person who had nothing to give back. I marveled that Alex was still in touch! I must remember to thank him next time we made contact. Grudges were always too cumbersome to carry anyway.

I loved ashram life.

I loved waking to the *bhakti* guitar serenade that an ashram brother offered on our stairwell at four each morning. To do that, his day had to begin even earlier. I loved the gourmet vegetarian aromas that wafted from the kitchen vents and made our saliva glands pump, anticipating the noon meal. How could we not remember to give thanks for such delicious fare? I loved the feel of fine white silky cotton against my skin as I wrapped into my sari for *satsangs*. I loved the sounds of the tabla drums and cymbals that accompanied our chants. I loved the fragrance of incense that permeated the ashram buildings and followed us wherever we went, as though we walked in the presence of God at every moment.

Morning yoga and meditation practices followed a jog in the icy air, then breakfast. Those with outside jobs took a delicious vegetarian meal to work, lovingly packed in their lunch kits by the morning kitchen crew. Those on the ashram staff began their work—editing the guru's writings, creating seasonal brochures, scheduling ashram programs, administration, accounting, gardening, maintenance, meals, and whatever else it took to run an ashram. Everyone shared a light supper of divine salads and soy yogurt, attended *satsang*, then returned to their quarters to meditate and sleep.

On Saturdays, everyone did home chores. I had chosen sewing without realizing it included mending everybody's clothing. I was never fond of mending. Saturday lunch, the only time we had dessert, was always and only dessert. Sunday mornings we cleaned the entire ashram. Since I was one of the Sunday sleepyheads, the only chore left on the list when I awoke was the huge dorm bathroom.

We did our home chores to *bhakti* chants. As we crossed paths with other residents, the greeting was always, "J'ai bhagwan," with eye contact and hands in prayer position. "I bow to the Divine Light within you," said the gesture, many times every day. It made a lasting impression on me.

My Saturday mending was often interrupted by sisters or brothers bringing a flower to thank me for repairing favorite jeans, replacing jacket zippers, or darning huge holes in yoga pants that they had no money to replace. Their smiles and their love made what to me was unimportant drudgery a vehicle of love and caring for many. I became a happy mender.

The women's dorm bathroom was enormous—six stalls, three tubs/showers, six sinks, a tile floor, and nearly eight feet of mirror. I was overwhelmed. A brother whose jacket I had repaired taught me shortcuts, techniques, and ways to speed my work. How I wished I had known him when my children were small! "When you're doing a tedious or difficult chore," he said, "first learn the techniques, then dedicate the chore to God with focus. Chanting helps, too."

His advice proved invaluable. I learned to do that bathroom in less than thirty minutes and I became an expert bathroom cleaner. What if my professors had walked in then!

We enjoyed daily gourmet vegetarian meals, with home-baked bread, grains, soy milk, soy yogurt and cheese, tofu, herbal teas and honey. We ate no meat, eggs, dairy products, or sugar.

I arrived with pain in my wrist joints and slept with ointment under my pillow to relieve it. In six weeks, several pounds had melted away and in three months, I was pain-free.

The healthiest, tastiest diet I had ever followed made the change. I happily committed to vegetarianism, as all residents were asked to do, and it became the healthiest year of my life.

Something else about the food had an impact. We rotated turns on kitchen crew. I looked forward to being part of that joyful crew. When my turn came, they asked if I were dealing with heavy problems. I wasn't then, but I was curious why they asked. "We try to eliminate all negative vibrations from the food," said the supervising brother. "Food is alive and plants react to emotions. Only those who love gardening work in the gardens, and we ask that all others who work with the food in any way be positive and joyful. If it's your turn for kitchen crew and you're depressed, unhappy, or angry, we'd rather reschedule you for another time. We want a lot of love and joy in our kitchen for our food to absorb."

I wondered if that was why ashram food was so fulfilling and healing.

I was impressed by the innocence I witnessed in young ashram residents who had lived there for several years. They were completely open about their feelings and would not stoop to even the smallest white lie.

Surrender was a big preoccupation. The guru gently urged us to be in constant surrender to God's will. It was easier said than done, so we practiced trust exercises. In one such exercise I climbed to the top rung of a five-foot ladder, then fell backward onto the "bed" of clasped arms of two parallel rows of sisters, trusting that they would catch me. Actually I trusted that God would catch me by making the sisters attentive and strong. Contrary to what I expected, the youngest were the most reticent.

The only outside work I found was for minimum wage in a sewing factory, sewing the same seam hundreds of times a day. The factory wouldn't hire college people, and I had already been warned that they suspected that ashram women comprised the guru's harem! It was like a nine-teenth-century nightmare. So I bit my lip, blushed before an onlooking brother, and lied on my application that I had completed third year high school. I had; I simply didn't mention how much additional schooling I'd had. I was lucky to get that job even though I arrived home every after-noon with such a terrible backache that it took an hour of yoga postures for my body to recover.

About four o'clock one Saturday morning, I was abruptly awakened for a telephone call. I stumbled in the dark to the hall phone and heard Dina mumbling something between sobs. I realized then that she was talking about Sandy— Sandy was in a coma in the hospital.

I got directions to the hospital and set about packing for several weeks' stay. I tried to be calm to answer everyone's questions, but my voice shook and my mind wanted to shut down. Word spread fast and two young brothers came to help. One gassed up my car and the other loaded a box of healthy foods he knew I liked.

We formed a prayer circle alongside the car before I left to bless me and the trip and to relieve my apprehension about driving fifty miles through a fresh six-inch snowfall before dawn.

As I drove out, I had a strange feeling that the car was full of loving companions. The sense of their presence in the car distracted me from the apprehension I'd begun to feel. I seemed to glide over the untended roads as if someone had plowed them flat. I arrived incredibly fast over a route that should have taken at least three hours to a building I'd never seen before.

As I entered the hospital, an onslaught of acrid medicinal odors offended my senses after the fragrances I'd recently left.

I made my way up to Sandy's floor with my stuff, intending to camp out there until she was out of crisis. Lisa and her husband and Dina were there. When they took me to Sandy's room and I first saw her, she looked angelic and beautiful, so healthy that I would have sworn she had just fallen asleep a moment before. I took her hand and began to whisper in her ear, urging her to please come back to us.

I was not ready to give her up. I knew I could pull her back by sheer force of will. This was my child. How dare anyone—even God—threaten to take her from me! I would not allow this to happen!

From the moment I knew something terrible had happened to her, I saw her as my child again. Although my eyes witnessed a beautiful young woman, in my mind's eye I saw the eight-year-old tomboy, full of life, full of fun, leading the neighborhood boys atop a fortress in the playground, winning sprints in school, pushing herself in swim competitions beyond anything she could possibly do and doing it. I remembered her struggle with studies, a right-brained child straining to absorb and express through the left brain, while her teachers unwittingly abetted by excusing her from classes so that she could paint spectacular murals on their classroom walls.

I remembered the year her ambitious gym coaches pleaded, "She won't compete any more. She's Olympic material. She must come back to be coached. Talk to her! Persuade her to come back! Make her come back!"

"She must follow her own heart and choose her own life," I had told them, refusing to influence her. How could I tell them she had just discovered boys?

She was my beautiful child, a gifted spiritual artist whose first one-woman show was less than a month away. She had founded an annual exhibit of spiritual art and wanted only the freedom to paint as she was inspired. She had planned to visit me at the ashram the next week.

All this flashed through my mind in seconds.

The nurses permitted me to stay in the intensive care family waiting room as long as I wanted and to go into Sandy's room any time, day or night.

I went ahead of the others and closed the door, while they made phone calls in the hall. I could feel it mounting. Sheer fury. What does He care what this does to Sandy! to me! to all of us! Betrayal! Indifference!

This was my biggest fear since they were little, the only thing that could destroy me.

"Don't you do this to me!" I put God on notice, pounding my fist on the wall. "I WON'T lose a child. This will NOT be so."

The room trembled with the terrible force of my will.

With the waiting room to ourselves, I cornered Dina for details of what had happened.

Sandy, her husband Jack, and son Jonathan had just come from dinner about ten o'clock. Jack returned to his office to finish some work and left Sandy putting final touches on a painting for her show. She planned to work late to get her paintings ready. Then Dina got a call from the lady who lives downstairs saying that Sandy was seriously sick and the ambulance was on its way.

"We rushed over to Sandy's," Dina continued, "and arrived as the ambulance was pulling away. Jack took Jonathan to our house, and I got the rest of the story from the neighbor, made some phone calls—that's when I called you—then came to the hospital. The lady said they were awakened by Jonathan's constant crying. It was unusual for Sandy to let him cry, so after an hour they suspected something was wrong and went upstairs to investigate. They found the door locked and asked Jonathan through the door where Sandy was. He told her his mommy was drinking orange juice and she fell down and went to sleep and wouldn't wake up. The neighbors told him how to unlock the door, and when they opened it, they found Sandy unconscious on the floor with the orange juice glass beside her.

"That's when they called the ambulance and the family."

The doctors said it was a cerebral hemorrhage that exploded in her left hemisphere. They weren't sure if they could ever rehabilitate her left brain if she survived this. I thought of all the times she had fallen at play. Maybe I shouldn't have let her be a tomboy. Maybe I should have restricted her more. Oh, God, how could this be happening to my child?

I went into her room at every opportunity to hold her hand and talk to her. I said only one thing. I begged her and ordered her to wake up, to get well. I promised to do whatever she needed for the rest of her life to rehabilitate her. I told her that she could still paint. I told her that Jonathan needed her. I told her she MUST get well.

When I spoke to her, I referred to myself as "Mommy," as I had done when she was a child. It was mother instinct—possessive, protective, always rushing to the sick or injured child, who became the temporary favorite until health returned to equalize them all. "Mommy" was the caregiver. "Mommy" kissed it and made everything well. When helpless or injured, they became my young again and, like the mother tiger, I would kill to defend them. I felt a surge of strength awakening from a slumber of eons back in time.

I would not allow this abomination!

Whenever I spoke to her, the monitor zigzagged wildly and her hand twitched in mine. I knew that she heard and tried to respond.

Lisa worried that I wouldn't be comfortable overnight on the waiting-room couch, but nothing could pry me away until Sandy woke up. Dina was as torn as I but equally as armored. I knew if I shed one tear, the dike would burst and my poor children would grieve for both of us. Rafi sat in stunned silence. Before the day was over, Jen had flown in and Jay was due momentarily.

I took my demands into Sandy every hour throughout the day as well as the following night. I was determined not to let up, even to force her back if I had to.

Each time I spoke to her I felt the twitch of her hand and saw the squiggle on the monitor.

By 4:30 Monday morning, I was exhausted. I had only catnapped since Saturday dawn. I rested my head for a moment on the waiting-room couch and closed my eyes. Five minutes later I got up to go into her room again. Something had changed during those five minutes. In a second I remembered all that I really believed about dying and "dying." I knew I had to say something important to her; I knew she needed me to say it.

I walked into her room and took her hand. I stroked her hair and told her softly how much we all loved her and how proud we were of her just for who she was. I told her how honored I felt that she chose to come into the earth through me and what a wonderful child she was. And then I told her what had to be said.

"We'd really love to have you back with us, Sandy, but if this is the time you've chosen to leave this plane and return to God, then I release you with my love and my blessings. I wish that you could stay, but only if that's your desire. I shall honor your soul's decision—whatever it may be—and no matter what you decide, I'll keep you in my heart forever."

I could have sworn that she gently squeezed my hand as I leaned to kiss her cheek, and the squiggle fluttered over the monitor screen.

I slept for a peaceful four hours. When I awoke, I brushed my hair and headed for Sandy's room. The nurses were changing the linens and asked me to return in fifteen minutes. Back in the waiting room, it was 9:15. I sat on the couch and closed my eyes for a second.

It is time to go back to Sandy's room. I stand beside her and take her hand in mine. As I stroke her arm, I feel movement coming from her shoulder. I look up and see her lying there wide awake with that impish smile she flashes whenever she teases me.

"Sandy," I exclaim, "you're well again!" Joy is about to explode inside me.

"Mom," she says, mischievously, "you didn't think I was going to stay that way, did you?"

My eyes sprung open at 9:30. Oh my God, I thought, another dream. I got up and rushed into her room, certain it was an omen and that I would find her wide awake, flashing her beautiful smile.

Instead, she lay lifeless.

Despite my disappointment, I took her hand and kissed her cheek and began talking softly, telling her about my dream. I noticed, however, that her hands were cold. I watched the monitor screen and, for the first time, saw a flat line where before there were squiggles when we talked. Neither was there a response from the hand that I held.

I asked the nurses if there was any change in her condition, and they said she was the same. I returned uneasily to the waiting room to await the arrival of the others.

Again, I dozed off.

I saw Alex's father standing there, smiling the smile he reserved for Sandy. His hand was extended, but not to me. He was smiling at someone just beyond me, as though he didn't see me at all. He smelled wonderful. He wore his black three-piece suit, and the shoulder that was injured in an old accident still hung inches lower than the good one.

I woke up, surprised that it was another dream. I knew he had been there. The fragrance still wafted faintly through the waiting room where I sat alone. What was going on?

Returning to her room, I found everything just as it was earlier: no response, her body colder, no more monitor squiggles. When I got back to the waiting room, the family had arrived. I excused myself to make a phone call to Nell.

I hadn't seen Nell since two weeks before I left for the ashram, but she had told me about her out-of-body travels to other dimensions at night. I had to ask the question.

"My daughter is hospitalized in a coma," I told her. "Something happened this morning or last night that makes me wonder if she is still alive. It's hard to tell with all the machines she's hooked up to. Can you find out for me?"

The hall was noisy with visitors going back and forth, so I didn't give details. She assured me she would try to get an answer for me. I gave her the number of the public hall phone and told her to let it ring. If someone else answered, she was to tell them to get me from the waiting room. She warned me that it usually took eight hours, maybe a day, to find people, so I shouldn't sit by the phone and wait.

I thanked her and returned to my family.

The doctors had scheduled another brainwave test for Wednesday. It would show whether Sandy would make it or not. I felt that I knew the answer already.

More of Sandy's friends came that afternoon. They were shocked to hear the news. Several had seen her only days before the catastrophe and came to tell about their conversations.

"She was excited about the change of date for her art show," said Kurt. "It fell on her birthday. She felt it was a lucky coincidence. She told me, 'It'll be my birthday, and my resurrection!' "

Marian said, "We lunched in a little cafe, talking about our lives. She said that her life was much better—the hard times were over. She had worked through problems about her father and was at peace with it now. She couldn't think of anyone she hadn't made peace with. She said, 'I feel I'm at a turning point. Life is good and getting better.' "

" 'I feel as if I'm on the verge of something fantastic about to happen in my life,' " she had told Bob.

Unconsciously I counted four rings of the hall telephone before I remembered Nell was to call me back. I dashed out to answer it. I heard Nell's voice before I could even say hello. Only two hours had passed since she'd warned me it might take long, so I thought she needed more information. I strained to hear her above the noise in the hall.

"... and I couldn't believe how fast I found her. I searched all over the first level but she wasn't there. I found her two levels beyond that. She's been there before, my dear. She knew exactly where to go without hesitation. If you could only see her—she's absolutely radiant! And she sends a message for you. She said she loves you very much. She said it was hard to leave with all of you in such pain, but when you released her with your blessings, she was free to go. She thanks you for that with all her heart. And she wants me to tell you that Grandpa was waiting with his special smile to help her over. She is in a brilliant white light, my dear, truly a sight to see."

Tears of joy flooded my face. How was it possible that my joy for Sandy overpowered my grief of losing her? For the first time since I embraced this philosophy, I understood. Grief is not nearly as painful if I know my loved one is not annihilated. If she thrives in another place, I have only to grieve my own sense of separation while I can rejoice for her. Loving her so, in the midst of my sadness, I could be happy knowing she lived on happily elsewhere.

I thanked Nell and told her I'd explain later. Then I called Jen aside and related the conversation to her. Jen didn't find it at all unusual.

Sandy's monsignor friend, for whom she had founded the Spiritual Art Exhibits, came. He looked in on her, but stayed close to me. I knew he wanted to be available when "Mommy" fell apart and I appreciated it, but how could he know what I had just learned.

We walked outside in the brisk, clean air and he started talking religion. I changed the subject to reincarnation, asking him point blank why the church had deleted all references to it in the beginning. He hedged, saying he wasn't responsible for what the church did, but he, personally, believed in it. From there we had a very nice conversation in which I told him that I felt Sandy had already left her body and was happy where she was.

"She's probably painting the most incredible art the heavens have ever seen," he speculated, surprising me, "and driving everybody crazy rounding up the artists to put on an exhibit!"

We evolved into a mutual admiration twosome. Despite our differences in background, our personal philosophies were comfortably close.

Sandy had opted for Catholicism in her teens. Later when she met him and they worked together, she always chose him to preside over her ceremonies, so we assumed she would want him to offer her own funeral mass. He had hoped I would ask, but because I discussed it without tears he assumed that I was in denial. I was not. I simply knew that she had left that body behind and was off somewhere else having a ball.

We went into Sandy's room again. My words brought no response. Her body never regained its heat and the monitor line remained flat. I spoke into her ear as if it were a speaker system through which she could hear me in whatever dimension she frolicked now.

"Be happy, my Sandy. Thank you for the time you gave us, and always remember how much we love you."

On Thursday they called us together to announce the results of the second brainwave test. It came as no surprise that she was brain-dead. They declared her death on Thursday. Nell had found her three levels up on Monday. We donated her organs. After surgical removal, they disconnected the life support, and we left.

I slept at Dina's almost the entire next day. I took a long walk to try to sort out the conversation with Nell.

How could she have known that I'd released Sandy from my demands that she come back to us? How could she have known that her grandfather waited to escort her over? There was no time to tell her any of this. And Grandpa's smile. Sandy was his favorite, and he had a special smile for her. He loved all the children and treated them well, but Sandy always melted his heart. When the girls were grown, we had laughed many times about his special smile for Sandy. How could Nell know that?

We buried her remains on Sunday. My bravado crumbled several times when I ached from missing her and never having her near again. What always brought me out of it was the certainty that she lived on somewhere else. If only I could stop missing her.

Days later I phoned Nell to thank her and share Sandy's story. When I confirmed the amazing revelations she had made, she wondered why I was surprised!

I needed to stay close to my children now. I couldn't imagine what it would be like having Christmas gatherings without Sandy. I wondered why it couldn't have waited another week so that she could visit me in the ashram. God, what difference did it make that she couldn't visit! That was so small beside what had really happened. My thinking got so mixed up that I hardly dared speak to anyone for fear that person would think I was losing my mind. I only wanted to sleep and dull the ache in my heart.

Nobody cried. I hated it. I felt as if no one dared let go for fear it would shatter me. As the days went by, I felt my energy depleting. By the end of two weeks, my life force had ebbed. I was like a battery that had run so far down that a supercharge was the only remedy. I packed, said my good-bys, and left for the ashram again to recharge my life force.

We had all changed a little. We were always close, but now we were more sensitive to each other. We made special efforts to see and call one another. We carried within us the scar of the surprises of time. How can we know how much time is allotted at soul level—for ourselves or another? In a nonverbal agreement, we determined to think of each other with love no matter where we were every day of our lives.

My guru brothers and sisters showered me with hugs and welcomes and a fantastic, unending stream of love when I returned. I thanked them for the card they'd sent with a zillion loving messages. I felt myself revitalizing in that energy, sure of the move I had made.

Slowly I recovered my vitality, surrounded by love, eating food grown and prepared in love, living in a fragrance of love, in the energy of my guru and his guru. I wasn't ready for chores yet, nor to handle food. I didn't want the sadness which sometimes crept into my heart to seep into the food that everyone ate. I would take my time to heal well.

In two weeks I was doing fine.

One night in *satsang* I closed my eyes to meditate and saw an image of a giant Christ standing before me with a chubby cherub leaning over His shoulder pouring blessed water on me from an urn. When I looked up, the cherub's face was Sandy's. I ran out of the room, crying. People came up to console me, but how could I explain? The image was beautiful, consoling. My joy in seeing her overflowed. I merely emptied my excess of tears.

The next week I was sewing at my factory job and suddenly burst into tears. It disrupted the work flow when everyone rushed to my rescue. I felt bad because distractions cost the pieceworkers money. It happened twice more. Each time there were no emotions, just tears spilling over.

An in-house intensive was scheduled for next week in the ashram. All residents were urged to participate. I welcomed the opportunity to therapeutically accelerate the mourning process and get on with my life, so I enrolled.

They requested we not focus on anything special. I decided that was fine for the younger residents. I, however, would cleanse all the emotional residue from my child's passing.

It was the most profound intensive I had ever experienced. All the feelings burst out, including my anger at God. We worked sixteen hours a day for four days. We meditated, slept, and ate very small balanced meals. The only rule was to get the feelings out and cleansed. By the fourth night, we danced a free-form finale with high energy, bright spirits, and squeaky clean slates. I felt like a newborn baby ready to begin living my life.

There were no more tears for Sandy, no more feelings of grief, and no apologies for God. God and I were close friends. I figured He knew what made me tick better than I did, and He knew all along that I never loved Him one iota less, no matter what I said. He always understood. He never let me down.

As I walked to the dorm that final night, I felt a presence again. I had my entourage back.

Life was good in the ashram. I enrolled in yoga teacher training and learned to teach yoga as we did it, to explain the postures and to use them therapeutically. My health improved. Part of my yoga training was to lead guided meditations and to compose the visualizations. Visualization scripts came easily to me without pondering a subject or an image. The sequence of images raced across my forehead as a movie; all I had to do was jot down key words. "Thank you" notes expressed everyone's appreciation for something I did to express love to them.

Wherever we walked on ashram grounds, we could feel that special energy permeating everything, making us feel like truly cherished children of God. We couldn't possibly articulate a love so profound and so constant, so we chanted it from our hearts and danced it with our energy. I lived for evening *satsangs*, beginning with *bhakti* chanting, and dancing our joy and devotion.

We dedicated everything we did to God, making it a gift offering instead of a competition. It made us do better and helped us through less agreeable jobs.

Different customs, professions, languages, education, ethnicity, and needs described the potpourri of our backgrounds. The point of unification of all our differences was knowing we were children of the same Progenitor, loved for our differences, cherished for ourselves.

We were each valuable and worthy, so we processed disputes until we set them right. We ended each processing with "J'ai bhagwan," acknowledging the Divine within each other. After a year of "J'ai bhagwan," how could I ever look into another's eyes without acknowledging that person's Divine Light, the God part of each of us? Living in His presence every day humbled us. Once I learned, I knew I could do it forever when the day came for me to leave.

Summer came, and I had to leave my sewing factory job. Earlier, my purse contents had spilled, scattering papers all over. A form for a class reunion reservation with my name and class year emblazoned on it let the cat out of the bag. The old "overqualification" glitch caught up with me. I felt complimented when co-workers hugged me good-by with remarks like, "You don't act like a college person. You're like one of us." It was time to move on.

I applied for a social service job requiring a bilingual person. They liked me. The job sounded interesting, the contract attractive, and the people nice. I really wanted that job, so I meditated and offered daily *japa* for two weeks. *Japa*, the repetition of a mantra using beads, was said to work miracles. I repeated, "I surrender myself to the will of God," on each of the 108 beads while holding the image of what I wanted—that job.

They called me for a second interview and asked me to

begin the next week. How wonderful to soon have a decent paycheck! I learned quickly, worked hard, and did more than my best. My record surpassed the set goals; the field directors liked me.

One morning two weeks after I had started, I unwittingly stumbled upon a major glitch and its culprit: the director. For the next eleven months and two weeks my job was hell.

I learned to be careful what I asked for; I'd probably get it.

I began getting dreams whose content I couldn't remember, but they ended with "time to leave." There were symbols of fours, church carillons, and fragments of a town I was passing through.

I tried to go about my life, but the dreams evolved to "time to leave to disseminate." I was puzzled.

As I set out one weekend to visit Lisa, an ashram visitor asked for a ride to Lanstown, a nearby town. It was on my way so I took her. She was going to Fourth Street to link with her ride to Ohio, so she directed me through town to her destination.

"You seem to know the town well," I commented.

"I used to live here," she said. "It's a quiet little town, not too large, and easy to get around."

I let her out at her friend's apartment and continued on.

When I talked to my daughters about my "moving" dreams, they reminded me that my ashram year was almost up. I had mixed feelings. I was reluctant to leave that loving energy, but the dreams pressured me to do more outside. When Sandy died, I had been there only six weeks. Was I guided there to be protected and cushioned for the big blow? How would I have survived if I hadn't lived in that energy when it happened? What would I have done had I not had that home to go to?

The pressure was on, undeniably. The message kept repeating.

Six months remained on my job contract before I could

leave the state and move back near my daughters. Who would rent me a place for six months? Would the timing synchronize to leave one place and move to another? So much to coordinate!

I decided to look around Lanstown for an apartment.

I set out one Saturday to explore and followed up three ads. They were already promised. A fourth, however, was encouraging.

"The address in front blew off in a storm," said the woman tenant who answered the phone. "Come to Fourth and Warren, the green corner house across from the church. It's more direct if you come up the side stairway and knock. That's my living room."

I followed the tenant's directions and went up the side stairway to her door. I was pleasantly surprised. It was small but ample for a short stay, economical, clean and quiet. It was close to everything I needed and would be available in two weeks.

The owner liked me and seemed fair, so I asked if he would lease it to me for seven months, explaining about my job contract and plans to move near my family. To my surprise, he agreed.

I remembered the dreams. The house was located on Fourth Street, it was the fourth house I looked into. The address, #202, added up to four, and the house was the color associated with the fourth chakra. As I left, carillons began to chime from the church across the street.

I must have found the right place, I thought.

6

DISCOVERING VIRGINIA BEACH A.R.E.: THE FUN BEGINS

Do I contradict myself?
Very well then I contradict myself,
(I am large, I contain multitudes.)
                              –Walt Whitman

SAYING GOOD-BY to the ashram was painful. My guru sisters said they had happily watched me grow into my own power there. My kitchen cronies were sad and loaded me up on ashram food. I accepted. I would miss that love-permeated food. Lots of hugs and tears sent me off with reminders that I was close enough to continue coming to *satsang*.

I began immediately teaching yoga and astrology in Lanstown evening programs, formatting the yoga classes after ashram morning practices with visualization, with postures, breathing, and meditation. Insomnia problems quickly disappeared. It went well.

Nell lived near Lanstown. I visited and brought flowers. I talked about how I loved ashram life, how it had deepened me—but she was obsessed that I would give up my power and never come back to my life. "Krishnamurti," she reminded me, "abandoned his own Center to teach that each carried God within and needed no go-between." I assured her that the guru did not use control games and I would not fall under anyone's spell.

Why was the "power" theme so prominent now? My guru sisters observed me growing into my power, now Nell was warning me not to give it up. I'd never thought much about power; I only knew how to consciously call forth the strength of a strong will when I needed it.

I put Nell's mind at ease while my own was in turmoil.

Rafi had developed a pattern of erratic, violent episodes. Hospital tests eliminated links with alcohol or drugs. They would keep him "manageable"—drugged—for three weeks, then release him. He would stabilize, find a job, an apartment, and repeat the episode three months later; he'd lose the job, the apartment, and most of his belongings while in the hospital again. Each time he was released, he had to begin anew. Each time, refusing therapy.

When I moved into the ashram, he moved to the same town, found work, and stabilized for a while. In Lanstown he visited every weekend.

He wanted to go with me to spend Christmas with his siblings, but the night before we were to leave he had his worst episode. He went into a violent hallucinatory rage and locked the doors. I was terrified! The violence was not directed at this mother; he didn't even recognize me. Whatever directed the hallucination goaded him to intense fury toward whoever happened to be there—me. His strength was formidable! I felt lucky to escape after midnight, unharmed but shaken, heartbroken.

Jay drove two hours to Lanstown to quiet my hysteria and

get Rafi to a hospital. His diagnosis was "undifferentiated schizophrenia." This time they keep him six weeks.

He stabilized for several months, then left therapy—despite our pleading—"to travel."

The memory of my narrow escape haunted me. I was too afraid to ever dare tell him my address when I moved.

Near the end of my contract I found only another waiting list for a New Jersey apartment near Lisa. What if when my contract and lease ended, I had no place to live! Uncertainty prompted me to seek a glimpse of my future.

A friend recommended a psychic who worked by psychometry. I arrived at her office one June afternoon prepared to let her hold my jasper earrings for my reading. She picked them up and flipped them out of her hand. "God, they're full of snakes!" she exclaimed.

I disowned the earrings immediately! My irrational fear of snakes sent chills up my spine. Snake scenes in movies filled my feet with fear, and I'd snap them quickly up on my seat and sit on them to keep them safe.

"Wait," she said, picking the earrings up again and closing her eyes. "The stones come from an area where many snakes simply pass over the stones on the way to find food. Don't worry. I'll cleanse the energy from the earrings." She cleansed them and tried again to read. "There are too many of their vibrations. I can't get a clear picture of you. Have you anything else I can use?"

I gave her a small leather change purse I'd made for myself, and she proceeded to read.

She insisted that my job ended mid-July. My contract clearly went until June 30, but I didn't argue. She said that a week before I moved I would hear that the New Jersey apartment was available. She told me more, but I was more focused on coordinating my move.

She picked up the earrings again and attuned to their energy. "No wonder you fear snakes," she said. "I see you in a pit of snakes . . . you've fallen or you've been thrown in. It's too deep for you to climb out. At some level you still remember it. That's why you're afraid ... "

I began to panic just imagining the picture she painted.

"Calm down," she said. "That's not for now. That's long past. You don't have to do that again."

I thanked her and pretended to forget the earrings when I left.

Two days before my contract ended, the director offered me two additional weeks of work at the same pay rate. I agreed. It brought me to mid-July, just as the psychic said.

The first weekend in July the superintendent of Lisa's apartment complex called. "You're tenth on the waiting list. We have a vacancy ready in a week, second floor with a nice porch, southwest exposure. I called the others and they've either found something else or can't move on short notice, so we're down to you. If you're interested, tell me and it's yours for next week."

"Yes, I'm on my way."

Shortly after moving back to New Jersey, I watched a late movie about a man returning from the army. He entered his cabin in the Everglades. Snakes hung from the rafters, crawled on his shoulders as he drank coffee, and slithered up his leg to his lap. He spoke lovingly to them. He had returned to his work milking venom for scientists to make snakebite serum.

An hour later I realized my bare feet were comfortably on the floor in the dark. I sat perfectly calm with no chills up my spine.

I could hardly believe it! What would have panicked me before was simply an interesting story now. I didn't have my snake earrings, so I couldn't test myself. Freedom from a phobic fear was a delicious feeling! I had finally defused and released a terrible hindrance from my life.

The next day I reviewed the movie scenes in my mind just to see if the fear would "hold." I was still free of it.

Dina had some time ago invited me to see *Raiders of the Lost Ark*, but I declined, reminding her of my fear. She'd said that she would sit through it again if I ever wanted to go.

I called her. "I'm ready, Dina, to see *Raiders*. I'm over it. I can watch the whole snake pit scene without flinching."

I sat through the entire scene, feet calmly on the dark floor of the theater, feeling no emotional response to the famous scene.

I was free.

I enrolled in an A.R.E. healing conference beginning Labor Day weekend. I was excited, anticipating seeing the place Cayce had founded, researching his trance readings, and relaxing on the beach.

Nell gave me the number of her past-life reading by Cayce and asked me to deliver a recent photograph of herself to Gladys Davis "to see if she remembers me."

I set out early Sunday, but before reaching the turnpike, I recognized the scraping sound of worn brake cylinders. I turned back to find a service station, but none had repair service available until Tuesday after the holiday. That meant I wouldn't arrive until Wednesday evening, leaving only two days of the conference.

Upset and disappointed, I went home and called A.R.E.'s registrar.

"Come down for next week's conference," she suggested calmly.

"But my housing arrangements," I said.

"Don't worry about a thing. We just took over a large house, and we have a room for you two blocks from A.R.E."

It gave me time to have my brakes fixed, regroup my forces, and leave the following Sunday. I forgot to ask what the conference was, but I was relieved that I would be able to go, whatever it was.

About midweek, I unpacked all the white blouses from my suitcase in an unexplainable urge to dye them purple. Some

I dyed solid and some I tie-dyed. What harm could it do?

I arrived in Virginia Beach on Sunday afternoon with purple blouses, white shorts and skirts, and a purple bathing suit. The registrar greeted me with, "Welcome to the Egypt Conference."

"Oh, well," I muttered to myself, half-bored, "I guess I'll have to sit through Egypt." I thanked her and went home with her to occupy my room.

Next morning as I sat dressed in purple and white, listening to a speaker say that priestesses in the Temple Beautiful dressed in purple and white for their healing rituals, I figured it was time to pay closer attention to this. Could I have had a connection with Egypt? This had not been my conference of choice, but God had apparently decided it was what I needed now.

One day during break, I went upstairs to deliver Nell's photo to Gladys Davis. Gladys had been Edgar Cayce's secretary who transcribed his trance readings since she was eighteen and she knew many of the people he read for. She graciously received me and was overjoyed to get Nell's picture, even more to learn that Nell was still alive and well at ninety-four. She gave me a note and a huge hug for Nell, and I knew that Nell would be pleased that she was still so fondly remembered.

Nell's reading surprised me. She had been a renowned Syro-Phoenician astrologer known as Zermada, who traveled enormous distances from her land to meet with the Essene Judith and consult with her about the education of the Child Jesus. Cayce identified Judith in the present and verified that they were again friends.

Recalling Nell's request to call her Zermada, I knew just how I could surprise her. I bought her a book from A.R.E.'s bookstore. *The Remnant* had a part where the author described Zermada's meetings with Judith. She would be thrilled to see yet another acknowledgment of a lifetime by which she obviously still felt powerfully influenced.

I relaxed on the beautiful beach with other conferees and enjoyed talking about past lives. Someone knew of a woman who did past-life regressions, so we lined up to get appointments.

As we anticipated the event, we considered ideas of what we would like to investigate. One man wanted to know if his girlfriend had been with him before. Another felt sure her husband had once been her father. I thought about the hard times the kids and I had been through and how we'd bonded. If we choose our families beforehand, I thought, they must have known what was in store for us. Why did they choose me? How many times were we together before? Were we always parent and child? And in which combinations? Those were the questions I brought to the regressions.

"Are you saying you would like to regress to times you were with the souls who are now your children?" she asked.

"Yes, that's exactly it," I affirmed.

I am in Japan, late teens, dressed in a fine brocade kimono and hand-carved wooden thongs. It is a sunny day as I play with my chubby little son, Umesh, in a fenced, pebbled garden. I recognize him as Jay.

Inside at the family table, I dine with my husband (Alex!), his parents (Alex's mother and my paternal grandfather!), his sister (Dina!), and his younger brother (Rafi!), while a servant girl tends my baby (Lisa!).

There is much animosity between my husband and his brother. My husband knows my brother-in-law covets me. I always fear it will bring me trouble through no fault of mine. My husband and his father spend much time in the provinces, and my brother-in-law always seeks opportunities to speak to me alone. Why does he pursue me like this? I do my best to avoid him.

Several years later I am sad because I long to spend

time with my husband—we are still young—but his work keeps him away a lot. We are a politically prominent family. The men constantly work to secure their position of rulership. I feel the wrenching loneliness in that time that I have almost forgotten in this life.

In old age, we all squeeze into a sort of carriage too small to hold us all, and we are racing somewhere to escape with our lives.

Suddenly I am slumped at the side of a road alone and very thirsty. I am dying of old age and dehydration. There has been a political coup and our family has been ousted from power. We are running for our lives. I don't know where the rest of them are. I am fading fast.

Many familiar details came up: my loneliness for my husband, his animosity for his brother (Alex and his alienation from Rafi), my commitment as a parent, my joy in my children (Jay and Lisa), my sisterly relationship with Dina, and my husband and his father having the same occupation.

It was uncanny.

The lessons? My husband and I were to learn to share a balanced life and nurture our own bond. His work absorbed him and I was left to deal with the children. Feeling the need to bond, I bonded with the children instead. Very reminiscent of this lifetime.

High status did not always bring happiness and security—all could be lost in a moment. Alex and I didn't do what we came to do. He didn't learn bonding. It had happened before. Perhaps I should not have been so passive when he left? Could I have stopped him? With the astrological placement of Mercury in Taurus, I tend to learn through repetition but, once learned, the lesson is etched in stone. Alex abused his power. We lived in a time and country in which women were powerless. I acted out powerlessness. I must have taken precautions at the soul level by creating the present "story line" that compelled me to take power for our survival. For me, it ended well; I learned many lessons.

We had time to do another regression:

> I am a dark-skinned waif playing near a dump in a crowded city in India. I go home for lunch to an abandoned, windowless, broken-down shop with mud floors. It is so dark even in daylight that I can only see my mother in silhouette. She stands at a makeshift coal burner warming lunch. The burner is propped on boxes, which also serve as our chairs and table.
>
> She spoons out the last morsel into my plate; there isn't enough for us both. She sacrifices her portion so that I can have lunch.
>
> I look into her eyes to see who she is (today). I see Sandy with her eyes filled with love for her child (me). I feel my chest full and tight with love for my mother. She is so good to me. I wish I were big and wealthy as the merchants in the shops so that I could buy my mother food and beautiful saris and sandals. She says I am enough to make her happy, for she needs only a little boy to love.

The lesson was above all to love and to nurture with love, to sacrifice for your little ones, if necessary, ever without complaint.

Sandy taught it by living it at that time. I saw her live it again in this life with Jonathan. I think I learned it. They were—are—such a joy. Who said you can't learn from your children! Often they were my best teachers when I paid attention.

I cried a few more tears of joy when I finished that session, remembering Sandy, missing her again, yet feeling her light so bright, so present.

During a break at the conference, someone invited a group of us to experience a reverie.

I recognized its similarity to the guided imagery we did at the ashram, only in this she led us to a place of our own choosing where we would meet with one of our guides. I had never done it that way before. It sounded exciting.

When I created my place and turned to meet my guide, it was breathtaking!

I saw before me, smiling, the most beautiful being I had ever seen. He stood about six feet tall with a thick layer of the softest white eagle feathers covering his brow, head, and shoulders, surrounding his neck and arms, and going all the way down his back. I longed to pass my hands over them, but I restrained the impulse.

In contrast, his skin was smooth, deep bronze. He had noble features and his eyes were the kindest and brightest I had ever seen. My focus locked on his eyes. I didn't notice his clothing, nor if he wore any. He stood tall and proud. When I couldn't understand his name, he printed it out for me on a large clay tablet.

As soon as I felt the glow of his energy, I missed the rest of the guided reverie. No matter. I had found this beautiful being, my guide. I had a constant companion whose countenance was now imprinted on my inner eye and whose energy I could feel wherever I went.

He never spoke in words or sounds, but his eyes and gestures spoke volumes in an instant, always with love. I understood now how children with "imaginary" playmates felt. He was always nearby, always encouraging and protecting. I became less fearful. I understood that we had been together for a long time, even before this time, and we had a long time to go. I liked that.

So many amazing experiences within days left me very introspective. These were precious moments, not to be shared with just anyone.

I spent time in the library browsing through Cayce's readings. The conference planners had skimped on our free time, so I arranged to extend my stay four days for extra time in the library and on the sun-drenched beach. Also, I wanted to integrate all that I had learned so fast.

Compared to the ashram, this was like a different facet of the same jewel. There was something unusual even about the energy I felt at the beach. The day that I went down to "The Strip" where the boardwalk and shops catered to the tourists, the energy was different. I felt as if I'd undergone some sort of initiation, so I didn't consider myself a tourist.

It was the energy at the north end of the beach that was so special. It was like a shot in the arm that accelerated spiritual growth. Even the dolphins seemed to know it, for they frolicked longer at that end.

I recalled feeling suddenly lighter, more buoyant, as I crossed the Chesapeake Bay Bridge to get there, but I didn't know why I suddenly felt so good. I understood now that it was this energy that I'd felt, and somewhere over that bridge was the turning point. It was almost like an alchemical change that took place either in the energy or inside me, enabling me to open more, to absorb more, and to grow infinitely.

So many wonderful, magical experiences happening so fast!

I loved lying on the sand by the sea, waiting for the dolphins to make their daily trek to the extreme end, watching my bolder peers swim out to meet them and frolic together with them before the sun went down. It was the ideal place to absorb and digest new spiritual truths and experiences. I felt that I was growing faster into insights and clarity than I ever had before and I never wanted to leave this magical place.

But, alas, I must soon return home to search for work and report to the unemployment office.

My impulse back home was to invite my guide to accompany me in meditation and to journal about the revealing experiences I'd had in Virginia Beach. I also had to deliver to Nell the book and Gladys Davis's message of love. I wanted to be in her energy again while I told her about Virginia Beach. I spent three days doing that, in denial about needing a job. There were no jobs in the university, nor in other nearby colleges, so I contacted my corporate friends who had provided such rave references when I left town. I was soon back on the course-designing/teaching track.

It wasn't as much fun as before. My mind was on other things. I could hear my grandmother scolding me about getting back to work regardless of whether or not I liked the job. "It's work. Adults must work. You're not supposed to like it. Life is hard," she'd say. No, Grandma, I don't feel it should be like that. I had bills to pay, however, so I did it for a while.

I might have been right about graduate school leading me to the ashram. The impact of that experience was so much greater even though I loved school. When I plunged back into the arena, I found A.R.E. and all the new experiences.

Unusual things began to happen. My intuition revved up again and I was getting all kinds of signals about things. When I denied or distrusted the signals before, I simply missed opportunities. Now, it was more blatant, more traumatic. When I first met people and my intuition screamed, "NOOOO!" I wouldn't listen. I'd go right back into the old denial of "It's not fair to judge them so soon. I just met them." And two weeks later in an ugly situation with them I would hear that little voice saying, "It's your own fault. You should have listened."

It was a wonder the voice still spoke to me at all. I did better in childhood but when I started school, ridicule engendered denial. It took several jolts for me to begin listening again. When I remembered to ask for help or guidance, it was always forthcoming. It never occurred to me that "it" knew when I needed help before I knew and it spoke spontaneously. It came like a thought in my mind. No pictures, no sentience. That was why I didn't trust it. I thought it came from my head. I thanked it and promised I would listen. I granted recognition to my ally.

My sensitivity to energies had increased. By trial and error, I learned first to listen, then not to hesitate or analyze, but to go with the first impression. The instant I got a second impression, there was confusion. Most important of all, I was learning to trust my intuition.

Despite living in a spiritual vacuum, I felt my interior energy spinning faster than I could move. I was insatiable. I went to workshops to learn every new age modality that I could find. At first it was like learning magic; later I would realize that these were all spiritual tools that help us to better understand and grow closer to God.

I had been practicing astrology since graduate school. Now I learned about amplifying energies using crystals.

I attended dowsers' conventions in Vermont to learn dowsing, an ancient divining art using rods or pendulums to locate water and lost objects or to get answers. The simple instruments respond to energy fields and the dowser's intent. I learned to transmute "hot spots" of negative energy in my living space. Later, in a radiesthesia course of medical dowsing and absentee healing, I learned to use herbal remedies. My interest in healing intensified.

The more dowsing I learned, the more it reminded me of Cayce's best line: *Mind is the builder.* Intent was everything in dowsing. The willfulness that brought me trouble in childhood brought growth and advancement in adulthood. I knew my will had to be used with extreme care and integrity, never to harm another.

I further developed the visualization techniques I had learned in the ashram, incorporating reveries I had experienced at A.R.E. I wrote original scripts and sampled background music. Ultimately I planned to record and market them. It was the perfect device to employ in order to program myself with constructive habits using my will with strong intent.

Having found music I liked, I sat at the kitchen table late

one night writing to the composer about his royalty require-
ments. I was tired and it was hard to start the letter. I felt a
surge of energy when I remembered that I had a brochure
with his picture. Seeing his picture would make writing the
letter easier.

I headed for the bedroom for the brochure, but midway
forgot what I'd set out for. I turned back toward the kitchen
to try to recapture the thought and just as I approached the
doorway, I sensed a shift in density of a crooked oval space
roughly five feet high. At the exact moment that I felt the
shift, the entire memory of why I had headed toward the
bedroom flashed back to me in total clarity, as if it were a
photograph in my mind. Like lightning I perceived that I
had just walked into a *thought form.* I had perfect recall of
how it felt on my skin.

The only person I thought I could discuss this incident
with was a new age minister who, I supposed, knew about
these things. But Cara wasn't very receptive.

"Why do you think it was a thought form?" I heard her
skepticism over the phone.

"Because *thought form* was the first impression that
came to me after I walked into the shift of density and instantly recovered the entire memory," I replied.

"What exactly did that shift feel like?" she persisted.

"It felt thicker, slightly heavier, but fluffy, like jello sort of,
only dry—yeah, like dry jello."

"Oh," she said, three decibels higher. "A dry jello thought
form! Well, that's clever."

"So tell me about thought forms," I ignored her sarcasm.

"Not about dry jello thought forms. But I will tell you that
I wouldn't go around asking about them."

I was disappointed. I'd assumed her ministerial status
added certain authority and knowledge about these things.
My feelings were wounded by her condescension, and I felt
angry because she'd ridiculed my honest question about a
real experience.

I didn't argue; I said good-by and hung up. I still remembered the feel of the shift in density and its size. I had not stepped into a different dimension because my conscious awareness was sequential and intact, with no lapses. The simultaneous recall of the thought I'd forgotten came as though a strobe light had focused on the scene. I refused to deny my experience just because someone ridiculed it. I had to own and defend my experiences and accept them as mine.

I thought about the many times when I forgot what I wanted to say or do and simply went back to the spot where I conceived the thought and instantly recalled it. Thought forms must linger in their place of origin! Even those that feel like dry jello!

The letter to the composer went off the next day.

I wrote a steady stream of scripts as easily as I did when in the ashram. Two weeks later the composer responded favorably, so I proceeded to refine two deep relaxation scripts and recorded them in a sound studio. In a modest marketing attempt I sent a review copy to A.R.E. I was thrilled the day they accepted my tape to sell in their bookstore.

After my first trip to A.R.E. in Virginia Beach, I returned every summer for conferences and beach time. I made friends among the people who lived nearby. Actually there weren't many locals in that area; most were transplants who felt drawn to move there. I looked forward to seeing my new friends during my A.R.E. visits.

One summer a MariEl Training Conference interested me. While browsing through the conference catalog, I'd felt very drawn to this hands-on healing modality. I followed my intuition and mentioned it to an acquaintance who said we could go in her car. When I reminded her of the limited enrollment, she offered to enroll us both on Monday morning.

Two weeks later I called to see if we had got in under the limit. The conference was filled. They found her name second on the waiting list but mine was nowhere.

"You'll be number forty-five on the waiting list now. It's the best I can do, though it's like not getting in at all. Half the conferees would have to cancel," the registrar told me. As the time drew near, I had high enthusiasm to participate in it, so I turned inward to see if the energy still drew me. It did, so I committed to go and surrendered to however the universe chose to do it. If I didn't get in, I would spend the week on the beach with new friends and discover why the universe wanted me there. A week before we left, I was seventeenth. Four days later I was eleventh—not close, but I refused to limit the universe.

We arrived to find that I had one last chance. I was first, but ninety-nine registered conferees had arrived. I was told to come Monday morning and simply hang out to see what developed. At ten o'clock Monday morning the registrar called the last person and was informed that the woman was vacationing in Hawaii.

I was in.

The training was intense. We had three initiations during the week and did some practice healing, using certain hand positions and symbols until we improved our technique. The initiations, however, were profoundly cleansing.

As I stood calmly watching a demonstration on someone else, I felt something rising as if from my toes, all the way up until it stuck in my throat, and in the next instant I was sobbing uncontrollably.

There I stood, still feeling quite happy, with Niagara Falls flowing out of my eyes, my nose running down to my chin, my chest heaving with sobs while everyone in the room focused on me!

The instructor sympathetically asked the question I dreaded:

"What is it, dear?"

All I could say between loud sobs and tremors was, "I don't know. I'm not even sad." It would have been a good role in a comedy of the absurd.

She put her hands on me and did some symbols and in a few seconds my crying faded out.

She announced that it was some old grief for a male that I had never been able to express and the MariEl energy was clearing it out. "Nothing recent," she said, "it came from too deep down. It might even have been from a past lifetime."

The trouble with these past lifetime things was that no one could ever prove or deny them. I had no idea for whom I grieved. It could have been my dad, my great-grandfather whom I liked, or Alex. It could have been someone from lifetimes ago. Who knows?

After the final initiation, the trainer suggested we each go outside to be in nature and meditate. When I finished meditating, I walked through the meditation garden to a small patch of roses near a stone wall. The colors of the roses looked so much brighter than when I'd passed that way before. Huge yellow bumble bees buzzed around them.

As I watched one of them, the feeling in my chest was similar to when my heart chakra opened wide in the ashram. It also evoked another memory that I hadn't recalled since Sandy, my second child, was born. I was already so attached to Jen that I couldn't imagine how any other child could be as lovable and precious as she was. I worried during the pregnancy about how I would love a new baby. How could another baby be as wonderful as Jen? How could I take from my love for Jen to give to the other little one? How unfair to both of them! The dilemma worsened when Sandy was born and I fell in love with her in the hospital. How could I face poor little Jen after taking some of my love away from her? The miracle happened the day I brought Sandy home. I stood by the door holding her in my arms, waiting for Alex's mother to open it for us; instead, Jen ran out, barely sixteen months old, and threw her arms around my legs, shouting, "Mommy, see my baby! See my baby!" In that magic moment I felt the shift in my chest as though something pushed at its boundaries, and what I thought was my limited supply of love expanded to infinity!

I felt such caring for that one particular bee that I reached out very slowly and gently stroked her back. She didn't move, except to slightly flutter her wings, so I did it again.

It was hard to believe that I could do that. I knew I could be stung, but I also knew I wasn't allergic to bee venom. I had learned that the hard way at sixteen while on a fishing trip. An entire swarm of bees attacked my back when I unwittingly moved the hollow trunk I stood on, disturbing them. Friends rushed me home, two hours away, while I threw up out the car window all the way. After having all 300-plus stingers plucked out of my back, I slept all day and pedaled back to school on Monday morning. I wondered why I felt no fear when bees later stung me.

Seeing this beautiful, healthy little creature reminded me of that experience. I felt very drawn to communicate peace and love to the entire bee kingdom through my touch, and her acceptance made me happy.

She allowed me to stroke her back once more before she flew off to another adventure.

I came away feeling I had learned more than I could articulate.

Each time I went to Virginia Beach, it became harder to leave. I was simply not ready to return with my friend when the conference ended. Another conferee, Susan, needed a ride back to New Jersey and could travel with my friend so I was free to stay.

I booked a one-way flight home and spent the extra week in contemplation on the beach and in the A.R.E. meditation room. I felt as if there was something I still needed to get. Strolling along the beach late one afternoon, I became very self-absorbed despite the many sunbathers I passed. I walked another block just past the crowd. I felt completely alone and came to a point where I stopped short, as though I had come up against a solid but invisible barrier. I just stood there. Suddenly I perceived—not knowing with what senses—an opening. At the same time there was a shift in the energy. I immediately sensed it to be a dimensional doorway. None of this frightened me, rather I was fascinated by a strong urge to step through. Just as I had almost convinced myself to go that extra step to explore, a thought stopped me. What if I did step through a dimensional doorway, then how would I get back! I paused as if waiting for an answer to my thought-question, but I felt no reassurances. I did not take the step. I couldn't bear not seeing the kids again. All grown and married, they didn't appreciate it when I still called them "the kids." Worse, I couldn't bear their sadness if I didn't return and they thought something terrible had happened to me. In fact, one day after daydreaming that I would summon that UFO again and tell them I was ready to go sightseeing, I had said to Lisa quite seriously, "If I should ever disappear for a while, or forever, could you please not worry or feel bad and trust that I'm O.K.?"

"Sure, Mom," she said, giving me a look that I had come to understand as pushing my credibility too far.

So I whispered, "Later," and turned back. I would do it another time when I understood it better. I had no doubt the opportunity would come again. I'd found in Cayce's readings that there are no missed opportunities. If they are not recognized when presented, they come again when one sees more clearly.

The result, for me, was an intensification of the pull to that energy. I had just left a stressful job and couldn't afford to move to a new place, especially jobless. I could barely pay my rent. True, I had already done it once and it had worked, with difficulty. It was not a pattern, however, that I wanted to repeat.

When I boarded the plane to return home, I felt a tearing

away from the energy; it was so poignant that tears streamed down my cheeks. The elderly woman seated next to me asked if I was leaving family.

Dina picked me up from the airport and commented on how relaxed and spacey I looked. After a short visit with Lisa nearby, we each went our separate ways home. I had an unusual stack of mail for my two-week absence, but left it to open later.

News came that my dear friend Nell had passed away just twenty-seven days before her hundredth birthday. What a void I felt! A thrashing of emotions! I contained myself, remembering how bored she was with this third dimension and how eager to make her transition. I could almost see her happy face, cavorting all over the universe with that twinkle in her eye.

I would miss our visits. I had learned so much from her, especially the day she talked to me about choice.

"We always have choices," she stated. "Except, we have no choice about making choices. We must choose, even when we think we can't or when we think there are no choices. Life is a series of choices, and we must listen carefully before we make them."

"Listen to whom?" I had asked.

"To the Inner You on the Inner Plane, your Higher Self, the same one your guru called the inner guru, the one Mr. Cayce called 'soul,' " she replied. "I will teach you how to see messages from that plane in an astrological chart. You can bypass the daily trivia most people come to ask. There are many at large who can tell about that. You will learn to focus on the important signs, the real things, the higher evolutionary astrology that shows their path and their direction. That's all that matters."

Whenever she thought I was getting overwhelmed with too much information, she abruptly changed the subject.

"Tell me, how do you feel about your parents?"

"Not too good." I didn't want to go into that.

"You made those choices," she interjected. "You might think you don't like them or what they did, but you chose them because they were the ones most likely to propel you on your growth."

"I read that in a reincarnation book, but I can't believe I chose those parents or that family. There must be some mistake, at least in my case," I had said.

"Well, relax. You're not subject to their rule any more. Whatever you're carrying, just toss it. Make your own rules now. You'll understand it. It isn't always obvious why you make certain choices but, eventually, the mystery reveals itself. You have time. You'll get it."

Her lessons were indelibly printed on my mind. I would never forget my dear friend Nell.

In my mail I found a flyer announcing a visit by a Filipino psychic surgeon. I called for more information and decided I wanted to experience it. A friend said I could stay over at her place and drive home the next day. Part of me really wanted to know how someone could put his hands through my skin, pull toxins out of my body, and close the "wound" with neither scar nor pain. All this in less than five minutes!

I spent time meditating and trying to put into meaningful context the Virginia Beach experiences I'd just had. Two weeks later, I headed for upstate New York for psychic surgery.

At the sponsor's home where the surgeon worked, people walked around in bathrobes and slippers awaiting their turns to be healed, while others sat in a line of chairs outside the room where he worked. Downstairs, some clients lay on sofas or on the carpet recovering from their treatments. They looked a little weak, but I heard no cries of pain.

When it came to my turn, I got on the table and he asked what I wanted healed. Friends who knew how Sandy had died had urged me to get a CAT scan, but I didn't feel intuitively that it was a congenital defect. I'd seen it as Sandy's plan to leave at that time and her means to leave fast. Just to be sure, I told him how Sandy had died and asked him to check out my head. He asked if I wanted my third eye opened while he was "in my head" and I said, "Sure."

I joined him in a short prayer, then he touched me between the eyes. I heard a "pop" and felt a spatter on my eyelashes and cheek. I heard a sloshing sound as his fingers moved in that area. He drew something out and showed me tiny clumps of bloody tissue. I couldn't believe that stuff came out of me! He dropped it in the waste container his wife held out, then he pressed the area between my eyes, stroked it upward, wiped it, and closed it without a mark. He then "drew" some symbols on the area and for the first time since I lay down, my eyes closed and I saw what looked like a brilliant sun inside my head with a light so dazzling and magnetic that I was subsumed by it.

Four minutes later I got up from the table and, much to my surprise, I went reeling almost to the floor. They caught me and supported me until I regained my balance, then called someone to help me to a couch downstairs. I remember lying down, looking through a window overhead at leaves blowing gently in the early autumn breeze just before I fell into a deep peaceful sleep.

I awoke twenty minutes later seeing a man staring at me from another couch. When he saw me open my eyes, he spoke softly, "I've been transfixed by your aura while you slept. Did he work on your head?"

"Yes," I answered lazily.

"The swirls of light and color around your head are amazing," he said. "There is an iridescent golden aura surrounding your head with light and colors shooting out from it like Fourth of July sparklers. The lights and colors reach upward as though toward higher realms. The gold spills into the rest of your aura in speckles, and I can see it through the soft blue and violet."

"I'm not sure what he did when he worked between my eyes," I said, "but I feel very lightheaded. It's as though I'm not all here in my body, like part of me is hovering above my skull."

"You need some grounding. I'll get one of the helpers to come over and do the grounding on your feet," he said.

A woman came and sat at the far end of the couch. She took hold of both my feet and led me through a visualization in which I imaged roots growing from my feet, longer and stronger, through the furniture and the floor, through the foundation of the house and to the earth beneath until the roots reached deep, deep down into the bowels of the planet, comfortable, warm, and firmly anchored. Then she brought me to a waking state.

The lightheadedness was gone, I could walk around, balanced, and my vision was fantastically sharper now.

In the restroom mirror I saw my cheek and eyelashes where the blood had spattered from the healer's "incision" between my eyes. It was true—not a mark or a sign of an incision.

At my friend's home we talked for a long time about the experience.

"Your eyes show that you're still in an altered state. Let me get my aurameter. It's a very sensitive dowsing instrument that measures the size of auras. Stay here, and face the window when you hear me coming back. I'm anxious to see if this experience has affected your auric field."

When I heard her coming down the stairs, I faced the window. Then I heard her saying, "O.K., you can look this way now."

"Did you change your mind about doing the measurement?" I asked before turning around. She sounded so far away that I assumed she couldn't find the instrument and gave up on the idea.

"No, just turn around for a minute," she repeated.

When I turned, I saw her in the middle of the next room

with the instrument bent straight toward her. She had started from the far end of the room to walk toward me with the instrument in neutral position. It had bent back toward her, moved by the force field of energy it entered, my aura, almost twenty feet from me.

I didn't know exactly what the healer had done, but I certainly saw and felt the wonderful effects.

I went to bed tired that night, but awoke with an energy surge the next morning. I went back to the home where the healer worked and waited to see him. When he came out for a glass of water, I cornered him and asked permission to observe a session. He did not object, but he said I must get the client's permission to observe their session.

Most were reluctant to be observed, but I found a Danish woman who permitted me to observe her session so that I could describe to her what he had done. She could not speak English nor could I speak Danish, but she felt certain we would understand each other.

I stood immediately next to the client and the healer, fourteen inches above where he worked. I saw every movement of his hands.

He made the "incision" on her lower back and took out several clumps of toxins, depositing them in a clean paper cup that his wife held nearby. He wore short sleeves and his hands never left the area he worked on. There was no sleight of hand possible such as the media had accused these healers of. He proceeded to work on her neck. It was very dramatic to see his fingers break through the skin without her feeling a thing, then to see them sink deep into the hole he had just made and slosh around until his fingers came up with clumps of bloody junk that he threw into the cup. Then more dramatic to see him clean his hand, often to the wrist, close the "wound," rub his fingers over it to erase any mark, and wipe smudges off the area. The patient then got up and left the room to rest on a couch or in a chair. I explained the "operation" to the Danish woman in words, signs, and gestures, and she understood and was very grateful.

I thanked her and the healer and set out for home.

How strange and wonderful! What attracted me so powerfully to unusual, magical experiences?

Since leaving the ashram, I'd felt a constant gnawing anxiety to get on with my soul purpose, but what was it? I seemed now to be on a roller coaster of experiences that appeared totally unrelated. It was a ride that I could not stop, and I often wondered where it would lead.

Soon afterward, I enrolled in Reiki training, an ancient Oriental laying-on-of-hands technique in which the healer serves as a channel of divine healing energy. It was very spiritually grounded and boosted the healer's growth as well. I practiced Reiki on myself and many friends, but I could not seem to generate enough clientele to focus my time on it. I had felt I was called to healing, but all the signs showed that spiritual forces did not support my doing it professionally, at least not now. I desperately wanted to work in a spiritual context, but I wasn't sure what area to focus on, so I had to bide my time and learn all I could while taking bread-and-butter jobs.

Whenever I got discouraged, I would take out the Cayce material and play the ashram tapes to raise my spirits. The Cayce readings offered much about attitudes and emotions that was similar to what I had read in Freemasonry. It seems that when one discovers Truth, one finds it in many places, and in places of high vibration it is consistent. I began to understand that by allowing negative attitudes to creep in, I blocked the flow of what good was on the way. Even having lived in the ashram, it was difficult amid the turmoil of daily problems. I was still thinking I had to solve it all myself.

Meanwhile the pull back to the Virginia Beach energy became stronger.

When I met Susan at the MariEl conference, we discussed

how we both felt drawn to live there. She wanted me to share a house with her, and it sounded good, but when I got home it seemed there were too many obstacles. Maybe next year, I thought, beginning to consider seriously her idea.

She called in October, saying she had already moved and was waiting for me in Virginia Beach. I couldn't believe it had actually happened. Living with her would be so economical, so I let myself dream about it again.

She wouldn't hang up until I gave her a tentative date.

I would need to break a lease. I would need to be here for Christmas with Dina, Jay, and Lisa. I would have to arrange help to move down there. I would have to . . .

"December," I said. "After the Christmas holidays. Right after that."

7

MOVING TO VIRGINIA BEACH: KARMA X 12!

... the Soul slays not, neither is it slain. It is never born,
and never dies, nor may it, being in Being, descend into
non-being ...   —*The Bhagavad-Gita*

I ARRIVED in Virginia Beach the night of January 3,
jobless, unemployment benefits ended, with my last $1,800
and two charge cards. Jay and his friend Bobby had borrowed a small van to help me move clothes, books, a sewing
machine, a bicycle, and a single mattress to the house I had
agreed to share with Susan.

She was out when we arrived. The key was not under the
doormat where she said she would leave it if she were out,
but I somehow knew it would not be there. I had a queasy
feeling in my solar plexus.

"Let's go eat seafood," I suggested to Jay and Bobby. "I
know a wonderful place and I'll call from there to catch

her when she gets home."

After calling unsuccessfully several times, I called Susan's former home. Her estranged husband ranted angrily, "She's not in Virginia because she changed her mind and won't be living there. She was having second thoughts and came home to think things out, but she's en route back to Virginia now."

The next time I called the Virginia Beach house, Susan answered. "My husband is confused. My mother and I are here to stay."

The feeling in my gut returned. What was this?

We unloaded the van and had a pleasant visit. Her mother was annoyed, however, when I said that Jay and Bobby could sleep overnight on the floor in my room. After all, it was past midnight and the trip had taken six-and-a-half hours.

The nagging queasiness in my solar plexus felt like the onset of a stomach disorder.

The next morning as I stood outside saying good-by to Jay and Bobby, I burst out sobbing. I felt depressed without knowing why. It upset Jay; he thought I was unsure about the move. I felt dark and threatened, but it wasn't connected with the move. I could neither explain it nor stop it.

I wondered if I was anticipating something negative or simply unloading earlier grief, as the MariEl teacher explained. "Tears could flow at any time," she had said, "whenever the body in its wisdom needs to expel them."

Over the next several days, my muscles ached less from the double move that brought me here. When my old lease expired in mid-December, what I hadn't sold I moved to Lisa's porch. Then another move to get here. Having stacked my belongings in a closet, I could now rest and focus on being fully in this magic energy without having to pack, move furniture, sell it, or move books or boxes until summertime. I had time to rest and enjoy life before looking for work.

One bright winter afternoon a week after arriving, I was

comfortably settled on the sun porch when Susan and her mother returned from lunch, appearing upset.

"I don't know how to say this," Susan said. "We ran into the landlord as we left the restaurant, and he said that the neighbors had complained that you brought too much stuff to the house. He said it would look trashy since it was already furnished, and he didn't like my having a roommate. He said either you have to leave by the end of the month or we all get thrown out."

My mind processed at computer speed what she had just said and compared it with previous conversations we'd had. I remembered drifts... "I have no idea who owns this place. I deal directly with the realtor... " and " ... just about all the people on this block are winter transients... "

Back in October she had pleaded, "Please come as soon as possible to share the house. I can't afford it alone. The agent said a roommate is fine—most renters have them."

I realized Susan's story was contrived to get me out, but I couldn't imagine why. I have never been skilled at such games, nor tolerant of them.

I gave her the last benefit of the doubt when I asked, "Did you tell him that the agent gave permission for a roommate? Did you tell him that most of what I brought were boxes of books and that they are put away in a closet for now?"

She danced around the issue with another lie. As I listened, alerted now to her lies, I felt another strange gut sensation. It wasn't depressive as before; it felt as though a tiny ballerina was in there dancing a joyous, exuberant dance!

How could I feel such joy while I was hearing the worst news I could imagine: that I would have to move again! This time in a strange, new town to which I wasn't yet accustomed, where the rent might be outrageous, the place might be horrible, and the location miles away from this energy vortex. What was this joy?

I missed much of what she said, distracted by the mixed internal message I was getting.

"I'm really sorry," I heard her saying, "but I hope you're not going to give me a hard time about this."

"No, no problem. I'll be out by the end of the month." I sensed that the little ballet was a signal that this was positive and, despite its appearance to the contrary, I conceded to it.

Afterward I spent a lot of time in my room studying housing ads, typing résumés, avoiding Susan and her mother, wondering why they had conspired to get me out when they couldn't wait to get me in, and praying to be led to the door of what would be my next home.

Within a week I had found a cozy room in a lovely house that I would share with Sarah, a nice, young woman with a small daughter. It was a short block to the ocean and to A.R.E. I returned to Susan's and began packing immediately. The next day, while they were out to lunch, I loaded my car and moved out.

Sarah and I were very compatible and our friendship grew over the next four months.

I had journaled my dreams since the "dream" about Alex. Two months before moving to Virginia Beach, I had an amazing dream or "dream" just before waking. Morning was the time when my most significant dreams occurred, so it was even more exciting.

Someone awakens me and beckons me to follow him. I recognize him and trust him totally, so I go without hesitation. He is quite tall, probably about seven feet, and wears a silver jumpsuit, much like an astronaut's. I say "he" because I sense a male energy, the only gender clue I have. He wears a helmet with a visor covering his face; only horizontal slits enable him to see through it. I, in pajamas, take his hand and off we go.

We arrive at a meadow with a rustic fence. It looks

like a western corral. There is a small out-building, a
picnic table, and a bench. He stands, one foot up on
the bench and the other on the grass, teaching, teaching, teaching. I pay close attention and strain to keep
up with him. This is very important material. I must
get it.

His nod signals approval, and I feel I've learned a
lot. We have finished this lesson. We return to my
room, he deposits me in my bed, nods approval, and
leaves.

I woke up totally frustrated, unable to remember anything he had taught me. It had all seemed so important. He
had even given his approval, but I didn't know how to retrieve it. I let it go, thinking, that's the nature of dreams.

Three weeks later, I had the identical dream. The same
man, the same jumpsuit, helmet, corral, the same intense
teaching session, the same trip back to my bed.

"What is going on?" I asked myself.

I had heard of reoccurring dreams, but most delivered
dire messages. I had never repeated dreams before, but
these had no fearful implications. I still could not understand what it meant, but I felt more frustrated because,
again, I couldn't remember the important lessons I had
been taught. He nodded, nevertheless, again in approval.
And again, I thought it was over.

The week after I moved to Virginia Beach, my teacher
appeared for the third time in a similar dream scenario.

He taps me on the shoulder to awaken me.

"Again?" I ask. He nods a yes and we leave for the
corral, he in the familiar silver jumpsuit and I in my
white cotton nightgown.

This is a particularly intense teaching session. When
it is over, I am ready to leave. He gestures no and points
beyond the picnic table to a crowd sitting in rows of

folding chairs, impatient for the show to begin. I'm not aware we are to see a show.

My teacher gently turns me to face the audience, steps away, and motions to me to begin teaching.

Me? I suddenly get stage fright.

"But I'm not ready," I plead, in thought transference.

He is determined. He folds his arms and gestures impatiently for me to get on with it.

I begin very timidly, glancing at his expression after every idea I introduce. He waves me on. Finally I have said all that I can say and the audience stands, claps, and whistles. They get rather loud.

It's very nice, but I look to my mentor for his reaction; that is what I most prize. When he nods a definite yes, I know I have passed the test. His warmth sweeps across all other energies in the corral.

The awareness that I have just passed an important test makes me glow all the way back home. But I'm also sad because I have come to feel very close to my teacher and we are parting.

We head home. On arrival, he deposits me in my bed exactly as before and leaves.

Well, I thought, a series of three. But what good was it if I couldn't remember a word or concept of what he taught me. It felt as though my brain was a huge room where it was all stored, but I couldn't find the key to get in to retrieve it. All I could do was record that third one, reminisce in fascination, and write it off to a strange dream series.

Shirley MacLaine, having emerged from the metaphysical closet, scheduled her first seminar in Virginia Beach. I had the opportunity to attend as a volunteer aide.

Most area volunteers were metaphysical counselors in their own right, astrologers, psychics, or channelers. During breaks, as we introduced ourselves and chatted, everyone was reading for everyone else. It was a mini-seminar within a seminar.

On the bright, blustery January morning of the seminar, I set out early only to find my car frozen solid from the unusual ice storm that had followed days of pouring rain. Nothing could keep me from the seminar, so I headed out to Atlantic Avenue hitchhiking, for the first time in my life, to the hotel.

There was barely enough time to thaw out with coffee when the conferees arrived to register. Half an hour into the job, a genial man registered as Jach Pursel from California. He resembled someone I'd met at a Capricorn birthday party, but I suddenly realized that he was the man who channeled Lazaris. When I told him I always enjoyed Lazaris's wise counsel and I asked for his autograph, he smiled and graciously took out a special memento card and autographed it for me.

I have always felt the energy of hands, and often the heart, that crafted things, whether a painting, an embroidered doily, a wood carving, a work in metal, a drawing, a letter, or a signature. When I taught and corrected many papers, the energies from my students' handwriting were often distracting. I delighted, however, in secretly touching museum clothing, jewelry, or leather crafted by ancient tribesmen. To me, it is touching the presence, the love, the patience inherent in the craftsman's art. Jach's autograph became one of my treasures.

Most students of metaphysics were already familiar with concepts presented in the seminar, except for a unique approach to a forgiveness meditation. Shirley led a guided imagery in which we were to meet someone we needed to forgive.

The only people I had a hard time forgiving were my grandmother for her harshness and my mother for abandoning me. I was accustomed to using imagery, but I was not ready to deal with them, so I didn't expect to gain anything from this exercise. We were packed like sardines in the seminar room, however, and I was a captive audience.

"Think of the person who most aggravated you in your life," she began, "or hurt you, or caused you the most suffering."

The imp who lives inside me began to wisecrack. "I know the answer to that one. Grandma," it shouted to me. I wanted to add Mother, but we were only sampling the technique once.

"In this meditation, you're going to thank that person," she continued.

"What??" hissed the imp. "She's really off the wall! You're still trying to heal the damage after all these years and you should thank her?"

"Be aware that it is this person who helped you the most on your path of growth, to become strong, to persevere, to strive for a meaningful life and to fulfill your purpose." She was gentle.

It was beginning to make sense in a strange way, so I quieted the imp so that I could hear the rest of it.

" . . . And to do this for you, this person had to take time out from his or her own path. Think about that. Don't you think this person loved his or her path and yearned for growth as much as you did? Don't you think he or she must have loved you an awful lot to take time—perhaps a lifetime—out of their own journey so that you could progress on yours? Think about that . . . "

The room was silent except for sounds of soft sobbing. Not mine this time, but it did sober me.

I participated as she guided the meditation all the way through forgiving the person for our anger at what we thought was a wrong committed against us, asking the person's forgiveness for forgetting their sacrifice and their love, and finally expressing to them our love and gratitude for the learning, the strengths, the strides on our paths that they had helped us to attain.

I was profoundly moved. I would think softly now whenever I remembered the thorns that Grandma stuck in my childhood side. Of all the forgiveness meditations I had ever heard, this was the best. I had just shed 500 pounds of rage, and I floated through the rest of the seminar sublimely light.

When the seminar was over and conferees left, the energy was so high that the volunteers stayed, chatting and hugging, trying to get grounded before returning to the material world.

People who didn't know each other were hugging first and introducing themselves later.

A psychic channeler to whom I'd been briefly introduced took my hand and said how nice it was to meet me.

Suddenly we couldn't unclasp our hands, and my arm began to vibrate from the shoulder to my hand and up through her arm.

"What are you doing?" she asked me, smiling suspiciously.

"I'm not doing anything; what are *you* doing?" I countered. "*You're* the psychic." I honestly thought she was kidding around with some hocus-pocus. She, on the other hand, thought I had a mysterious power to vibrate her arm.

Suddenly, with our hands still "glued," her head dropped to one side, her eyes rolled back, lids closed, and she began to speak in a strange Oriental accent, so softly that I had to lean in to hear her. Our arms continued to vibrate while I was being addressed by the Asian entity she was known to channel.

"Entity, you have asked many times for the power to conduct healing energy, have you not?" he was asking.

"Yes," I replied.

"Are you ready to accept this gift?"

"Yes, yes," I said.

"Are you aware that you must use this energy responsibly for those in need?" he continued. "And are you ready to do that?"

"Yes. Oh, yes," I committed myself.

"Then receive, entity, and blessings on your work."

Electricity, whose source was neither one of us, ran through our arms for long minutes, painlessly.

"Thank you. Thank you," I heard myself saying, as the psychic began to move her head and wake up, sleepy-eyed.

"What happened?" she asked.

"Oh, come on. You know what he did." I thought that she had been aware of the entire exchange.

As we spoke, I looked around and saw a group of volunteers staring at us. I could hardly believe that I was standing dead center in a public place having a conversation with a disembodied entity. Yes, I did it. I experienced it and, again, I would allow no one to deny my experience.

A week later, I learned from a friend that whenever the psychic went into a channeling mode, she was not aware of the messages given. I tried to make up for my ignorance by sending her a copy of the interaction that, of course, I had recorded as soon as I returned home that day.

My heart was in the right place, but I had no idea what to do with the healing energy I had been given, so while I would not permit others to doubt my experience, I began to doubt it myself.

Living with Sarah was much nicer than living with Susan. I settled in and enjoyed the peace. All I needed was a job.

Area colleges and stores had no openings. I didn't know where else to look, so I stayed close to home. I became a beach bum and frequented the A.R.E. Library. I was fortunate to live close to both, and they brought me great joy at no cost.

One morning I awoke surprised. I'd had another visit. It didn't occur to me to call it a dream. My teacher in the silver jumpsuit had begun to feel more real than flesh-and-blood friends. This visit took a different turn.

He awakens me and I look up, surprised but happy to see him.

"I thought we were finished," I say.

"No," he responds, " . . . second phase."

We go to a place that at first I can't see. I know it is not the corral. It is not the same planet, perhaps not even the same dimension.

After a time we are inside a huge, ultramodern, dome-topped building or ship. It is not another teaching situation. I'm not sure what we are doing.

It feels like a large meeting. Many different life forms mix in friendship.

Suddenly I am aware that I am the only one in night-clothes and barefooted and, for a moment, I am embarrassed. As soon as I wish I were dressed appropriately for this gathering, I am beautifully dressed.

My mentor walks with me at his side, nodding at those we pass, while they nod cordially at us both.

It feels like introductions. All conversations are by thought transference.

Then it is time to go.

Now we are at my bedside. He tucks me in and leaves.

This was no less fascinating, but still more frustrating. What had just happened felt even more important, yet I couldn't remember what the meeting was about, who the people were, or why I had to be there. What exactly was it!?

It made me think a lot about the earliest dreams I'd had.

Between these new sensations, signals in my solar plexus and the dreams, I was beginning to confirm that I walked with unseen companions. I had joked about having an invisible entourage, but now I felt the energies more strongly. I knew now with certainty that I constantly lived in company, and my entourage followed wherever I went. It was quite nice to never feel alone.

My sensitivity to energies became stronger. Not only could I tell instantly the kind of personality before me, I could now sense the intentions. Like an early warning system, I sensed hostility and dishonesty from strangers or acquaintances. I was learning simultaneously to trust the impressions and to make a fast getaway from negative energy. It was interesting.

Finally in May I found a part-time job. I was glad I had carefully budgeted my meager savings. It was also time to move again. As I packed books, I found the folder full of letters Nell had written to me the year I was in the ashram. I missed her. I sat browsing over them in date order. Although she discussed many things, there emerged a continuity of theme. In each letter there was a sentence, phrase, or some reference to power, empowerment, giving my power away, claiming my power, carrying my power like a dynamic ball of brilliant light. Was this the "something" she still needed to teach me? She had never specifically told me it was about power, but I suspected it was.

By June 1, we vacated the house Sarah rented and went our separate ways. The only room I could find was not available until July. I spent June living in a corner of a friend's living-room floor until my July rental became available. I was happy to have my mattress and grateful for the floor space.

When my old car threatened to die, I remembered the fateful words of a man I'd met when I moved to the Beach:

"Hope you like roller coasters! The energy in Virginia Beach is very intense and when you come here to live, karma speeds up. You get six year's karma in six months, so fasten your seat belt!"

"Not me," I thought smugly. "That might be your case, but I've already dealt with most of my karma."

My words bounced back to haunt me, while his were coming true before my eyes. I felt as if I lived in a cauldron of problems and I grabbed every opportunity for psychic advice, though I was unable then to discern the authentic from the contrived.

One Sunday, a visiting psychic from Chicago gave a local workshop. I had no money for it, but when she offered a sample group session to anyone interested, I attended. Among twenty seekers, I sat at the far left on the front row. She spoke about conditions on the planet and how we must all try to raise the consciousness of light; then she began at the opposite end of the row to give each person a minireading.

Halfway through the row, she announced that a Lemurian guide wanted to convey a message to someone in the room. Her head dropped to the side, her voice became deep, loud, and mean as she channeled the message.

"You, entity . . . you in the color blue with the flower in your hair . . . "

We took furtive looks down the rows to see whom the guide addressed. I assumed it was a woman because of the flower in the hair, but I didn't see anyone dressed like that.

Suddenly I felt the flush creep up the sides of my cheeks and burn my ear lobes as I realized I was the only one in the room wearing blue—a blue dress—with a flower in my hair! I had rarely ever blushed, but the mean, scolding tone in her voice hinted at a public reprimand that promised to be embarrassing.

"You are here to work, entity, not to play. Why are you not about your work?" the guide spoke emphatically. "You are here to learn thirty lessons. When you have learned those thirty lessons, you will no longer be here. You will be in another place, teaching what you have learned. You are wasting time in play. It is time to be about your business."

Her head straightened up, and she continued reading for the others as though there had been no interruption.

I kept a very low profile and wondered why the Lemurian guide was so annoyed at me. I was trying my best to emerge from my density. Was he referring to my joblessness? I had tried to get back into teaching, but there were no openings. I felt undervalued having to take a minimum-wage job, but it was all there was. When I got home I immediately took out a pad and wrote down all the problems I'd had since I moved here and what I had learned from them. They felt endless but, in reality, they didn't approach thirty. I figured I was here for a long haul.

I recorded the experience and filed it away for later reference.

I kept thinking about the angry Lemurian guide and the thirty lessons. Days later while I was washing dishes, I remembered having seen something about thirty lessons in a Cayce reading. I called a knowledgeable A.R.E. librarian to see if she was familiar with it.

"No," she said, "it was thirty incarnations, not lessons. Something about needing a minimum of thirty incarnations for the soul to complete its experiences before it was ready to be in the presence of God."

Was that what the Lemurian meant when he spoke of thirty lessons? I had thought of literally thirty lessons. Would each lifetime represent a lesson? When he urged me to get to work instead of playing (on the beach!), I thought he meant literally career work—the job situation really had me crazy. The more I thought about it, the more I realized he meant spiritual work.

When I moved to Virginia Beach, I was too far from my grown children for an afternoon visit. I was lucky that everyone who rented me a room welcomed them when they visited. Dina, Jay, and Lisa had visited from New Jersey, keeping their promise to help in my adjustment by frequent visits and calls. Jen, however, was living in southern Kentucky and Rafi was somewhere in the Midwest. I worried about him and missed him, but I was still too frightened to let him know where I lived.

My sensitivity to energies grew faster than ever, and my dreams were giving good advice for the glitches in my life.

I liked working in A.R.E.'s bookstore. I enjoyed helping people find the perfect book, sharing their wonder as they recounted the breakthroughs at conferences and telling them of the legends of Seashore State Park in our back yard. I liked steering them upstairs to the most unique spiritual library in the country, to the garden where they could commune with nature, and to the third-floor meditation room where they could find an other-dimensional oasis of peace. It was particularly exciting to see so many navy personnel searching the shelves as though hunting for treasure and taking the grand tour of the grounds. I was content here.

Contentment, however, did not spur me on to return to the competitive world for a more lucrative job. I was happy just being in this intoxicating energy. I had no place better to go, nothing better to do just yet, no big plans to pursue. It was a good place to be while I made up my mind or received inspiration.

Meanwhile, I took on the chore of ghostwriting a book. What I first thought would need only proofreading turned out to need major editing and rewriting. It surprised me that it came so easily to me, like correcting student compositions, and it felt much like the rediscovery of a latent skill from an earlier time. It was hard work but fun. I treated it as a rehearsal for my own future book.

I was surprisingly able to save a small stash from my bookstore job because of my lengthy apprenticeship in stretching income. I began to feel crunched in the small, expensive room for which I had to put in sewing time to make up the part of my rent I couldn't afford in money. When my children visited, we barely fit, spread out camp-style in sleeping bags across the floor. I didn't mind being cramped temporarily, though I yearned for larger quarters and time alone.

A week after I completed and delivered the rewritten manuscript, a late call came from a Louisville hospital announcing Rafi's death. They needed my permission to do an autopsy, but it appeared to be a suicide. My vision blurred and I became cold.

I remember the woman telling me names, addresses, and details to write down, and I remember how patiently she repeated them several times before I got them correct. I tried to call my other children, but even their phone numbers blurred in my mind. I was grateful when Jen called to say that she had already called everyone with the details. She suggested I try to sleep and think about it tomorrow, and I agreed like a robot. I was in shock and couldn't think for myself. I needed someone to tell me exactly what to do.

Dina planned the itineraries to fly us all to Kentucky to identify and bury him. Mostly I remained in a zombie state.

On the plane to Kentucky I thought of how hard his life had been from the very beginning. I wanted so much for him to capture a little happiness in it. A week short of nine months since I moved here—the time for the gestation of a life—my youngest son had ended his. How did he feel living as a schizophrenic on the road, landing in this shelter or that, never knowing for sure whether those who peopled his world were real or hallucinations?

I had tried so hard, particularly with him, to be both parents to compensate for Alex's indifference to him. Could the Japanese past life I had uncovered really have caused a rift between Rafi and Alex that carried over to this time? Sandy once said she thought for years that Alex had left to escape Rafi's whining. Were my constant tears and despair for my marriage during that pregnancy the root of his condition? I remembered what a frail child he was, clinging and whining for everything.

Jen and Jay had taught him to play chess so well that by five he could defeat the recreation supervisors at school. Jay would take him along, at nine, to calculate change as he collected from his newspaper customers. Rafi loved showing off his math acuity, but in school he mostly daydreamed.

The sad, dehumanizing schizophrenic episodes he endured after he returned from the army were heartbreaking. Fearing he would come crashing through my door during

an episode, I kept my address secret. He sent my letters to
Lisa's address, and I sent his to various homeless shelters in
different Midwestern states. I saw from his handwriting his
cycles of episodes and stability. I knew when he was going
into the abyss and when he came out. I yearned to reach
out to him, to hold him to my heart, to heal his hurt as I did
when he was small, but fear held me in a vise.

Now it was too late.

We fertilized a young tree with some of Rafi's ashes on
the Kentucky farm that belonged to Jen and her husband. I
contained my grief to avoid upsetting the others, and I think
they held back so that it wouldn't upset me.

On my lonely return flight to Virginia, I relived the scenario complete with the fear, now changed to guilt. I should
have been there for him. I was his mother, his only real parent, the one who had always solved the children's problems.
Why couldn't I solve Rafi's problem? Why couldn't I *make*
him go for therapy and tests? Why couldn't I make him well?

My heart was tearing to pieces.

It was not like Sandy's passing—no dreams, no reassur-
ing messages, no final anecdotes from friends. That I would
regret my cowardice till my dying day nagged at my heart.
Never would I permit anything to cause a rift between me
and my children, never again would I ignore unfinished issues with loved ones. To lose a beloved without closure was
unspeakably painful, like living with a festering hole in my
heart. I longed to have it healed.

Maybe I was hard on myself. I couldn't accept my inabil-
ity to devise a solution before it resulted in death or even to
think of something that would make his life easier. I had
reassured countless relatives of suicides that a loving God
would never punish one already so mortally wounded, but
when it came to my own son, I begged that he not be punished, for I knew better than anyone that he had already
suffered enough punishment in his young life.

I knew by his most difficult astrological chart that he had

brought in too much to work on, as if he had decided at the soul level to balance all his karma now to get it over with. How could any soul bring so much to do in one lifetime, knowing it must begin as a helpless infant with its soul memory veiled? I blessed his courage and asked for mercy for him.

I seesawed between acceptance and peace when I remembered that he would never endure again the cycles of schizophrenia, then guilt and self-recrimination when I recalled being so caught up in my own fear that I couldn't feel his. Two steps forward and one step backward.

I forgot to ask for help for me.

Then anger burst forth. "Did you think I would wait like a sitting duck with the wind knocked out of me to see all my children struck down one by one? NO!!! SO STOP! This is not what I brought children into the world for! Whatever this lesson is, I have learned it! I will NOT TOLERATE this happening again!"

I shouted out my warning to some vague being in the universe.

Who was the target of my angry dialogue? Was it Sandy, for leaving? Was it Rafi, for leaving? Was it the old theme of abandonment still not healed?

Externalizing my anger relieved pressure, helped me to set aside the guilt and anger of old beliefs and reclaim my new truths. I centered into calm, recognizing that each of my children was an individual sovereign soul with an individual agenda to pursue and a chosen time to leave this plane. I focused on the joy that was my reward for channeling them in and helping them during the early years on their own path. I treasured our bonding, but I must release them in love when they choose to go. My grief, I remembered, was for my separation from Rafi, not his end, for there was no such thing.

Back home, friends were wonderfully supportive. We had long been students of metaphysics and *knew* that there is no "death," only a transition, much like birth. We *knew* God is not vengeful. We *knew* all these things, but when chaos ripped through our lives, we lovingly reminded the wounded one of these truths in order to regain a healing perspective, to return to being centered.

Six of us created a simple "bon voyage" ceremony on the beach and sent Rafi love, as I scattered the rest of his ashes over the ocean. He loved freedom; now he could fertilize the earth and go wherever the dolphins carried him.

I needed solitude.

I moved into a tiny cottage surrounded by pine trees, set far back from a quiet street. Pines to soothe a broken heart, said one of my teachers. After a few months huddling under the back yard pines after sunset, inhaling their calming fragrance in the early dark, my heart began to heal. I preferred the neighbors not see me dressing my wounds in this embrace of the pines. Eventually, though, I began to feel a little lighter, a little more energetic, a little less isolated from life.

I wrote a short note to Tom Baker about Rafi's suicide. Tom was a young priest from Indiana with whom I'd made friends at an A.R.E. conference before I moved to Virginia Beach. He sensed my fears and my guilt through my news-item report and wrote immediately, saying exactly what I needed to hear: "Rafi is in the company of angels now . . . " I thanked him for his consoling imagery when we met on his next visit to the Beach, but he can never know how crucial his words were for me the day I received them. More than language, they were alchemy—a spark of life that awakened me to my Selfhood again, but so much more that I couldn't express my gratitude in third-dimension language. I promised myself that someday when we met on another dimension, I would express it in its proper glory.

I waited every night for Rafi to communicate some message, but instead, one night I dreamed fragments of the dream about visiting Alex. It made me remember it had taken fifteen years to "meet" with Alex after his death. Rafi might need time to process and resolve his confusion, to get back in touch with *who* he really is—a divine sovereign child of a loving God—before he could move on.

I blessed him and released him to the angels, who could help him better than I. I released self-blame and promised to be patient. I prayed I would not have to wait fifteen years to hear from him.

In January my job dissolved. I barely eked out winter expenses doing astrology readings and a dowsing workshop. March rent and heating bills were due in five days with no prospects for March income. My flippant joke with friends I'd left behind—"I'm moving, job or not, even if I end up a bag lady"—echoed in my mind, tormenting me with an anguish I could not quiet. I sat, paralyzed with fear, staring blankly out the window at the melting snow, wondering where I had gone wrong. Hadn't I listened to my heart and trusted my guidance, leaving everything behind to come here? The message had seemed so clear after years of agonizing pressure to get on with my soul's purpose and frustrating attempts to divine what exactly it was. Hadn't I verbally committed to do God's work? Was I being fired? Were my efforts unsatisfactory? Were my friends right when they said it was all my imagination and that I was getting pretty flaky?

The telephone snapped me back into this dimension.

It was strange to hear Ursula, a close friend from graduate school whom I hadn't seen in almost ten years. She had found me through the Virginia Beach Directory Assistance after remembering a note on an old Christmas card saying that I planned to move there. After discussing how successful she and Vince had been in their consulting business and my chaotic path since my move, she got down to business.

"We've just figured our taxes and we've had such a great year that we have surplus money, and instead of donating it to unknown charities, we've decided to make gifts to friends who need a boost to do their thing. All I need to know is if you will accept a gift check from us to use for anything that will enhance your life or your business ventures."

I was profoundly moved. I almost slipped back into old programming and rejected it, but recovered in time to accept. Her last instruction was to watch for it within five days.

I was grateful.

I imagined twenty-five dollars. I could buy some food. With fifty dollars, I could pay the heating bill before they turned off the electricity. Ursula's gesture had uplifted me and restored my faith in Spirit.

Two days later, the mail carrier delivered it. Her check was for $500! It covered rent for the cottage, bills, gasoline, and food. I was safe through March!

I blessed my friend many, many times since then and continue to do so.

Winter broke early that year. The cottage and the quiet street I had come to love were the perfect prescription for healing. The air filled with bird songs, and the dogwood and forsythia burst into bloom. Daffodils and tulips broadened their smiles in the gentle sun. The ocean water warmed my bare feet as breakers edged on shore. The gulls seemed less ravenous. It was sweet to watch the sandpipers racing ahead of the waves to keep their feet from getting wet. Walking on the beach became my morning routine.

A neighbor caught up with me during a walk and told me of a firewalk she was sponsoring. When I asked what a firewalk was, she explained it to me.

"But why," I asked, "would people want to risk scorching the soles of their feet walking a twenty-foot path of burning coals?"

"Well, it's a mind-over-matter process. Most people don't even get a blister. You see, most of us impose limits on ourselves, sometimes from childhood conditioning, that we carry unconsciously. The firewalk begins before we even get to the bed of coals. We work on new conditioning first. Sort of like Cayce said, 'Mind is the builder.' We build new attitudes. Then we focus on our feet feeling very cool, and we hold that focus throughout the walk. When we walk without burning our feet, we realize that our limitations are only in our mind. Then we can move beyond those limitations with more freedom."

"I don't know," I said. "What if my feet get scorched? I wouldn't enjoy that. It sure would feel good, though, to be free of some of my old conditioning—all those ghost voices that repeat '…you can't do that…' every time I get a great idea."

I ruminated about that conversation when I got home. The very idea of feeling freer made me aware of how I had improved since Rafi's death, but I knew in my heart that I showed a much freer face to the world than was true. Part of the old conditioning was: *Don't let the enemy (world) see how scared you are or how wounded.* I was tired of coming to the threshold of success in a project and sabotaging it. I wanted to be free of that. I wanted the ghosts obliterated so that I could move forward with my life.

I remembered a time when, after much flying, one scary experience made me very fearful of airplanes. It lasted for years, then for no reason that I could pinpoint, the fear lifted one day, like a garment rising up over my head. It was so freeing. After that I could fly anywhere without fear, settled into my seat, sleeping during most of the flight, feeling as if I were curled up in the lap of a loving angel. The new fears were vague, but I could sense congestion in my body from all that I had allowed others to keep me from doing. This, compared to burnt feet, was much more devastating. The promise of the firewalk far outweighed the fear.

I decided to do it.

The afternoon of the big event, I was on my knees installing a carpet remnant in the hall when someone knocked. As I got up to answer the door, my right knee sent a pain shooting down my leg. I knew I had done something to my kneecap. I opened the door to an acquaintance who had decided to visit. When I told him about my knee and the upcoming firewalk, he laid a pronouncement on me.

"Are you crazy? Why do you want to walk on hot coals? It's crazy. You'd better heed the signs. Your knee is telling you not to do it. Whatever it is that you keep yourself from doing, you probably shouldn't be doing anyway. You women! You have such cushy lives and you're never satisfied!"

That was it! I told him I couldn't visit now. I needed to rest my knee so that I would be ready for the experience. He protested my determination; I protested his pronouncement.

I could have been furious at his patronizing attitude, but I knew it wouldn't help my knee, so I released it. So far, so good. I wrapped my knee in a castor oil pack, took some homeopathic arnica pellets, and did a Reiki healing on it. I was so psyched up to do the firewalk that I would allow nothing to interfere with my plans. I created a special visualization, then took a nap until the alarm clock woke me an hour later. My knee was perfect.

Prior to the walk, Tolly Burkan, the father of firewalking in the U.S., rehearsed fifty of us in affirmations and visualizations. Many said their fear was gone. I intellectualized all the techniques and sat terrified.

Downstairs in the Radisson parking lot, our twenty-foot strip of glowing 1,200-degree coals had been burning for two hours. We formed a circle around the fiery path. Tolly instructed us to walk when we felt inspired to and not to walk if we weren't so inspired. He said he would call for those who wanted to do a second walk as soon as everyone had walked once.

I stood terrified, thinking: How many people are going to get burned? When they talk about it, it sounds like a statistic instead of individuals, each with two burned feet. What if my feet burned and I couldn't go to the family reunion in New Jersey in two weeks? They would never forgive me. I would never forgive myself. What if I walked halfway and got so burned that I fell and burned my hands, too? What if ... what if ... what if ... ???

"Second time around," I heard Tolly shout. I panicked. I had dawdled too long, watching to see if anyone writhed in pain. I was about to lose my chance. If I didn't do it now, could I ever again get to this level of determination to do it? It was now or never.

I ran up to where the "second-timers" were already lining up. They moved fast and suddenly it was my turn.

My mind blanked out and refused to retain the techniques we were taught. I had only a moment to bring my determination up to my power chakra, then to my heart, before I looked up and whispered in love and desperation, "This is it, guys. No turning back. Help me to do this. Walk with me."

Guys? It had nothing to do with gender. It was the way I had come to think of my entourage. I felt their presence again in that moment. Unclear faces, but I knew there were guides, angels, and various helpers—the same gang that always hung out with me.

I proceeded to walk as fast as I could and found myself halfway through the path of coals with my feet feeling no different. Then I was at the end and still not a blister. When I fully realized I had walked the coals without even so much as warming my feet, I was so excited I couldn't resist getting in line to do it again.

This time I was much more cocky—I knew I wouldn't get burned, but I wanted a blister, a souvenir to prove to me tomorrow that I had really done it. I ended up with a tiny blister between my third and fourth toes and an enormous smile. "Thanks, guys," I whispered, as I felt my heart and my courage expand.

Back in the circle, as I waited for the others to finish, I began to question my experience. "It probably wasn't very hot," I secretly told myself. "I must have waited so long that the coals had cooled. I must have stepped on ashes that were already cooled by those who had gone before me."

I turned to respond to a tap on my shoulder and recognized a friend. She asked if I'd gotten burned. As I answered, "No," I noticed her teary face. She confessed that her feet were badly burned and she was in terrible pain.

"I'm so sorry," I said. "Were you one of the first to walk?"

"No," she replied. "I went right after you."

I felt really bad for my friend. At the same time, it told me that if she walked behind me and got so badly burned, the coals had to be hot when I walked. I became a believer! I had really broken past my terror and walked barefoot over 1,200-degree coals, twice.

Excitement filled me for having successfully done this outrageous feat. I stood unharmed and triumphant, but worried. Would I be expected now to conquer more fears and forge past further limitations? All I needed was a red and blue suit with a cape and a big "S" centered on the shirt!

The first thing I did to break through limitations was to send résumés to nearby colleges. I'd had enough of this financial diet to dull the memories of academia, so I would brave it again for the fall semester. It was mid-May, and I had to vacate the cottage by the thirty-first. I'd had no luck finding a place to move to for the summer. Winter rentals at the Beach were reasonable, but rents rose astronomically with the temperature, and the cycle of moving began again. Part of the karma here was to learn to be a good nomad.

How I hated moving!

This next move would be the sixth in sixteen months as a Virginia Beach resident. It was more confusing than complicated. The first move took two carloads. Later, after accumulating books and items and bringing back cookware from each New Jersey visit, a move took four carloads. I feared it would be worse this time.

Each move meant pack, load, unload, and unpack. It was backbreaking and mind-boggling. I couldn't remember the new places for items because they changed so often. I was constantly looking for things in places where I'd kept them two or three moves earlier, then the next time I moved I'd find what I thought I'd lost. I had reached a point where I was afraid to completely unpack.

I had two weeks. Confident that I could pack in seven days, I spent the first week searching intensely for new quarters. All my friends were helping in the search, so I was optimistic. To my dismay, however, by the end of the week we had found nothing. I knew why. I had become attached to the cottage, and its vibration was one that I wanted to remain in. I had felt cared for and nurtured, rocked and pacified, as if in a mother's lap. But the reality was that it was not a mother's lap; it was a house, and its owner wanted it back for the summer. I couldn't blame him, but I knew I would have to be routed out. That evening I decided it was time to begin packing.

The phone rang when I was in the midst of labeling countless boxes of books. It was Sarah calling to invite me to a Gemini birthday party. "Just in time for your birthday," she coaxed.

"Well, I'm packing books now. I have to move in a week. It sounds good, but it depends on how my packing goes. You know how it is. When you have to be out, you have to be out. But thanks for inviting me. I'll really try to come."

"Can you use some help?" she asked. "I know where to get boxes and I can ask around and get some strong backs to help."

"Yeah, both might be a good idea. I'd appreciate it."

"I'll call and let you know," she said before we hung up.

Packing books again, I came across the Cayce book I'd bought at the campus Swap Shop. I sat for a minute to rest, groaning about moving. I opened the book to a place where two lines almost jumped out at me . . . "*For that which ye hate has come back upon thee. Don't hate anything in the present.*" I felt really creepy—as though someone were reading my mind and talking to me through a book! How easy for whoever it was, when I was doing all the work! How could I heed Cayce's warning about hating things when the lords of karma had decreed that I would move, move, move, since the day I arrived in Virginia Beach!

Twenty minutes later the telephone rang again. I nearly tripped over floor clutter trying to reach it. Why can't Sarah let me make a little headway packing, I thought. Why can't she tell me tomorrow that she found helpers. How could she have found help so quickly?

I picked up the phone and heard my Uncle Lucas's voice, calling from New Orleans.

" . . . we didn't know she was sick either," he was saying, "but when I got there and saw her, I told her she had to go to the hospital. She didn't want to go, but I insisted, and when they admitted her, they put her right into intensive care. She could hardly breathe. You'd better drop everything and get down here if you want to see your mother alive. We don't know how long she'll last. It could be a week or a day. You should hurry."

8

MOTHER IS DYING: TRUTH UNCOVERED

*You cannot be other than where Love has placed you
to learn its holy lessons.*   –Alan Cohen

I WAS stunned.

The timing was terrible.

How could she be that sick? She was always so robust. She hadn't mentioned being sick in the birthday card she sent me last week.

We communicated through letters because every time we talked we argued. She would insist that I was her baby and she still knew best, the what-was-I-doing-in-my-life interrogation and critiques followed, then the review of events I should have handled differently as far back as childhood.

Finally, " . . . why aren't you looking for a rich elderly man to marry who could set you up for life?"

It wasn't enough to tell her that wasn't my idea of living my life. She always responded, "No, of course not, it always has to be *your* idea, *your* way! And look where it gets you." We could never agree about my life, and the confrontations were always ugly. Letters worked better for us.

"Well, are you coming or not? I can't hear you." My uncle's hearing was impaired. He thought he couldn't hear what I was saying, but I had gone into a brief reverie.

"I can't come now. I have to vacate this house in a week, and I don't even have my things packed yet. I haven't found a place to live either. Can't I come after my move?"

"Not if you want to see your mother alive."

"Why is she getting sick now, of all times?" I assumed it was a ploy. "I can't stop my life to come running there. How am I going to get packed, moved, and suddenly be down there? What do you think I am?"

"Well, we don't always choose the times for these things." He sounded sincere. "She didn't ask me to call you. She's terrified of planes, and she'd only worry if she knew you were flying here. I just thought you should know. If I called to say she had died, you'd be angry because no one told you before."

He was right. I started to panic. I was just healing after losing Rafi nine months before. How could I do all this in so little time? Where would I put my things? My head was so tangled in details! I couldn't face calling airlines.

"You're right," I tried to sound calm. "I'll do what I can and get back to you about the arrangements."

I felt my energy seeping out. I wanted to escape into a peaceful sleep with wonderful dreams and wake up two years later with all these problems gone.

"Please, God," I prayed aloud, "help me to get through this. There's so much to do, and I don't know where to begin. Please send me the help I need."

I sat at my meditation altar with candle and incense

burning and chanted a Sanskrit mantra about twenty times. It meant: *I surrender myself to the will of God.* I slipped into a short meditation and when my eyes opened, I was centered and clear. I whispered another plea for guidance and help.

I called Jen in Kentucky, explaining the situation. She offered to make airline inquiries. She called back saying the only flights available to New Orleans were during the next two days. Everything was booked until after Memorial Day.

I reserved the latest departure—4:00 p.m. two days later—and worked through the night packing.

Sarah dropped off boxes in the morning and made a pot of coffee before leaving.

Word had spread and angel helpers came from everywhere! Jerry called to say that I could put my things in his friend's basement until I returned and found a place to live. "Leave everything on the sun porch and I'll bring it there."

I took two catnaps during the day and worked again through the second night, forcing myself to stay awake with caffeine.

Around ten the next morning as I pushed myself through exhaustion, someone knocked at the door. I opened it to a woman named Jane whom I knew only slightly from potlucks and seminars. I thought she was dropping in for a visit and I was not very polite. I told her it was a bad time for a visit; I was in an emergency and had too much to do.

"I heard about your emergency and came to help. Two of us can do it faster than one." She stood there with the most loving smile I had ever seen. I couldn't believe how she had just appeared on my doorstep to help. I showed her the kitchen, now a disaster from my frenzied efforts, but she didn't even wince! I explained that I'd work until 2:00, then shower and dress for my ride to the airport to catch my 4:00 flight.

We worked steadily until 2:00. Finally everything was packed and moved to the sun porch, rooms vacuumed, and the bathroom cleaned. Only the kitchen was unfinished, but I had neither strength nor time to finish it.

"Go on. Get ready to go," Jane urged. "Tell me where the realtor's office is. I'll finish the kitchen, lock up, and drop off the key to the realtor. Hurry so you'll be ready when your ride comes."

How could I ever thank this woman! Or any of them? Had it not been for these helpers, I could never have done it.

My plea for help was heard, and a crew of angels came. I marveled at how help always came from sources I couldn't have imagined. All I had to do was ask. But, ironically, I still hadn't learned; I always asked as a last resort! I promised myself to remember to do it first from now on.

How could I not feel gratitude? How could I not feel loved?

I wasn't aware when the plane left the runway. I awoke in a choppy cloud bank five minutes after takeoff. I slept through most of the trip, partly from exhaustion, partly from resistance to returning to the painful haunts of childhood. When I arrived, my uncle met me with a warm welcome and took me to the hospital.

He drove through old neighborhoods I'd been through on foot, on skates, on my bike, or in streetcars. In conversation with Uncle Lucas, I relived brief vignettes of some of the worst scenes of my childhood, as well as some of the sweetest.

Mother lay disoriented. She couldn't see me clearly and insisted that Lucas had brought someone who resembled me as a joke. Finally she recognized my voice and hugged me, tearfully.

"I never expected you to come all the way here to see me," she kept repeating.

It angered me when she coughed. She could hardly breathe, but would not stop smoking. I cringed when she hugged me in a cloud of smoke, but despite myself, I was moved. I brought up all the armor I had, lest I feel too much sympathy for this woman. I had learned to raise my armor years before during daily spankings. Once, unarmored, someone cried out in pain, and I discovered that I felt pain empathetically in my body where the person was injured. Thus armor again became helpful. After Sandy's birth, when I heard women groan in labor, I got contractions. Oddly, I could deal with wounds, blood, stitches, or incisions as long as I didn't hear cries of pain.

In deference to Mother's condition, I was pleasant. My uncle suggested we leave early so that I could catch up on sleep, but not before Mother made me promise a daily visit.

We toured the city on the way home. Uncle Lucas pointed out the shocking deterioration of the Garden District and Canal Street. I saw the once-grand department stores lining Canal Street now empty, as well as the baroque theaters that once featured vaudeville shows and first-run movies, abandoned to a failing economy. There were few signs of progress. Tchoupitoulas Street, once a dirt road that paralleled the freighter tracks along the Mississippi docks, was now a busy boulevard. Remnants of hobo-cooking fires no longer blew in the wind along the tracks. The Louisiana Avenue ferry that we used to ride to cool off on torrid summer evenings was larger, more modern. Air-conditioned buses replaced streetcars, except for the St. Charles Avenue line that traced the most affluent section, and Audubon Park now housed an open wilderness compound opposite the old caged zoo.

It had always been a skin-deep beautiful city. Beneath its surface beauty, however, festered a corruption carried over from French and Spanish political intrigues and slave-masters' exploitation.

We arrived at my uncle's frame house to Aunt Iris's welcome, and we chatted endlessly before I fell asleep. Eleven hours later I awoke refreshed from my long exhaustion.

Aunt Iris served shrimp stew and rice for lunch. The exquisitely maddening aroma reminded me of the first time I'd left the city; people wouldn't believe I grew up there because I didn't know what *shrimp creole* was. Our everyday fare had simple names for cuisine the world called gourmet. To get recipes I had to stand over people and write as they cooked. Little measuring and much tasting were their instinctive creole cuisine secrets. I had almost forgotten the aromas that permeated the neighborhood from noon on. Shrimp creole returned me fast to my roots.

But I didn't come here for food. I reminded myself that my life and my heart were in Virginia now and this was a temporary interruption.

After lunch, Uncle Lucas and I toured another section until visiting hours.

I knew my city well, despite its enormous size. Instead of a family car, I remembered that we had an enviable public transportation system that reached every part of the city and was safe at any hour. For a dime we could transfer between four linked streetcars. Going everywhere on foot, on my bicycle, or on streetcars imprinted upon my memory streets and routes and all manner of intricacies of the city. I rode the Desire Street streetcar many times through the neighborhood in which Tennessee Williams set his play, *A Streetcar Named Desire.*

As we drove down St. Charles Avenue from Louisiana to Canal Street, my uncle complained about the racial strife while I phased into reliving my own private memories of earlier times. We passed the old Walgreen's Drug Store where Benny Parks took me after our first movie date. We had malteds so thick that they came with half-inch straws, and we were both sick the next day.

We moved down Royal Street through the French Quarter, then circled Jackson Square alongside the St. Louis Cathedral and the old Spanish *cabildo,* a major magnet for school field trips, where my teachers delighted in showing us dungeons and cells barely two feet square into which prisoners were jammed for months or years. Legends of haunted mansions, ghosts of tortured slaves, and voodoo spells burdened my childhood in this city of dark magic realism. It was not until high school that I discovered curio shops filled with delightful crafts, the symphony hall, museums, flower shows, and similar light-filled places in my city.

The tour relaxed me to face the hospital visit.

We arrived at snack time to find Mother eating two desserts. She was so happy to see me that she put them down, but all I could see was that she had no respect for her health, preferring instead what would surely harm her.

"Why are you eating that sugar?" I snapped. "You know it's not good for you. You do everything that you know will make you sick, then you expect everybody to come running to help you."

As my words echoed in my head and blasted through my ears, I was shocked to hear my grandmother. God, I didn't want to sound like my grandmother! I feared my scolding would upset her, but only because I didn't want to be responsible for upsetting her.

"Don't be mad at me," was all she said.

I couldn't find any compassion for her. I stood at her bedside seething with anger for her manipulation and abandonment.

I did my best to be inoffensive during the rest of the visit, but I was relieved when my uncle said it was time to go home. Mother was steadily improving since I arrived.

The visit that night went better.

The next morning we rode past the house Grandma's father built, where I grew up. Several interns and nurses who worked in the hospital where Mother was confined now shared the house. I wondered if the swings of my gym set were still in the back yard or if the rattan glider still stood beside the overgrown oleander tree, but the new owners had blocked the view with a fence.

Later while my uncle and aunt watched the news, I sat on the back porch stroking the cat, recalling my childhood in the other house. The neighbors used to make embarrassing jokes about the daily spankings that rewarded my active imagination, my choice of friends, my ignorance of Grandma's whimsical rule changes, and my bed-wetting. I could almost feel those spankings again from Grandma's Popeye arms. Every day brought new angst. Punished on the back steps, I'd bare my soul to Tootsie, my truest collie friend and confidante, as she licked the tears from my cheeks.

My childhood Saturdays were my great escape. I was either sent by taxi to visit my mother, who was never harsh, or my dad would bring me to his neighborhood where I would be passed down a line of affectionate, doting Italian grandmothers who commented, "She's getting so big" or " . . . so bright" or " . . . so cute."

On Daddy's Saturdays, Grandma would order me to demand my overdue child-support money and to sass his new wife. I was constantly spanked for being sassy at home; now they were telling me to do it! I was much too timid to parrot Grandma and too fond of my daddy to talk mean. And his new wife was nice to me; I liked her. Grandma said it meant I loved my mother less, but that wasn't so. She interrogated me after every visit and when I hadn't obeyed, I became a "bad, ungrateful kid."

Grandma's austerity permeated our house. Her dominant personality ruled everyone. Her bachelor brother, her spinster sister, Mother's younger brother Lucas, and I lived in her domain. My great uncle supported us and bestowed my recreation allowance—four weekly movie fares for me and my teen-age chaperone to get respite from "the willful child" for a while. Lucas went to high school, then business school, then married and moved out when I was thirteen. I called him "Lucas" then. Years later when I took my children to visit, I took on their habit of calling him "Uncle Lucas."

My gentle great aunt Nan was as different from Grandma as sisters could be. She worked in a large downtown hotel for a pittance and contributed what she could. She was the eternal buffer in family conflicts. She never married, but I suspected she carried a youthful crush long after her sweetheart returned from war and married another.

There were dark secrets in my family, many of which I could never penetrate. When I was bored without playmates, I would investigate every closet and drawer in the house to see what interesting things I could find. Grandma called it "rooting." She saved everything and I hadn't seen half of it! Rooting became my favorite remedy for boredom and a frequent cause for punishment.

One day while rooting, I discovered a cache of exquisite old-time Valentines addressed to Nan with loving messages signed by "Ike." I was so taken with their beauty that I could hardly wait till she came home from work to ask about Ike. When she saw me holding her treasures, she paled, grabbed them, and refused to speak to me for days. I loathed having hurt the most loving person in my family. My curiosity didn't justify hurting her, but I couldn't help feeling a nagging curiosity about this maiden woman's real life.

Secrets offended me even in childhood. The family expected me to cooperate in its endeavors, but did not allow me to participate in its history, although part of its history was my history. I still didn't know the biggest secret of all about me—why I was sent to live with Grandma at age two. Every time I asked, they frowned, as though I was meddling into someone else's business. Was not my life my business? The more they withheld, the more I wondered what they were hiding.

Evenings when it was too late to be outside but not yet bedtime, Nan entertained me with card games. By third grade I knew how to play blackjack, poker, gin rummy, casino, three kinds of solitaire, and Chinese fan-tan. We played for match sticks or tiny scraps of paper which she called "chips." In school when I spoke of a new game I had learned, the teacher asked what other card games I knew. When I told her, she asked, "Who's the gambler in the family?" I didn't know what "gambler" meant so I didn't answer. I never caught the fever to play cards; it was just something to do on cold winter nights. It was not until I was married that Alex told me they were all gambling games and that fan-tan was an especially high-stakes game. Another mystery about my beloved Nan.

When she came to the island for Jen's christening, I asked where she had learned those games. "Never mind" was all she would say.

It rang of a salty past for such a homebody. She had once owned the corner house and opened a small grocery store in front while living in back, but she lost everything after granting credit to jobless neighbors needing food for their children. She swallowed her pride and moved to her brother's home amid "I-told-you-so's."

Sundays, when I was four, Nan walked me three miles to Sunday school, where we sang about Jesus and colored pictures of Him loving little children. I fell in love with Him then. I couldn't get enough. Grandma loved it when I got certificates, "evidence" for the neighbors of her superior mothering. I brought her eight years of perfect attendance certificates from Sunday school by the time I was twelve. It included times I was sent to church with bronchitis and fevers. After confirmation, I graduated to the regular service. No more Sunday school. The minister pounded his fists at the congregation and raged about someone who was angry and vengeful, thrusting his fist out of the heavens and threatening with a sword.

This wasn't Jesus. I wanted no part of it.

I walked out down the center aisle of church during such

a resounding sermon and refused to go back. Grandma grounded me forever. Having been overexposed to her tactics, I had learned to turn them against her.

"I don't care how long you ground me," I sassed. "I can wait longer; I'm younger. You won't have me to do your errands any more, and you'll have to stay home to make sure that I remain grounded."

Nan always came to my rescue. The grounding was lifted. After Nan coaxed me to return to church, I did, never taking seriously the minister's rantings. I didn't like his God and, when I said so, they expected me to be struck down. Instead, I walked away and went about my business.

In her teens, Sandy had spent two weeks visiting Mother and Grandma. When I picked her up at the station, her first words were, "Mom, how did you stay sane?"

I wondered if the nurses and interns who now lived in the old house felt its intensity.

Mother stabilized. I could have come a week later instead of going through those incredibly hectic two days.

One day I arrived to find her hospital room empty. I felt an achy catch at my gut. She died, I thought! But they had moved her to another room. I sighed with relief. My feelings were more mixed than ever.

A social worker asked me to attend a meeting for relatives of seriously ill patients. I was uneasy among dutiful daughters whose mothers had lovingly reared them. I listened to them tell how they loved their mothers, and I heard the social worker advise them how to deal with the situation. It embarrassed me.

I searched inside myself and couldn't find feelings like those. When it was my turn to speak, I felt my armor stiffen. "I don't have that kind of relationship with my mother. My mother abandoned me when I was two and her mother brought me up very harshly. I wanted my mother to raise me and love me and care for me like yours did, but that was not my experience. She didn't want me to live with her. I owe her nothing, and I'm jeopardizing my only job and income by being here this long." I left seven shocked faces staring at me.

How many brick walls had I run into pursuing the secret of Grandma's guardianship! I persistently asked it. There were three versions. Grandma said she had legal custody because my mother was too young. A next-door neighbor said that when we came home from the courthouse after the divorce, Grandma unlocked the front door, took me from my mother, put Mother's suitcases out, and told her to leave because she did not want a divorced woman under her roof. I couldn't believe this, for Grandma was also divorced. The woman swore it was true. The third version came during a visit five years earlier when I asked Mother for the real story. First she inquired warily what I'd been told, then she angrily snapped that my grandmother never had legal custody of me, but would fly into a rage every time she tried to take me back, so she gave up.

Gave up? It had only intensified my anger. She couldn't have wanted me. I knew how I would fight anyone who attempted to take a child from me! I would never allow it! I couldn't see how this strong, forceful, aggressive woman would allow it either unless she didn't want to be bothered. She was gentle and loving when I was small, but later became as unstable and harsh as Grandma.

The family tried to hide a lot of ugly stuff. I had known since childhood that Mother attempted suicide, but talking about it wasn't permitted. She'd eloped at fourteen, and Grandma had angrily opposed the marriage. Grandma's opposition was not open to discussion; Mother's elopement, however, was abundantly criticized.

"Oh, thank You, God," I whispered at my mother's bedside, "for granting me the strength and insight to leave this festering sewer of intrigue to struggle through my own problems in peace."

I sat watching her sleep, listening to her erratic, labored breathing. I knew there was a hole in my armor when I began to feel sad for her. She had been reduced to such a helpless state, in itself, sad.

When she awoke, I did little things to make her comfortable. I brushed her hair, rubbed her feet. She liked me to stroke her hair while we talked. She said it made her feel pampered.

Her speech slurred as in times when she'd been drinking and had phoned me to bicker, but even that didn't bother me now. I noticed that I could now sit with her for a long time with my armor down.

I remembered a "dream" I'd had years after Grandma and Nan died. They were trapped in an open garage with a bright light in back of them that they didn't see. When I walked by, they stretched out their hands in a desperate gesture, begging me to pull them over to where I was. It appeared that they didn't know they had died and wanted to come back instead of going into the light that was right there. I had heard that when people don't understand the transition of death, they could spend years wandering in confusion.

I decided to approach the subject with Mother in a way that might make it easier for her, should it be nearing her time to pass over.

"Do you ever think of Doc?" I asked. Doc was her adoring second husband who had died of cancer years earlier.

"Yes! A lot." She immediately brightened.

"Does he ever come to talk to you?"

She gave me a funny look. I told her then about Sandy's communications and how real they were.

"Oh, I wish Doc would do that. It would make me so happy. I miss him so much."

I told her how I saw Sandy's grandfather waiting to receive her just before she passed.

"Do you think Doc will be waiting? Oh, but he died."

"They say they don't really die," I explained, "they just slip out of their broken bodies and pass to a different dimension, where they continue learning and doing what they do. Every now and then they come back to help a loved one who's arriving in that dimension. But nobody really 'dies.' Remember how much they talked in church about our souls? Well, that's the part of us that never dies; that's the real *us*, and that's what slips out and goes its merry way. Isn't that neat?"

"That's wonderful!" She was excited and smiling. "I hope that's the way it is. I hope I see Doc again."

When I left, she was more relaxed and content.

It was steamy that night at Uncle Lucas's. Lying directly under the fan didn't help. I thought I'd toss till morning, but at some point I suddenly saw my mother at seventeen. I knew it was she but it was as if I were living in her body at that time in her life, feeling her feelings, living her life.

In the mirror I see my hair like Marlene Dietrich's, soft and blond. I see a fair, blue-eyed beauty. I am painfully frightened and lonely for my baby who was torn away. I am so desperate; I might never get my child back. I can't find a job. Where will I live? How can I earn money for rent? Either I'm too young or I haven't enough school for the jobs I try for. My mother has turned me out, I'm divorced, and no one will take me in. God, what will I do? What will become of me alone?

I awoke crying. Feeling every wrenching emotion she had. I perceived this was her frame of mind just before her suicide attempt when I was four.

Nan once told me during my teens, "Paul's chauffeur was on his way to the airport at five that morning to pick him up from a business trip when he saw a young girl in a gutter, unconscious. He rushed her to the hospital and called Louise to tell her what had happened. Louise called the airline, told them to page Paul and tell him to take a taxi home, then she went to the hospital. Louise gave her own address and paid your mother's bill, saying she would live there after her discharge. They thought your mother would die. She had swallowed a lot of poison. She finally improved and went to live with Louise and Paul in that big house on St. Charles Avenue until she completely recovered. They sent her to nursing school but she didn't finish. She stayed with them for two years. They loved her like she was the daughter they never had, I think more than your grandmother did, and they remained friends for many years."

I remembered Grandma taking me to visit her there. Louise and Paul were so kind to me that I cried when it was time to leave. Small as I was, I saw that Grandma resented Mother's rescue and wanted her punished for some unnamed sin, but instead Mother "ended up like a princess." Again I felt caught between two opposing forces. Later when Mother completely recovered, I visited often. There was such joy and good will in that family that I would always wish I never had to go home.

Something had shifted now. I had felt Mother's feelings. For the first time, I saw her and felt her as a teen-ager, helpless, rejected, without allies or education, vulnerable, frightened, abandoned by her own mother. God, I can't stand her pain, I thought! The pain I felt was of longing for her child. She was hardly more than a child herself. I felt her desperation and terror when she reached the limit of what she could bear. I sensed the fear behind the smart-aleck mask she presented to the world. We had been taught not to show fear or disappointment, for if the enemy saw that we were hurt, it would know how to attack us. It was always we and they, attack and defense. I wondered who had

passed this on to her. I shrugged it off years later; Mother
took it for the entire journey. She was scarred first, I came
after. She succumbed and repeated the pattern, I grew more
willful and strong; I escaped. If only Mother had recognized
her vulnerability and asked for help.

Was this a "dream" like the one about Alex? A glimpse
backward on the time line? Someone was directing this.
Every time I needed to process something, to resolve or release it, a dream told me the entire story in feelings. I
thanked my helpers and forgave the time I had lost in anger.

I visited early next day, pulled the chair up to the bed,
and leaned my head close to hers. I felt softer. She sensed
the change. I asked if she remembered all those fights we
had through the years, and she did. I asked if she would feel
better if we could forgive each other for that and start over
from here. "That would make me feel real good," she said.

"You know, all my anger came from feeling that you had
abandoned me to Grandma's harshness, and no one would
ever tell me why. Even when I asked you, it sounded like you
just didn't want me enough to fight it out with her."

Her eyes were watery and she couldn't speak for a moment, so I went on. "I had a dream last night that told me
exactly how it was. I still don't know the details, but I do
know that you loved me and you suffered when you couldn't
get me back. I know what you had to deal with and how
hard it was. I know how you felt. And I need you to forgive
me for all the harsh things I thought about you all those
years. Can you do that?"

She cried as she nodded a yes. When she could speak,
she said, "I can forgive you anything. I love you."

"And I forgive you," I said, "for keeping secret all this time
the true circumstances of that arrangement and for not telling me the truth about it. It has dogged me all my life and
robbed me of my self-esteem. I really thought I must be so

terrible that you just couldn't stand me. I can forgive you that, even if I still don't know the story, because I understand now what it cost you and I love you. Part of my anger was that I always loved you and wanted to be with you and I thought you didn't want me. I release that now because I love you."

We hugged by the side of the bed and cried softly together.

I could feel a surge of love rushing in to fill the place where hurt and anger had festered for so many years. I felt 500 pounds lighter by surrendering my armor.

The next day I tried to tell her gently that I must return to my job in four days before they replaced me. I already had been away ten days. She became very sad. I held her as if she were my own child and promised to go and secure my job and return in three weeks. I needed to earn money to pay bills and buy a plane ticket. She perked up, anticipating my return, and promised to stay well until I got back.

Two days later, a nurse said that her x-rays showed no growths. Her lungs were very congested, however, and they would have to hook her up to a suction device to remove the mucus to help her to breathe. She had severe emphysema.

Minutes later several aides arrived with the device. It had tubes to go down her nostrils, through her throat, and into her lungs. They asked me to leave the room while they inserted it, but I stood there. This was happening too fast.

"Come on, hon," the nurse coaxed my mother, as she readied the device, "we're gonna set you up so you can breathe easier. It'll be a little uncomfortable going in, but you're a big girl—it'll be all right."

It offended me to hear her talking to my mother as if to an impaired child, while Mother lay helpless.

"You won't be able to talk," she droned, "with the device in place because the tubes will obstruct your vocal cords.

But you might get more rest that way. You can watch TV or listen to your radio. Your button is here so that you can signal for a nurse, and you can write your messages to your family on a pad."

Mother's color drained. Her surprise turned into panic, as betrayal and fear swept across her face. She broke out in tears.

I realized that no one had told her about this. She had no time to adjust to the idea or to the inevitable, or to say what she had to say to everyone.

"Wait a minute!" I blocked the nurse so that she couldn't reach Mother. "Did anyone tell her this would have to be done?"

"I just told her," she said, coldly.

"You just told her! She gets five seconds' advance notice? No, I'm sorry. It's not like that," I said. "If you waited this long, you can wait a few hours longer. If she's grave, why hasn't there been a nurse in here for two hours? Did anyone make sure she understood how long she wouldn't be able to talk? What if she has something important to say? What if she wants to chat with her family a while before you shut off her communication? Is that so terrible? Do any of you give a damn how *she* feels about this? How frightened she may be? That you might just destroy her will to live? What doctor ordered this done without consulting her family? What exactly is *your* name?"

The nurse backed off after mumbling something about families interfering. The aides removed the device. We had bought time.

I was livid. The nurse returned to announce, "The doctor said he'll explain tomorrow afternoon."

Mother appreciated the extension. I told her to gather all her thoughts to speak all she wanted to say because the device might have to be in place for a while.

Happily, she did not suspect how long it would be in place.

Part of my anger was subjective. I had just gotten my

mother back and we had so much to say to one another. I could not allow them to abruptly cut us off.

She pulled me close and whispered, "You know, I've always loved you even when we argued through the years. I had just weaned you four months before I had to give you up and I was heartbroken. I could never tell you what you wanted to know; I was too afraid you would hate me. Even if I could have fought hard enough to get you back, I couldn't have provided for you. If only I had stayed in school instead of eloping at fourteen, I might have been able to get jobs that would provide for us."

I reminded her that if she had done that, there might not be an "us." She smiled and shrugged it off.

"By the time I could provide," she continued, "you were in your teens and I came on too strong. By then, you were resentful and I was defensive, and all we did was fight. But I loved you through it all. Later, you were all grown up, handling problems I could never have handled, and you hated to hear me say it, but you were always the baby I lost."

"I never understood that, Mother, until Sandy died, and I caught myself saying to her, 'Mommy loves you, Baby.' I'm so sorry I didn't understand it then."

We had to stop talking to dry our faces and blow our noses. We looked a mess, but we were both so happy.

"You know, I dreamed about Doc last night." She brightened. "He looked wonderful. Like when we first met, before he got cancer. He just stood there all dressed up and smiling at me, like when he used to come to take me out! I felt so good this morning when I woke up and remembered it. It felt as if he were really here."

Just then they rolled a respirator past her door.

She looked off in the distance for a moment. "They rolled one of those things into my room this morning by mistake. They said it was for another patient. I asked what it was, but I forgot the name. It's one of those machines that keeps people alive. Well, not alive—they breathe for them until the doctors disconnect them and let them die. I was sad for the poor fellow who was being put on that thing. Don't let them do that to me. Stand up for me like you did today, honey. I don't want any machines. If I get that bad, I'd rather just die. I'd go right to where I could find Doc. Do you think I could find him?"

"I'm sure you could," I said. "I'll bet you wouldn't even have to look for him. He'd be there waiting with a big hug."

"That would be nice." She calmed. "I really love dreaming about him. It was the first time since he died. It felt so real, as if he really were here in the room. I'd love to get well and keep dreaming about Doc. As soon as I get this thing that will help me breathe better, I'll rest a lot and eat well so I'll be a lot better when you get back from Virginia."

My talk had altered her outlook and given her hope. She looked really cheerful now, like she could indeed rally.

The next afternoon they inserted the device, and Mother communicated as best she could with a pad and pencil. She could breathe easier, but I saw the torment of her frustration when she needed attention and the nurses couldn't understand. I was also concerned about the notes she wrote. Her proud spelling was falling apart, rendering her words illegible. Even the note in my birthday card bore no clue of her downslide.

Every two hours they had to empty the accumulation of phlegm so thick that the suction device barely managed to pull it out of her lungs. Every two hours the container was full again. How could lungs hold so much putrefaction? As fast as the device extracted, her lungs produced more. How could there be room for air amid all that?

It tore at my heart to see this beautiful, powerful woman reduced to helplessness.

I spent my last two days at her side all day, trying to entertain her and make her comfortable. When it was time for me to leave, she cried hard and held me close, as though she forgot everything we had discussed about my return. She looked so helpless, trying to cry with tubes down her nose and throat. I tried to lighten it by reminding her that I would hold her to her promise to get better for the time when I got back, but she clutched at me so hard that I could barely get loose to leave before my own dam broke and flooded the universe.

All the way to the airport I cried. My face was a mess. I checked in with red eyes and a runny nose. I slept fitfully on the flight back, seeking unconsciousness.

Sarah picked me up and took me to her place. She invited me to stay the two or three weeks until my return to New Orleans. I was spared scurrying for living quarters.

I reported late to work. Oversleeping became the norm. I was too tense to sleep well and couldn't get my energy moving. The more I went in late, even if only by five minutes, the cooler my reception. I worked as many hours as I could and read astrology charts after hours to earn money to return before Mother got worse. The manager was not receptive to talking about job security. I gave up in exhaustion and did what I could without expectations.

Two weeks later, my uncle called to say that my mother had died that afternoon.

Why didn't she wait for me? I would have been there in another week. I knew at some level that she wouldn't stay long. I understood the appearances of Doc and I saw her surrender to frustration with the device, but I felt cheated. I wanted more time. After so many years of misunderstanding we had finally come to know each other only to be abruptly cut off.

They had found her will, and Uncle Lucas was executor. He needed us there to meet with the lawyer. Jen and Jay flew down to meet me in New Orleans, and we stayed at Lucas's house.

It depressed me to remember how things were when I last saw Mother. She couldn't talk. She had no visitors except Lucas, Iris, and me. Not even her minister would visit—she had been dropped from the membership for not sending pledge money. After calling three churches, we found a minister who would come, but it angered me to see her become so childlike, asking him to forgive her "for being so bad." I wanted to tell her that she didn't need a go-between, that God knew she wasn't bad. But I decided not to interfere.

Jay returned to his job when the legalities were done, but Jen and I stayed a week longer, helping my aunt sort through Mother's things.

As we sorted, we chatted about old times, the neighborhood, the city, the changes, the racial issues, how I could leave my birthplace, my children, how I got through college, and my work. Aunt Iris told what a wonderful childhood she had as one of ten children. Jen agreed that it was fun having lots of siblings. I said I was not fortunate enough to have that experience.

" . . . maybe next time around," one of them said.

"Oh no, no next time for me," I said. "I never want to go through childhood again. It was terrible."

"I'm sick of hearing what a terrible childhood you had," my aunt snapped. "Your grandmother was a good woman. Where would you be if she hadn't taken you in? You had a wonderful childhood. You had three hot meals a day, a clean, warm bed, and nice clothes for school. What more could you ask?"

"Maybe some love, some affection, and understanding, the basics for any child."

"Don't think you were an easy child! Always sassing your grandmother, making her worry when you didn't study enough to get A's, always badgering her about your mother, ungrateful for what she was doing for you. She's the one who reared you and nursed you through your illnesses. You had a wonderful childhood, but you're too blind to see it."

"Let's forget it. You get as upset about it as I do. It's over, I'm not a child any more, so let's just skip it."

"No, let's not skip it. You have to get the story straight."

"Please," I said, "I've heard everybody's story. With all due respect, you didn't live my childhood. How can you know what the experience was? I was nearly thirteen when you came into the family, engaged to my uncle. My childhood was lived before that. You've never asked me. It was, after all, my life, and only I can tell you about it. That is, about all but the biggest question in my life—why I was ever left with Grandma in the first place."

"I know the answer. Why didn't you come to me?" she gloated.

It took me totally by surprise!

"I'm sure you do—yet another version!" I snickered.

"No, I have the official one—on paper." She was so smug.

"Sure!" I couldn't stand anyone knowing the most closely guarded information about my life when I didn't know it. She was bluffing, spreading hearsay again, but what about the paper?

"You were the only one who left the family," she raged. "Do you know how that hurt your grandmother, after she took you in and reared you?"

"That's the second time you said my grandmother 'took me in,' as if I were an orphan. I had two parents who cared about me, then suddenly someone has to take me in? How can you have proof of something that happened before you were part of our family?" I boiled. How dare she know more about my life than I.

I baited her.

"O.K.," I said. "Tell me the story and show me your proof."

"Your grandmother was convinced your mother was too immature and flighty to rear you, and your daddy wanted to get back at your mother," she said. "So they hatched a plan between them."

"It sounds like a Monday night movie plot," I egged her on.

"The judge was all set to give your mother custody. Your grandmother went to your daddy and offered to testify that your mother was seen at the beach embracing a man and was morally unfit. On one condition—that when the judge awarded custody to your daddy instead, he would turn you over to her to rear.

"That's some plot," I said sarcastically. "You've been watching too many movies."

She went into her bedroom and came out after a minute. "The proof." She handed me a folded paper.

It was an official decree awarding my father full custody.

I froze. It was true. It explained everything. I stood stunned. Could this be the secret behind the mystery?

My head was whirling. The good guys became the bad guys, the bad guys became the good guys in this sick wonderland. My poor mother. She had been ruthlessly betrayed by her own mother, stripped of her rights, her child, her dignity, turned out into a world unsupportive and coldly indifferent to her needs and her fate.

I wasn't surprised to find Grandma's finger in the pie. The master manipulator demanded her pound of flesh. It soothed her conscience to collect my church attendance certificates, report cards, achievement awards, spelling bee prizes, to flash before the world as justification for her treachery. The whole neighborhood must have known what I didn't know. I thought I had finished forgiving her after Shirley MacLaine's seminar. Now I would have to begin again. Was this a retest to see if I really had learned it?

How relieved and grateful I felt for the insights between Mother and me during those last days at the hospital, for the dream and the understanding, for the healing that ended the terrible thing between us all those years and let our love come forth in its fullness! How devastated I would have been had we not forgiven each other before she died and I had learned this afterward! I was certain now of the intervention of a helper. The dream had turned the tide.

Disappointment was all I could feel toward my dad. I had really loved him. I would not have believed him capable of the heinous thing he did out of hurt pride. He deceived me for years into thinking he was a loving, benign, decent man. How would I forgive him the deception that cost Mother and me so much?

The test of forgiveness that I thought I had passed erupted again like a spewing volcano. It made Alex look snowy white!

I felt nauseous as I realized the range of the parameters. How many people hid this secret? How many would I have to forgive for this lifetime of deception?

No doubt Nan and my great uncle knew. They lacked the courage to disobey Grandma. They kept the peace, at any price.

"Did Lucas know this all these years?" I asked Aunt Iris.

"Of course, he knew."

"Oh! And you knew, too, of course? For how long?" I tried to mask my wounded heart with impudence.

"I knew since we got engaged. We had to keep the secret for your grandmother. She was the one with the responsibility. It really was none of your business," she said.

"Of course not, it was only my life." I was beginning to lose control. "How nice that all knew because they were in the family, and you all got together to protect Grandma, but what about me? Aren't you all co-conspirators in a master deceit, a contract from hell, to deprive me of my mother and her of me? Would you like to suffer lifelong deprivation of your only child as my mother did or have your self-esteem trashed as I did from thinking I was so unlovable that my own mother didn't want me? Had I known earlier, I could have charged all of you with conspiracy. That's why my grandmother needed your secrecy. It would have been

smeared all over the papers. It could have meant jail. You
would all have been infamous as you deserved!"

She shrunk from my gaze as I raged on.

"Think about this. When you spoke of all those meals and
clean beds I had in childhood, did you think how you would
have felt with your belly full, your sheets sweet, and your
self-esteem stunted? A child has much more than material
needs. I had to leave home because I had needs that
couldn't be met there. Think of how maimed I walked
through life until I mended slowly by trial and error, and
wear *that* image as your badge of achievement."

On the trip back to Virginia Beach, I ruminated about
how my family thrived on dissension. No wonder I hated
intrigue. It had been like living in a Tennessee Williams
novel set to operatic melodrama. Grandma's ire often
reached high C. I wondered how all who knew the big secret
could keep it so well hidden all those years.

Lucas reminded me of my dad, smiling up front while he
hid his part in the secret. I was furious at him until I realized
he was only twelve then and too young to participate. He
was caught between his mother and his sister. He loved
them both. The choice was: smear his only sister's reputa-
tion by revealing his mother as the merciless conspirator
who had cut down her own child or maintain silence. Stories abounded of similar dramas our family's women had
set in motion. Judgment overflowed. It was the only way
women gained power then. Did he think I would judge his
sister as others had if I knew the story? Couldn't he see that
I was a misfit in that family since the first day, that all my
problems resulted from seeing things through different
eyes, my eyes?

I couldn't alter this. I needed to get clean of the muck,
release it, and move on. It would take great effort to do another round of forgiving, but I was well rehearsed and the
taste of freedom profoundly lured me to sever the past.

My willfulness proved to be my salvation. It had led me down a different path and taught me much. I would heal my self-esteem and emerge the winner in this, for I had learned strength and the value of love over pride. Also, my conscience was clear.

An image of the Star Trek episode I had seen the night before Iris's revelation clicked into my mind. Spock was making his symbol, saying, "Live long and prosper."

"Yes, Mr. Spock," I whispered, "I will."

I would leave the others to "meet self," as Cayce said.

9

Healing My Wounded Child: Moving into Post-Grad

> "I could tell you my adventures—beginning from this morning," said Alice a little timidly; "but it's no use going back to yesterday, because I was a different person then." —Lewis Carroll, *Alice in Wonderland*

WHAT TIMING this was! Learning the truth from the custody document was a blatant call to forgive my persecutors. I was being tested again for forgiveness at another level!

I turned to the One who had already done it, asking that He be my Mentor for this most difficult test I had ever undertaken. I determined to get beyond it. After having my power and rights stolen and being negatively programmed and manipulated by a dysfunctional family, learning the truth, paradoxically, restored much of my self-esteem.

Within nine months—the time it takes to form a new life—my youngest son had ended his, my mother's had faded away, and the truth was about to restore mine.

I reached back into childhood to a time when I couldn't hold anger. I saw myself calling to a schoolmate to wait so that we could walk to school together, then her strange look reminded me that we'd had a spat two days before, but in anticipation of the fun we could have I had forgotten. Vengeance was never attractive either—it would take too much energy and time and keep me from my next great adventures.

I could hate these people, stew in this festering mess, and drag them around for more years than those already damaged by their deceit, or I could forgive them, delegate their "sentence" to God, and free myself to move on with my life.

My life was too valuable to forfeit. I made the harder choice—forgiving—so that I could walk clean into the light. I would find a way to release them and sever the tangled karmic threads.

A letter awaited me in Virginia. I was granted an interview for a college teaching position. I danced around Sarah's kitchen at the prospect of getting a job.

Walking on campus the bright sunny morning of my interview, I could feel my confidence running high. I wanted this job, I needed this job, I would get this job.

The director's feedback was positive. They said they would let me know, so I expected a three-week delay.

The next day they asked me to begin in September.

I rented the cottage again until spring and quickly settled in, retrieving my belongings at my leisure from Jerry's friend's basement. I felt wounded, but lighter. I'd begun most of the difficult adjusting, forgiving, and healing using the soul-contract insights, but in this cozy cottage something was missing. I liked living alone, having total freedom of movement, but I yearned for something to cuddle and love.

The lease prohibited pets, so I browsed through several shops to find the perfect stuffed animal. I fell in love with a

furry baby tiger. When I brought it home, I held it on my lap
pretending it was a kitten. I almost thought I heard it purr
one night.

Hail on the glass and a draft from the open window woke
me at dawn one Saturday morning in the middle of a dream.

I am a very small child, running around playing until I'm tired. My mother takes me on her lap and covers
me with her sweater and rocks me. I feel her love and I
fall asleep.

I wake up, still on Mother's lap. I look up at her and
smile when I recognize her. But she has my face, the
face I have now as an adult. It seems she is a larger me.
I am me and I am mother.

Now I can feel what she feels as she holds me, and I
feel her heart expand when she feels love for me.

I am wide awake now and full of energy. I jump up
off her lap to run around again. She's watching me, and
I can see me through her eyes.

What I see, as me, is the stuffed tiger running
around, loving my mother. It becomes all mixed up. I
am me and the tiger, and she loves both of me. I am
also mother.

What a weird dream! I played all the characters. I jumped
up to close the window and ducked back under the covers
to sleep longer. I grabbed the tiger from the floor and pulled
it to me to stroke its fur and cuddle it while I slept.

I tossed and turned. I couldn't get back to sleep. I decided
to stay in a cozy reverie, holding the tiger, until I either fell
asleep or got up.

After five minutes, I had a sudden insight about the dream.

"I was the mother and the baby," I said aloud. "The baby
was also the tiger. That makes me the mother, the baby, and
the tiger, too, right? So we're all one and the same, right?
Right!"

I was doing really well having this conversation with myself out loud and answering myself! Obviously I was acting out being all three. Some element of the dream kept trying to force its way into my conscious mind.

Suddenly I remembered! Someone in a seminar had once suggested using a stuffed animal as a surrogate child-self to heal the inner child.

I traced my motives from the time I bought the tiger. I needed some little creature to love and to feel loved me. I felt that love when I cuddled the tiger under the covers. Then in the dream we were all three: the mother, the child, and the tiger.

"That's it," I realized. "At some level of my mind I had accepted the suggestion and the dream showed me how to do it."

It was as simple as acting. The tiger would play the surrogate child-me and I'd play the mother I wanted. As the mother, I could lavish all the attention and love on the child that she missed in childhood, and I was accessible to playing that role until she had all she needed.

It wasn't logical—and I would be laughed out of town if I talked about it—but it clicked at gut level and it couldn't hurt anyone, so I would try it. It made perfect sense to me.

I called her Tiger when I spoke of her, but when I held her as a surrogate me, I called her by my own name.

Tiger sat in a chair or atop my bed during the day. In the evening I would take her on my lap, stroke her, hug her, call her by my name, and speak to her as a mother to her small child.

I let her speak out all her hurts and fears while I held her close, so that her anxieties would melt away. It came very naturally. I had done it so many times with my children when they were small.

She complained about how Grandma restricted her play and drove off her playmates, and a myriad of other things. "It's not fair that I can only play with my toys when she has time to watch that I don't break anything! It's not fair that she won't let Weezie come back to play because she made fingerprints on the window! It's not fair that I can't play at their house unless she has time to stay with me. It's not fair that she makes me read and spell big hard words so that I'll be smarter than other kids when I go to kindergarten, then threatens to let me fall off the dresser when I get tired and want to stop. It's not fair that she spanks me after the principal beat my hands with a ruler for picking the spitball off my neck that Henry threw at me. It's not fair that she never believes me. It's not fair that she makes me read all my library books aloud so that she knows I really read them. It's not fair that . . . "

The complaints were all from early childhood.

I would rock Tiger and hum a nursery tune to quiet her down and tell her, "That won't happen any more. Mommy's here with you now and she loves you. You'll have wonderful playmates and all the time you desire to play. If ever you break something—no big deal. And I believe every word you say. You don't have to read anything aloud, and you can choose whatever you want to read. And best of all, you don't have to be the smartest one in school because I love you just as you are, even when you make mistakes and get F's and spill your soup. Simply because I couldn't love you less. You don't have to worry any more. Mommy is here to stay, holding you close and loving you forever."

Soon it began to feel as if Tiger could sense what I was doing and sent those feelings back. Every time I stroked her to show my love, I would feel very loved, very cherished.

I would tell her how wonderful she was, how bright, how cute—just as the Italian grandmothers spoke to me in my childhood. I would tell her she could achieve anything in the world she wanted to do, and slowly I saw my self-confidence rise.

Then I took a bold step and told her how fortunate it was to be a little kid with God for her daddy, how very much God loved her, how she could have anything in the world that belonged to Daddy-God just for the asking because Daddy would gladly share anything He had with her as long as it was good for her. Sometimes I could almost feel myself inside the little tiger's body, curling up and cuddled in the lap of Daddy-God.

I brought up all my theater skills from college days and all my ashram training in visualization to create this energy and found it to be sublimely empowering.

My inner child was healing. It was working. I was reclaiming my stolen power and sloughing off a lot of negative fear, anger, and self-sabotage.

It was not as though I could set the child aside now. I understood that she remained a part of me and would be with me forever in the same way that the young woman in the sad marriage would always be a part of me, as well as the other who explored the realities suggested by her dreams. I had no problem accepting all these identities. They were all me. After all, I was born with the sun in Gemini and had joked many times about there being at least ten of us in here! What surprised me while working with my tiger was how very much it felt like multiple personalities, except that the person I referred to as "I" always consciously directed the action.

Best of all, if I ever slid back, I now knew how to get myself back to center.

There remained some fine-tuning to do, but I was ready now to confront and demystify whatever old myths surfaced. I had a tool that made me the creator of my fate. I now sat in the driver's seat and claimed the reins and the full responsibility for this trip. I was so excited that I wanted to shout out to the world, "Look, it's working. I've found a way to heal myself. Anyone can do it . . . " but I could not speak generally of my rehabilitative techniques for the same reasons that I could not speak of walking into a thought form!

I sat in the A.R.E. Library one weekend afternoon, chatting with Al, a friend very knowledgeable in Chinese astrology. I commented about the cuddly stuffed tiger I had recently bought.

"Why a tiger?" he asked. "Why not a teddy bear or a kitten?"

"I don't know," I responded. "I guess it was the cutest animal there that day. I fell in love with it."

"Did you know that you are a tiger?" he asked, laughing.

"Excuse me?" I didn't understand what he meant at first.

"You were born in a year of the tiger in Chinese astrology."

I tossed off a casual smile, but privately I felt once again the subtle synchronistic hand of God directing the action to heal my life.

How little we realize, at the conscious level, the many little synchronicities and significances our Higher Selves offer up to us to help us on our paths.

I continued working with Tiger. Every time I would sit and rock her, I saw myself at a different age. I watched a panorama of scenes go by, some brief, some detailed.

In one scene I was seven and Mother arrived at Grandma's with packages. A delivery had arrived minutes before. She said they were for me—early birthday presents—and that after I opened them, we would go to the drugstore and have a sundae. In the boxes were three beautiful dresses from Louise, the lady from St. Charles Avenue who had rescued Mother three years before. Mother insisted that I try them on as Grandma grumbled about where on earth I would ever wear them.

"Louise says every little girl should have some magic princess dresses, Mama, to set her dreams afire, even if she only wears them to make mudpies," my mother answered.

We had to call the man next door to pry open the heavy box containing Mother's gift. I was so happy I could hardly contain myself when I saw the picture of its contents: a gym set, complete with swing, chinning bar, trapeze, and see-saw. A neighbor assembled it in the back yard, and I had years of fun with it. Again Grandma grumbled, but she came to appreciate the hours it entertained me.

I wore one of my brand-new princess dresses with a scuffed knee as we traipsed off to the drugstore for ice cream. I felt so proud every time we went out together. Even though she wasn't mine for keeps, no other kid I knew had a mother as beautiful as mine.

In another scene I saw Mother's boyfriend, Pepe, with his silk shirt-sleeve pinned up with a diamond stud. He bought her lots of pretty clothes and one day, when she came to school to pick me up early, she went into my classroom and all the kids gasped. I was so proud that this beautiful woman was *my* mother. Even the teacher stared at how beautiful she was. When she picked me up to kiss me in front of everybody I was ecstatic. All the world knew now that my beautiful mother loved me.

Another day I remembered dancing school. A girlhood friend of Mother's taught dance, and Mother enrolled me in ballet at seven. Ballet was too disciplined for my energy, so I switched to tap and acrobat. Learning to move my body to different rhythms helped dissipate the anxieties built up in my stressful home life. I loved the recitals, the stage, the lights, the costumes, the magic. By the time I was twelve, Mother had no more money for dancing lessons, but I had already derived great benefits from it. High energy and an adventurous spirit led me to other outlets like dare-devil bicycling and skating. I felt the joy of soaring into the wind on skates, brimming with health and with friends at my side.

I flashed back to my last sad visit to New Orleans when

Uncle Lucas took me down St. Charles Avenue toward Canal Street. He had followed the route of the queues we
formed after the Mardi Gras Day parade. We had joined
other masqueraders snaking toward Canal Street to frolic in
the French Quarter. Mardi Gras, the highlight of my young
life, meant Fat Tuesday in French, the final day before Ash
Wednesday when Catholics could last eat meat and drink
before the Lenten fast began. Revelry was the order of the
day. We could drop out of the queue anywhere along the
route to satisfy our hunger or thirst at friendly open houses,
dotted within a block of anywhere. Tables of homemade
creole delicacies were spread out to welcome us. We could
pick up the queue again to continue on to Canal Street, to
the Quarter, or even across the Mississippi via the Canal
Street ferry to Algiers to watch the Zulu parade.

In my middle teen years, I spent the day with classmates
from our all-girl high school, following the queue into the
Quarter where we reveled and danced all day. Months before the big day, the struggle began between Grandma and
me. I wanted to masquerade as a gypsy again or an Oriental, and she wanted me in a period costume. Usually I won,
but one year she insisted I wear a colonial costume. As soon
as we said good-by, I raced to my friend's house where I had
stashed last year's gaudy, sequined gypsy costume and changed
into it. I felt so happy in that old costume. We preserved the
mystery by staying true to the custom of never removing
our masks while we flirted and danced with masked "older"
men of nineteen and twenty. The masks allowed us to assume exotic names, strange accents, and storybook identities as we party-hopped through the Absinthe House, Pat
O'Brien's, and The Court of Two Sisters. As long as we reported home before dark, there were no penalties. We never
revealed the sights we had seen in broad daylight! There was
no end to the fun on Mardi Gras. We played out our fanta-
sies all day, uncensored, and created a lifetime of memories. Happiness filled me when I relived that time.

Once I remembered crossing Canal Street approaching the French Quarter, smelling the seductive aroma of French Market coffee. I clutched Tiger close as my mouth watered for a beignet with coffee. Suddenly I was older. I proceeded deep into Bourbon Street to the Mexican nightclub, where I had danced the nights away with my Latino boyfriends and where Alex and I first met and fell in love. Four blocks farther stood the quaint blacksmith shop of the pirate Jean Lafitte's brother, converted to a patio restaurant and bar. The bar housed a classical music jukebox and an array of instruments inviting visiting musicians to perform. Outside, tiny lanterns hung from fragrant trees, and sandalwood scented candles melded their drippings in blown glass wine bottles, softly lighting the tables. From the kitchen wafted indescribable aromas of Creole seafood that teased the senses, though we all took it for granted.

I remembered taking Jen and Jay, after Mother died, to see those landmarks of my life. The nightclub no longer existed; the blacksmith shop was rundown. The weatherworn sign "Lafitte's" hung outside. We went in to satisfy my curiosity. It was only a tavern now, so we sipped icy draft beer inside the thick, insulated walls—much like old Spanish fortresses on Alex's island—that protected us from the sweltering heat. I told them how, early in our courtship, it was our favorite place to dine.

Artists around Jackson Square still worked alfresco, some on the Square itself and some in shaded alleys between the buildings, like a scene from Utrillo's Paris. Unlicensed street vendors freely sold their ethnic edibles during my childhood. Chinese vendors sold tamales that Grandma swore were made from kidnapped dogs, Japanese sold sweet rice cakes—a nickel a dozen—that I ate until my stomach ached, Cajuns sold steamed crawfish with fiery dips, and Germans sold frozen cream cheese, a unique ice cream that I could never find anywhere else.

I flashed back to good times with Alex, tender moments still poignantly alive in my heart, moments that never would die. And the time when the kids woke up and caught me playing with their toys as I set them under the Christmas tree. And those summer afternoons when it was too hot to go outside, and we played on our bellies on the living-room floor in front of the fan—that was when I recovered my lost playtime and found the most wonderful playmates in my children. There was no one to tell me that adults don't do such things; I was free to follow my intuition.

Happy things I'd forgotten so long ago now flooded my mind in a blaze of joy.

After working several months with Tiger, I noticed that few hurtful memories ever came up any more. What came up now were the happy times, times that before had been buried beneath the debris of malice and deception. The debris was cleaned up, the residues released, and the joy unfolded unobstructed.

Was I witnessing a miracle?

How wise I was as a child! If only I'd had the power to express my promptings. I was eight when I recognized the destructive manipulation in my family. I secretly vowed to preserve my own values until I was free to live them. I first fell in love the same year, as intensely as I ever had in adulthood, but with limited outlets of expression. I quickly perceived the untruths adults used to maintain a safe status quo. I tried to remember this when my children were very young.

Do a child's unseen guardians provide the necessary insights, or is it the child's own acuity?

At eleven, still innocently in love, I promised myself I would leave family patterns behind and not perpetuate the dysfunction into further generations. I had needs that couldn't be met there. I knew as surely as I knew the sound of my voice or the color of my eyes that I would one day claim the power to do it. And I did.

I remembered the words of a psychic channeler: "Sometimes a father who leaves early in a child's life is not really meant to be part of that life, but comes only to lend the seed to create the vehicle for the soul's entry." It could apply to me. Did my father lend his seed, then leave? Was I only to be ushered into that family for training, but not connected? Did they feel like misfits as I did and did the best they knew? Was the entire scenario a group-soul contract played out in the great free-will arena of Earth? Whichever it was, the speculations enabled me to release the past and move forward.

Teaching college proved disappointing again. I left institutional teaching forever after one semester. The confines of academic regulations rankled me. I could no longer teach like an obedient robot, and I disagreed that competing for grades was healthy. I preferred teaching experientially—at least balancing data with experience. I was happiest teaching yoga, meditation, visualization, and astrology. Students learned at their own pace, everyone benefited without grades and judgment. They were happier, too. I opted now to do only work that made me happy.

After final exams, my class met at a Spanish restaurant to experience authentic Spanish food and flamenco dancing—a small taste of the culture to match the language they had just struggled to learn. I would have preferred to take them to Mexico, rent a villa, and assign them chores in town each day. If they failed their chore, maybe there would be no food to eat and peer pressure would get them on track quickly. Within three months, they would absorb culture and communicate fluently. Then they would be ready for literature.

Academia exhausted left brains and deplored right-brain

"interference." To me, the only way to learn was whole-brained.

It was late when I took the expressway home. We had parted in good spirits after the Spanish night out. Halfway home, someone entered from the ramp and slightly bumped the car in the adjacent lane about six car lengths ahead of me. That car spun to avoid a harder hit and bumped another. That one spun and hit two more. Six or seven cars were spinning all over the road as I approached. I couldn't exit the expressway to avoid tangling with them, and I knew I would inevitably get hit.

Automatically, I spoke out, "God, where are You? Help me. I don't want to be part of this. Get me out of here, please!"

My car was in the midst of it now, but suddenly it took a slalom course, weaving in and out of spinning cars on all sides. Quickly I had passed them to safety and found my hands at both sides of my head. A very eerie feeling crept over me as I wondered who steered my car through that slalom course! My hands were not even on the steering wheel! Even if I had tried, I could not have judged how to dodge the spinning cars. I had to assume God took the wheel, and I was profoundly thankful, but reluctant to take that route again for months.

I didn't want to take anything for granted.

The next several years in Virginia Beach proved more comfortable than the earlier ones. As a result of the self-healing work I had done, I felt freer and had a new attitude. I became more aware of my thoughts and actions and thus could alter certain patterns to bring about creative outcomes. I no longer ran after every little available job for an income. I learned instead to honor the ancient talents my Higher Self had brought to help me attain my soul purpose this time. I added to my repertoire of spiritual tools to accelerate my growth. I stopped living at a running pace and began to catch up with the accelerated vibrations. When-

ever my inner child felt wounded, I worked with Tiger again.
Whenever I became aware that I'd slid back into blocking
my own progress by losing faith and enthusiasm, I'd remember all I had to be thankful for and get myself back on
course. The flow would begin again.

Claiming my power was the first sign of breaking through
limitations following the firewalk.

I enrolled at A.R.E. to study massage therapy, an idea I
had twice postponed because I feared studying anatomy. It
did not come easy, but I learned it. The benefits far outweighed the struggle, and the massage experience proved
invaluable. Massages sometimes triggered dramatic spontaneous emotional releases in different places in my body
where stuffed conflicts hid out. It would occur with sudden
overwhelming sadness or anger, without understanding,
with about five or ten minutes of hard crying, then relaxation into softness, warmth, and peace. The related body
site became supple and relaxed as well. It was the easiest
way to release stuck emotions.

Initiation into Reiki II promptly brought up more stuck
issues and speeded their processing. By now I resisted nothing. I wanted every bit of excess baggage purged from my
psyche. I was now addicted to lightness, clarity, and freedom. Eventually I integrated massage with Reiki II and the
best of other energy healing modalities I had studied to create a special technique.

During the same year my anxiety about computers lifted,
just as the earlier fear of airplanes had lifted. I developed a
strong attachment to computers and bought one before I
could articulate questions about its operation. No doubt I
added much healthy laughter to the boring days of helpline
technicians, but eventually I managed to formulate questions they actually understood. Today I enjoy a close
relationship with my computer, though I long to eventually
abandon it for a younger one.

During the same year I tracked some of my past-life

haunts in the Yucatan region of Mexico. Of my studies in pre-Columbian history, the Mexican Yucatan was the place to which I'd felt most drawn for a very long time. Being bilingual and bicultural made navigating through the Yucatan easy. I did not go to break through limitations, but to embrace a land I strongly felt was a significant part of my past. I was certain it would be sheer pleasure, and I wasn't disappointed.

Toward the end of the visit, I began to wonder why I had felt so intimately connected. Every part of the area felt thoroughly familiar from the moment I arrived, but I couldn't pinpoint any one site as truly mine, where I had once lived. The day before Jane and I were to leave, we toured Tulum, the only site of ruins by the sea. Our enthusiasm and expectations were not high.

On arriving, we grouped outside the stone wall surrounding the fortress city. At the tiny tunneled entrance, the Mayan guide instructed us regarding the time and location of our return bus. We then walked through the six-foot-long tunnel and came out to behold a magnificent panoramic view of the main pyramid and surrounding buildings.

I felt a huge goose bump form at the top of my head. It seemed to break into millions that spread down like a wave through my arms, my torso, and limbs and returned to my head. I stood captive by an inexplicable force for almost five minutes, while Jane stared and wondered what was happening. It was hard to speak when I tried. My energy seemed immobilized in goose bumps. The impact of familiarity was clear.

When I felt a release, my words tumbled over each other as I tried to tell Jane what had happened.

"As long as you're O.K., I want to climb up that pyramid." She pointed to the big one and I ran behind her.

She climbed up fearlessly. It was not very high but, with my fear of heights, it was awesome. I yearned to follow her to the top and look out on the blue Caribbean, but fear paralyzed me at the pyramid's base. I lingered until I could no longer stand the yearning, then I pulled myself up the steep steps, one by one, carefully, until I stood beside Jane at the top. What could have been a triumphant moment was one of great anxiety. With my fear of heights, panic set in when I saw how high I was. Climbing up was not bad; getting down would be dizzying.

In the midst of my panic, however, a stronger image suddenly took precedence in my mind. I "saw" a twist in the path at the pyramid's base that wound around to the side that we had not yet seen, past a group of large rocks to an opening where the breakers splashed against a strip of beach. I told Jane about it, but we couldn't see in that direction to verify it, so we decided to go down the pyramid, find the path and follow it to see what was there.

How would I ever get down!! Every time I looked at the steps, my stomach ached and my vision blurred. I waited again to get up my courage until I noticed almost everyone had gone down to explore other parts. "Where are you, guys, when I need your help?" was my plea to my helpers. I knew that only I could get me down, and if I didn't do it, no one could, so I simply had to go. I turned to go down backward so that I could clutch the steps closely, feel each one with my foot, and not look down. I started down.

I had gone down four steps when I froze. I had allowed for that. I didn't care how long it took.

Just then a middle-aged gentleman and his wife passed me on the way down. He realized I was having problems.

"Do you need some help?" he called.

"I sure could use some," I squealed. "But how can you help me? You have to get down, too, and the steps are so narrow."

He thought out the problem for a minute.

"Well," he said. "I can get one step below you and support your back end as you come down."

I was embarrassed, but recognized a limitation I could not overcome.

"That's fine," I said. "I appreciate it." And I was infinitely grateful, beyond embarrassment, for the help in getting down.

I caught up with Jane and we found the path. It twisted around exactly as I had imaged it and just past the large rocks splashed the bluest water I had ever seen. I leaned against the rocks with the waves breaking on my legs, drenching my clothes, but I was content, knowing I had found what I'd come searching for—my point of contact.

A mile or two from Tulum was a natural lagoon, clear and deep, called Xel-ja. The sun was hot that day, so we looked forward to dunking in the water. We had borrowed snorkel gear when we heard how beautiful the tropical fish were. Jane jumped off the pier and swam out with her snorkel gear in place. I couldn't swim, so I stood yelling to her to keep an eye on me. I wanted to snorkel, but couldn't touch bottom after the last step off the pier. She was so engrossed in her experience that she couldn't hear me. I would either have to do this on my own or miss the experience completely.

I stood on the pier step holding myself above water and waited for Jane to look my way, but I couldn't see her and our time was running short.

With one more signal to my angels, I set out to the nearest reef about sixty feet away, determined to reach the reef and see the sights. I paddled feverishly with the fins every time I felt myself beginning to sink. I reached it, but there was yet another fear! What would I do now? If I viewed the fish through my snorkeling mask, I couldn't hold on to anything. I would be taken by the water in any direction. I was getting short of breath from paddling so much to stay above water. Then I noticed what looked like a bowling ball hole in the reef, just large enough and deep enough for two fingers. How accommodating! I inserted my fingers and anchored myself to stay in place, while I enjoyed the most spectacular display of tropical fish in varieties I had never seen. I wished

I had rented an underwater camera. When I'd had my fill, I retrieved my fingers and pushed off less fearfully to paddle back to the pier.

I was happy with a sense of fulfillment for having gotten what I went to the Yucatan for, and more. I had found my point of reference in Tulum and a bonus! I had broken past two fears that I had forgotten I had. I climbed the pyramid despite my fear of heights and snorkeled at the reef despite being a nonswimmer.

I spent the last night lying on the sand studying the stars, something I never do at home, but that I felt I did there many nights long ago.

Before moving to Virginia Beach I had begun experimenting with past-life regression hypnosis after my own first regression. Friends were eager to explore. I closely observed other techniques, but I resisted building a practice because clients often seemed to become dependent on the hypnotist. Since I had always been attracted to modalities that empower the individual rather than disenfranchise one, I held back.

I discovered Ericksonian theory. I realized the scripts that I'd composed for ashram visualization exercises were almost identical to hypnosis inductions. The primary difference was that visualization scripts did not incorporate post-hypnotic suggestion. I began writing scripts that strengthened the client's hold on his or her personal power. Both the client and I got better results moving therapeutically through past-life issues, and I became more confident. After all, writing came easy to me, I had been through the power-surrender and back, and I was deeply grounded in spiritual teachings and practices, enough to know that ego could not be allowed to enter into this guidance.

I became a certified hypnotherapist in Virginia and witnessed dramatic breakthroughs by using recently developed therapeutic techniques.

Hypnosis has proved an invaluable spiritual tool for me. I have had quite amazing personal breakthroughs serving as the "client" in practicums during my formal training. Personal issues that had become stalemated after years trying every known therapy suddenly opened to new hypnosis techniques and clarified within minutes. I know its value experientially. If I'd had access to those techniques during the hard years of learning, I could have grown faster and begun earlier to pursue my higher goals. But all is a learning process.

I use these techniques now in my practice which, together with teaching a variety of metaphysical/spiritual tools (with no grade evaluations!) and writing, are the most fulfilling work I have ever done. All that I have learned are spiritual tools that catalyzed my own self-restoration to spiritual consciousness. I use the tools now to teach others in "Empowerment" courses that I design to help students move forward in command of their lives.

Over the past two years an astrological transit had opened the way for me to purge old unresolved emotional residues. I have been unusually open to doing this and it has been made quite easy for me, at times with dream forerunners that reassured me of its safety and its promise of greater growth.

A pleasant surprise came last year, perhaps a reward for persistent hard work, in the form of a dramatic kundalini experience that cleared my channel from the root chakra to the pineal. I felt it like an electrical charge rising steadily up my spine to the pineal. A few seconds later, it repeated, this time going up, then down, then up again. Although I could hear an inward electrical buzz as this occurred, no one else could hear it, and it caused no pain or discomfort. This time it involved all the chakras. For several days there were feelings of heat from my neck up, then there followed a dramatic resistance to cold weather, more vibrant energy, self-healing, and spontaneous body cleansing, especially of the sinuses. There was also a strong pulsating at the third eye during meditation and sometimes upon waking, with colors swirling into each other. I continue to experience as well greater clarity, a sense of power, and sublime contentment, along with a need for more time alone and frequent meditation. I am infinitely grateful for this breakthrough.

The Chicago psychic passed through town again several months later and her first impression when she attuned to me was "a profoundly peaceful aura, getting ready for a major inner change, finding a temple of peace . . . already in the throngs of it now, a strong spiritual connection . . . feels like God is right beside you, with you wherever you go . . . an incredibly lifting feeling . . . "

Yes, I feel God there.

I reached a new understanding of my life. I knew that I would always be supported in any endeavor in my life. Every time I asked I had received assistance, despite my density and my reluctance to believe myself worthy. Finally I had to accept the truth of how much I am loved.

As I've said before, I walk with an entourage. I remembered a Cayce reading saying that when the soul forms a pattern, it attracts "many, many, many souls" of similar pattern from other dimensions to assist in soul growth and they could sometimes be felt. I feel more of their energy with time, and I am comfortable with it. I know it was O.K. to be a willful child. Will, one of my great strengths, is necessary in all important work and I have more to do. I know it was my truth to abandon church affiliation, for orthodoxy never filled my needs, and I would bow to no authority except my Creator. My contact was always within and the Creator was always available to me. Krishnamurti, the great Hindu teacher, avoided traditional approaches to emphasize awareness on finding God within self. I found Him there early. How wonderful our world would be if that were everyone's experience!

I know I needed all my traits: my naïve childhood trust made learning surrender to God easy for me; my intelligence, honed by my grandmother, has always served me well; my armor protected me against the worst and still lies available for my use if need arises; my inner experiences have always moved me forward and continue to do so; and the strong will that heaped trouble on my head in childhood has brought me triumphantly through many battles—it is a special gift.

I have grown to understand what it is to be a child of God, a divine soul. I have been here many times and networked among friends in many dimensions. I am a cherished member of God's family—God-seed. I meet my Father/Mother-God at a special contact point within, so I carry God around with me. I try to maintain that awareness, but some days are better than others. On a bad day, one of you might come by and, as I remember the ashram greeting, "J'ai bhagwan"—I bow to the Divine Light within you—I will be reminded by your light, for you are His child also and He lives within you as He lives within every one of us. I have heard it explained as the Prime Intelligence we call God, dividing His essence among all the souls He created and imbuing part of that essence into each soul. That is why we are reminded to love each other, for we are all part of the same soul. Knowing this fills me with pride and humbles me at the same time, for the inherent power is awesome, as is the karma for its abuse. I understand what Jesus meant when He said He must be about His Father's business. It is the most exciting and fulfilling business I have ever found to do, and I seek ways in all that I do to make this my purpose.

The past continues to influence my life today through ongoing studies and teaching—metaphysics, Eastern wisdom, hypnotherapy, astrology, co-creation, and the Cayce wisdom of *mind as the builder.*

My opinions, outlooks, and methods have changed, but never my values or integrity. My personal integrity means never allowing my values to be compromised or violated.

I believe with my whole heart that we all know these truths at a cell level, for they have been part of us for eons. When we enter Earth's dimension, however, we bring only a fraction of that awareness to the conscious level. It is as if we grow by playing an intricate game on a huge game board. At certain points we regress somewhat; at others we leap forward following an "Aha" experience. We arrive at many junctions where we encounter those we allow to drag us backward and those we allow to propel us forward. We grow unevenly for a grand purpose. We pass what we have learned (remembered) to others who have not yet remembered those particular facets of truth and, by doing so, we balance the karmic debt to those who have helped us to remember. At some point in our remembering we come to understand the rules of the game. Ego is what drags us to regress; Spirit's help propels us forward.

There are indeed no accidents; everything is as it should be. We are growing—at whatever stage—exactly as we should be.

Back when channeling was "new" and the first tapes were circulating, I heard many references to "runners," the people who come into our lives to bring messages, lessons, help, or rewards.

Seeing the main cast of players in my life as runners has helped me to make peace with them and feel deep gratitude as well.

Alex was the seed-donor of five precious children who were my companions in growth. I feel honored and grateful that they chose me to usher them into this plane at this time and to be their early caregiver. People joke about children being a twenty-year sentence; they are actually a lifetime of joy. Alex was also the catalyst of my mind.

Mike was seed-donor of a beautiful child and incomparable birthday present for whom I have given thanks every day of her life.

Sandy made easy the lesson in releasing. She remembered to call home to say she was O.K.

Rafi brought a harder lesson of releasing and accepting that he, too, is God-seed and empowered to his own decisions, including that of his transition. Since other dimensions are governed by thought, I hope that I have learned to process my grief and not create obstacles to any soul by sending any grasping or discordant thoughts.

I have thanked my Higher Self countless times for the dream of Mother that led to our mutual forgiveness and for the opportunity to share with her hints of why Doc came back so that she could leave with awareness. My mother lightened my childhood with gifts and dancing classes that brought magic in the midst of austerity. Would I have become the mother I was had I not yearned so for her?

My dad was seed-donor for me. Thank you, Dad; it's a great time to be here and I'm looking forward to every minute of it—the millennium, I mean. Apocalypse, though, was never part of my reality.

Beloved Nan was the buffer in all home conflicts, the first teacher of unconditional love.

Great uncle provided the movies that fired my imagination.

And Grandma. How would I have done what I had mapped out for my soul to do without Grandma? Without her rigid training, I would not have a well-honed survival sense, nor could I have summoned the grit to do what it took to raise a large family alone. I would not have learned to read library books at four, nor whetted my strong will by opposing her. I would have gone to college much earlier and perhaps missed discovering the ashram, finding Cayce in the campus Swap Shop, and meeting my wonderful undergraduate teachers. I might have missed being acquainted with my Latino friends, meeting Alex, and not having the particular children I had.

Not having my grandmother might have unraveled my whole life. If it is about soul contracts, since my grandmother was a major player, I owe her an enormous and humble debt of gratitude for her sacrifice of time out of her own path, her determined training, her tough love—for I do believe she did love me—and her meticulous care.

With each act of forgiveness, I emptied my chalice of anger and it filled with joy.

And certainly not the least, I am grateful to the precious souls—my children—who stayed to share the adventure and help me learn, for without these beloved companions in the flesh, life would be bland indeed.

I cherish the child who struggled to survive to follow her heart, I cherish the very young woman who put her whole heart into everything she did to do her best, and I cherish the woman she has grown to be whose unrelenting courage and drive to understand experiences through personal trials led to her inner knowing and spiritual growth.

I like who I am, aware that I have been sculpted by all my experiences. Each experience was valuable. To reject any one would be to diminish who I am. To alter one detail, one comma, one period, of my life would be to alter the outcome. I am in the perfect place on my path, the perfect outcome, pointing in the right direction and moving ever forward.

Mine is not the only breakthrough. Many are breaking through fears, limitations, dilemmas, and blocks in greater numbers than ever before. Unseen help always awaits, without judgment, to be invited.

In this most exciting time to be here on Earth, I am beginning to understand the dream that repeated with variations, four times, of the being in the silver jumpsuit, and I am feeling very close to comprehending what the "second phase" is. It gets better, and I plan to stick around to experience it.

For those restless to arrive at their spiritual goal, be patient to arrive. Enjoy every minute of the fascinating trip.

To focus on the tragic is not my nature. Knowing that I proceed ever forward, I confess to a curious fascination anticipating the marvels of dimensions to come!

About the Author

Dorian Caruso received her B.A. magna cum laude and M.A. from Rutgers University in New Jersey. She taught college for several years while independently teaching astrology and designing specialized courses for professional groups. Following a year's residence in Kripalu ashram in Pennsylvania, she began teaching metaphysics, yoga, and meditation, as well as creating visualization tapes for stress reduction. She is a certified master hypnotherapist, specializing in past-life therapy, stress management, behavioral reprogramming, and phobia elimination. She is also a writer and creator of Empowerment I and II—courses that teach spiritual tools to facilitate reclaiming the students' own power—which she offers through classes, lectures, and workshops in and outside of Virginia.

She currently resides in Virginia Beach and may be contacted at P.O. Box 1267, Virginia Beach, VA 23451.

What Is A.R.E.?

The Association for Research and Enlightenment, Inc. (A.R.E.®), is the international headquarters for the work of Edgar Cayce (1877-1945), who is considered the best-documented psychic of the twentieth century. Founded in 1931, the A.R.E. consists of a community of people from all walks of life and spiritual traditions, who have found meaningful and life-transformative insights from the readings of Edgar Cayce.

Although A.R.E. headquarters is located in Virginia Beach, Virginia—where visitors are always welcome—the A.R.E. community is a global network of individuals who offer conferences, educational activities, and fellowship around the world. People of every age are invited to participate in programs that focus on such topics as holistic health, dreams, reincarnation, ESP, the power of the mind, meditation, and personal spirituality.

In addition to study groups and various activities, the A.R.E. offers membership benefits and services, a bimonthly magazine, a newsletter, extracts from the Cayce readings, conferences, international tours, a massage school curriculum, an impressive volunteer network, a retreat-type camp for children and adults, and A.R.E. contacts around the world. A.R.E. also maintains an affiliation with Atlantic University, which offers a master's degree program in Transpersonal Studies.

For additional information about A.R.E. activities hosted near you, please contact:

A.R.E.
67th St. and Atlantic Ave.
P.O. Box 595
Virginia Beach, VA 23451-0595
(804) 428-3588

A.R.E. Press

A.R.E. Press is a publisher and distributor of books, audiotapes, and videos that offer guidance for a more fulfilling life. Our products are based on, or are compatible with, the concepts in the psychic readings of Edgar Cayce.

We especially seek to create products which carry forward the inspirational story of individuals who have made practical application of the Cayce legacy.

For a free catalog, please write to A.R.E. Press at the address below or call toll free 1-800-723-1112. For any other information, please call 804-428-3588.

A.R.E. Press
Sixty-Eighth & Atlantic Avenue
P.O. Box 656
Virginia Beach, VA 23451-0656

the Wealth of Insights Contained in the Edgar Cayce Material...

Throughout his life, Edgar Cayce (1877-1945) was able to display powers of perception that extended beyond the five senses. He was guided by one solitary goal: to be helpful to people, and he used his talents of psychic perception to provide practical guidance for thousands of individuals.

The Edgar Cayce legacy contains information on more than 10,000 different subjects in the areas of healing, holistic health, spirituality, meditation, philosophy, reincarnation, dream interpretation, and prophecy. He has been called a philosopher, the most gifted psychic of all times, and the father of the holistic health movement. More than 300 books have been written about his work!

In 1931, Cayce founded the Association for Research and Enlightenment, Inc. (A.R.E.) to study and research this information. Today, the A.R.E. is an open-membership organization–made up of thousands of individuals around the world–that offers conferences, seminars, research projects, newsletters, and small group activities. For information, call 1-800-333-4499, or use the card below.

☐ Enroll me as a member of A.R.E. (Edgar Cayce's Association for Research and Enlightenment, Inc.) I enclose $40.00 (Outside U.S.A. add $15.00 postage.)

VISA or Master Card CALL TOLL FREE
1-800-333-4499, 24 hours a day, 7 days a week

You may cancel at any time and receive a full refund on all unmailed benefits.

OR Make check or money order payable to A.R.E. (Non-U.S. residents must make payment in United States funds.)

☐ Check or Money Order   ☐ MasterCard   ☐ VISA

If payment is enclosed, please use envelope for your privacy.	**Expiration Date**		**Charge Card Number**			
	Mo.	Yr.	☐☐☐☐	– ☐☐☐☐	– ☐☐☐☐	– ☐☐☐☐
	1712		Signature_____			

(Important! Sign here to use credit card.)

Name *(please print)* _____

Address _____

City_____ State _____ Zip _____

Phone   (_____) _____

☐ I can't join right now, but please send me additional information about A.R.E. activities, publications, and membership.

How Can I Participate in A.R.E.?

Although A.R.E. Headquarters is located in Virginia Beach, Virginia–where visitors are always welcome– the A.R.E. is a global network of individuals in more than seventy countries. The underlying principle of the Edgar Cayce readings is the oneness of all life, tolerance for all people, and a compassion and understanding for individuals of all faiths, races, and backgrounds.

In addition to Headquarters, hundreds of study groups and Edgar Cayce Centers exist world-wide. Regardless of your location, individuals are invited to participate in group activities, explore new publications, or simply enjoy membership benefits through the mail.

For additional information about the organization's activities and services, please use the card below or contact:

A.R.E., 67th Street & Atlantic Ave.
P.O. Box 595, Virginia Beach, VA 23451-0595

The Wealth of Insights Contained in the Edgar Cayce Material Includes:

Alternative Healing Principles	**Universal Laws**	**Global Community**
Dreams	**Attitudes & Emotions**	**ESP**
Spiritual Healing	**Mysticism**	**Self-Hypnosis**
Study Groups	**Karma & Grace**	**Death & Dying**
Earth Changes	**Meditation**	**Prophecy**
Psychic Development	**Spiritual Guidance**	**Astrology**
Atlantis & Ancient Civilizations	**Reincarnation**	**Akashic Records**
Discovering Your Soul's Purpose	**Angels**	**And Hundreds More...**

EDGAR CAYCE FOUNDATION and
A.R.E. LIBRARY/VISITORS CENTER
Virginia Beach, Virginia
Serving You Since 1931

NO POSTAGE
NECESSARY
IF MAILED
IN THE
UNITED STATES

BUSINESS REPLY MAIL
FIRST CLASS MAIL PERMIT NO. 2456, VIRGINIA

POSTAGE WILL BE PAID BY ADDRESSEE

A.R.E.®

P.O. Box 595

Virginia Beach, VA 23451-9989